T0358215

Our Long Walk to Economic Freedom

Our Long Walk to Economic Freedom is an entertaining and engaging guide to global economic history told for the first time from an African perspective. In thirty-five short chapters Johan Fourie tells the story of 100,000 years of human history spanning humankind's migration out of Africa to the Covid-19 pandemic. His unique account reveals just how much we can learn by asking unexpected questions such as 'How could a movie embarrass Stalin?', 'Why do the Japanese play rugby?' and 'What do an Indonesian volcano, Frankenstein and Shaka Zulu have in common?'. The book sheds new light on urgent debates about the roots and reasons for prosperity, the march of opportunity versus the crushing boot of exploitation, and why it is the builders of society – rather than the burglars – who ultimately win out.

Johan Fourie is Professor of Economics at Stellenbosch University, South Africa, where he coordinates the Laboratory for the Economics of Africa's Past (LEAP). He is a National Research Foundation-rated scholar, co-founder of the African Economic History Network and former editor of *Economic History of Developing Regions*.

Our Long Walk to Economic Freedom
Lessons from 100,000 Years of Human History

Johan Fourie
Stellenbosch University

CAMBRIDGE
UNIVERSITY PRESS

CAMBRIDGE
UNIVERSITY PRESS

University Printing House, Cambridge CB2 8BS, United Kingdom

One Liberty Plaza, 20th Floor, New York, NY 10006, USA

477 Williamstown Road, Port Melbourne, VIC 3207, Australia

314–321, 3rd Floor, Plot 3, Splendor Forum, Jasola District Centre, New Delhi – 110025, India

103 Penang Road, #05–06/07, Visioncrest Commercial, Singapore 238467

Cambridge University Press is part of the University of Cambridge.

It furthers the University's mission by disseminating knowledge in the pursuit of education, learning, and research at the highest international levels of excellence.

www.cambridge.org
Information on this title: www.cambridge.org/9781009228466
DOI: 10.1017/9781009228503

First published 2022

A catalogue record for this publication is available from the British Library.

ISBN 978-1-009-22846-6 Hardback
ISBN 978-1-009-22848-0 Paperback

To my teachers

Contents

Figures

Acknowledgements

Our Long Walk to Economic Freedom was first published in South Africa in April 2021. It was a team effort. While I was writing the book during the first few months of lockdown in 2020 it was Helanya, my wife and best friend, who shared in the delights and despairs that came with colonising the living-room table in a tiny apartment. My undergraduate students, who were the first (and most critical) readers of the initial draft chapters, were only too happy to comment and to offer critiques, as did several of my graduate students and postdoctoral fellows subsequently. I dedicated the South African issue to them; they were superheroes during a time of immense upheaval.

My South African editors, Gill Moodie and Russell Martin, turned the text into an easy and fun read, not the easiest of tasks for a topic as serious as global economic history. They did such a good job that *Our Long Walk* attracted the attention of Cambridge University Press.

Michael Watson of Cambridge University Press was instrumental in making this edition happen. I've known Michael for many years. He has always encouraged me to write – even inviting me to breakfast in New York in January 2020, just before the world went into lockdown. I promised him then to write a book. Never could I have imagined that I would keep my promise – but write an entirely different book! There are few editors who care so much about their subject area as Michael. It is a privilege to work with him.

That trip to New York was partly sponsored by the Andrew W. Mellon Foundation, which supports my team and the work we do through the Biography of an Uncharted People project (uncharted-people.org). My own research, reported in Chapters 13 and 14, has benefited from the generosity of the Swedish Riksbankens

Jubileumsfond and the Cape of Good Hope Panel project (capepanel. org). Principal investigator Erik Green of Lund University is a great collaborator and an even better friend. There are many who support the work we do at the Laboratory for the Economics of Africa's Past (LEAP), the research unit I coordinate at Stellenbosch University (leapstellenbosch.org.za). Supporting economic history research is not an obvious choice on a continent with many other pressing issues. Although it is unfair to highlight only one individual, the invaluable, no-strings-attached financial support of Keith Meintjes, a retired engineer from Michigan, has provided my students with the resources they need during times of crisis or allowed us to digitise and transcribe material that would not have been otherwise possible. Thank you, Keith.

Just as humans thrive through collaboration, I have benefited from a strong network of supportive scholars. In November and December 2019 I was fortunate to visit the Becker Friedman Institute at the University of Chicago and the Paris School of Economics on short research sabbaticals. Despite bitterly cold weather in Chicago and protests in Paris, I met several scholars who would later contribute their time and energy to improving the manuscript: a big thank-you to James Robinson and Pierre-Cyrille Hautcoeur for the invitations. Emmanuel Akyeampong (Harvard), Belinda Archibong (Barnard), Gareth Austin (Cambridge), Jörg Baten (Tübingen), James Fenske (Warwick), Price Fishback (Arizona), Ewout Frankema (Wageningen), Leigh Gardner (LSE), Vincent Geloso (George Mason), Leander Heldring (Northwestern), Alfonso Herranz (Barcelona), Tony Hopkins (Cambridge), Kris Inwood (Guelph), Peter Lindert (UC Davis), Martine Mariotti (ANU), Anne McCants (MIT), Alois Mlambo (Pretoria), Nicoli Nattrass (Cape Town), Johannes Norling (Mount Holyoke), Nonso Obikili (UN), Sheilagh Ogilvie (Oxford), Karin Pallaver (Bologna), Elias Papaioannou (LBS), Mohamed Saleh (Toulouse), Marlous van Waijenburg (HBS), Jan Luiten van Zanden (Utrecht), Marianne Wanamaker (Tennessee) and Leonard Wantchekon (Princeton and ASE) read and improved parts of the manuscript, gave encouragement when needed, pointed me in the right direction, or invited me to give a talk or seminar. A presentation to the expert team of African economic historians at Wageningen University in the Netherlands – and the detailed feedback of Felix Meier zu Selhausen – saved me from several blunders. My two colleagues, co-authors and friends, Willem Boshoff and Dieter von Fintel, have helped to shape the text, often inadvertently, through our many conversations and collaborations.

The purpose of *Our Long Walk to Economic Freedom* is to tell the story of why humans have prospered. I do so from an African perspective. I rely almost entirely on the fascinating research of my colleagues in the field of economics and economic history. But disseminating research also requires other skills: Mike Cruywagen of Nudge Studio has done a great job of building a website – ourlongwalk.org – where additional resources are available. Philip du Plessis of Blindspot Films created the attractive and informative explainer videos. As I write in Chapter 33, Africa's economic prospects hinge on service exports. I highly recommend these two South African companies!

The lessons we learn from economic history are relevant and important to us all – especially at a time of rapid change. 'Those who cannot remember the past', the philosopher George Santayana famously said, 'are condemned to repeat it.' But this sounds all too pessimistic. Yes, there have been (and are!) many egregious abuses of power and privilege throughout human history – things that we have done wrong and that we should have avoided. But there is also much in our history that is worth celebrating – and repeating. No one can deny that today humans are more numerous and more affluent than ever before. Economic history is a profoundly optimistic story. Our long walk to economic freedom has not been easy, but it is undeniably taking us forward.

I've been fortunate to learn from some of the brightest minds in the field of economic history. I dedicate this book to those who act as guides on my own long walk. I would like *Our Long Walk* to contribute to a conversation, one that is frequently revised as new evidence emerges. In the words of the Coldplay song, I want to be a comma, not a fullstop. We are all students, all the time. May this book introduce a new generation of (African) scholars to these ideas, and may they be inspired to continue the search for understanding the roots of prosperity, in order to build a better world.

A Note on Sources and Terminology

This is a book for non-specialists. I've tried to steer clear of endless footnotes. The articles that I refer to in the text are cited in the endnotes, but I do not identify every single source I've consulted.

I am an empirical social scientist. Throughout the book I rely heavily on open-access GDP and other development statistics. For the sake of consistency I rely on the 2021 version of the Maddison Project (GDP per capita at constant 2011 US dollar) and World Bank's World Development Indicators (GDP per capita at 2010 US dollar) wherever possible. Both maintain online repositories that are freely accessible. Because of different ways that the World Bank and Maddison Project calculate GDP per capita estimates, countries are comparable within these datasets but not across them. I also owe a huge debt of gratitude to Max Roser of ourworldindata.org. His data, figures and maps are freely downloadable and provide a wonderful public resource for the social science community. For anyone still in doubt about the astounding progress humankind has made over the last two hundred years, just spend a few minutes on this site. For figures published in copyrighted journal articles, I have downloaded the replication data from the authors and redrawn the graphs in R. I was ably assisted by former student and data science whizz Jonathan Jayes. Find him at interludeone.com.

As is still the case in South Africa, I use lower case when referring to race and upper case when referring to ethnicities or nationalities. South Africa still classifies its population into four race groups, for example: black, coloured, white and Indian/Asian. To identify as 'coloured' in South Africa does not have the same derogatory connotations as it may have in the United States and elsewhere.

Although this book is aimed at an audience outside the classroom, I will continue to use it in my undergraduate, graduate and MBA courses. It would be great if others were to do the same. Visit ourlongwalk.org for freely downloadable teaching material such as lecture slides, explainer videos, test banks and translations.

How Do We Thrive?
An Introduction

Since the board game *Settlers of Catan* was first released in 1995 it has sold more than 25 million copies. It works like this. Play starts after tiles of different land types – mountains producing iron ore, pastures sustaining sheep, and so on – are laid out – and numbers between 2 and 12 are randomly assigned to each tile. Every player picks a spot on the board to establish his or her first village. When the dice is rolled, a player receives a resource that matches the number on the dice if his or her village is located next to that resource. So, if the pasture next to my village has 9 on it, and the two dice thrown add up to 9, I receive one sheep. Those resources I then use to buy roads and villages and cities – and so expand my empire. If my resources are not quite appropriate, I can also trade them for other resources with other players or with the 'bank'. The first person to reach a specified empire size wins. But here is the key takeaway: by the time the game ends, everyone has a flourishing network of towns and cities, some just more so than others.

The game of *Monopoly* offers a very different challenge. You are a landlord, acquiring titles to property and charging rent to those who are forced (by the dice) to visit your property. The game starts with every player having an equal amount of cash. It ends with one player owning everything.

The world can be divided into two types of people. The first group believes the world is like a game of *Monopoly*: only the strongest, smartest or most fortunate survive. For this group, life is a zero-sum game; for you to win, I need to lose. If you have a world view like this, then you will inevitably also believe that wealth is acquired through the acquisition of something owned by someone else, whether it is their property (as in the game), their land or their forgone wages. The second group, by contrast, believes that the world is more like a game of *Catan*. They hold the belief that you can prosper while I prosper too. In fact, those in this group might even believe, as do the best *Catan* players, that you *have* to prosper for me to prosper, that our fates are irrevocably joined together.

Unfortunately, *Monopoly* is the board game most associated with wealth and prosperity. It is unfortunate, because the real world is nothing like a game of *Monopoly*. Let me give one example, very close to my home. I teach at Stellenbosch University, in a university town about an hour's drive from Cape Town. The population of Stellenbosch increased by a factor of eight between 1911 and 2016 – from almost 22,000 people to more than 170,000 in little more than a century. Back in 1911, according to the census, there were only ten people who owned cars in the entire town. Today that number is at least 62,000 – we don't know exactly how many cars that is, as the census only counts one car per family. The point is that the number of car owners has gone up from 1 in 2,000 inhabitants to 1 in 3. If Stellenbosch was a game of *Monopoly*, then only one person would have ended up with all ten initial cars – and the game would be over. But because it is more like *Catan*, because our prosperity depends on that of our neighbours, there is far more wealth to go round. Instead of just one family monopolising everything, thousands of Stellenbosch families now own cars.

We find it hard to believe that the modern world is less like *Monopoly* and more like *Catan*. One reason is that we are constantly bombarded by negative economic news – of tech billionaires and their ballooning fortunes; of company closures and job losses; of debt and deceit and destitution. Our world view is also informed by our experience. Behavioural scientists have identified that we have a 'negativity bias', that negative things have a greater impact on our psychological state than positive things, even if the two are of equal proportion.[1] It is therefore very human to focus disproportionately on the negative and ignore the positive.

A third reason we find it hard to believe that the world is not a zero-sum game is that our education curricula have shortcomings. History courses focus almost exclusively on political and social history. Economics courses focus on formal models and technical tools. Economic history courses have almost disappeared from university programmes. The shift towards postmodernism, as we will see in Chapter 1, has not helped. Topics that deserve our attention, such as slavery and colonialism, have been appropriated by fields of study where empirical fact has been displaced by subjectivity, relativism and a general suspicion of evidence and reason. Power and ideology, instead, are touted as the only tools to understand the past. While there is ample reason to doubt the 'objectivity' of colonial sources of evidence, that is no reason to throw the baby out with the bathwater. The only way we can uncover what happened, and why, is to construct a theory, collect source material – sometimes using innovative new (statistical) methods – and test whether the hypothesis holds up against the evidence. This book is based on research that uses such an empirical approach. Alternative approaches, I would argue, can only result in reinforcing the researcher's own beliefs and biases. History, then, becomes the study of our own fantasies.

Having self-reinforcing fantasies rather than solid evidence of how the world works has consequences. If we believe that everyone is competing in a zero-sum game, that I can only become successful if I overpower and subdue you, then that will make us dislike rich people, the implication being that they could only be where they are because they took advantage of others. But if we believe that success requires cooperation and interaction, that we can only be successful because we depend on and trust others, then we will come to appreciate that wealth creates more wealth. You don't have to worship at the feet of Bill Gates, Jeff Bezos or Elon Musk to appreciate their companies' contributions to the profound improvement in our standards of living. Recognising that wealth requires a shared dependence also allows us to identify where wealth is unsustainably, unethically or illegally obtained. A government official misappropriating taxpayers' money or a business manager cooking the company books breaks down our trust and cooperation, weakening our economic freedom; whereas an entrepreneur who builds a thriving business increases it.

The good news is that economic history suggests that it is the builders rather than the burglars who ultimately win out. The empirical evidence is unequivocal. Over the last two centuries, our economic freedom – the ability of every human to work, produce, consume and invest in the way they please – has increased exponentially. True, the process has not been uniform. In some places, such as South Africa and many other parts of Africa, economic freedom for most was suppressed until quite recently. Where economic freedom was, on the other hand, allowed to flourish, it has created immense prosperity. The economic historian Deirdre McCloskey calls it 'the great enrichment'.[2] The average human is today at least eighteen times richer than in the year 1800.[3] To put that another way (and here I borrow from McCloskey): the average person in 1800 could only possess one pair of shoes – probably of shoddy quality. That person's great-great-great-grandchild today can own eighteen pairs of shoes, one for every occasion.

This prosperity allows us to buy not only shoes but also health and happiness. Today, we live much longer and healthier lives than previously. To give just one example: 43 per cent of babies in 1800 died before they were five years old. Today that number is 4.3 per cent, a tenfold decrease. Although we do not have measures of 'happiness' dating back to 1800, we do know that general happiness, measured by surveys, has increased over the last half-century. What is more, people in countries with a higher GDP per capita are also generally 'happier' than people in low-income countries.[4]

How and why this incredible increase in human prosperity happened – and why it has been slow to take off in some places – is the topic of this book. We begin in the distant past – 100,000 years ago, to be precise – and, in thirty-five chapters, cover all of human history. This can never be a comprehensive global economic history, of course. It is, rather, a personal and somewhat eclectic selection of the economic history topics that, I believe, are most informative about our long walk to economic freedom.

The book is unashamedly written from a South African and African perspective. Africa usually receives little treatment in global economic history courses – and when it does, it is usually as an afterthought or, worse, as an example of where 'things fell apart'. There are valid reasons for why Africa is pushed in this way to the periphery. Africa is indeed the continent with the lowest levels of income. Whereas the average global citizen is eighteen times more affluent than their great-great-great-grandparents, the average

African is only six times more affluent. We live better lives than our ancestors, but it is clear that there is still much room for improvement. Another reason for the neglect of Africa in economic history books is that, in contrast to the rest of the world, the economic history of Africa is generally poorly understood. This book, informed by an exciting new research agenda in the field of African economic history (as Chapter 1 explains), hopes to enlighten.

By the very end of the book we turn from the past to the future. It is very possible that the world will become a much more prosperous place over the next decade. But it is also possible that growth will stagnate, and average living standards will decline. There is no guaranteed outcome. This is especially true for Africa, the continent I call home. The difference between the optimistic and pessimistic scenarios will depend on whether we can secure the economic freedoms many Africans still do not have. And that will depend on the policies we implement, the politicians we elect into office and, ultimately, the stories of prosperity and wealth creation we tell ourselves and our children.

Join me on this epic journey through our history – and the story of our long walk to economic freedom.

1 Who Are the Architects of Wakanda?
African Economic Historians and the Stories We Tell

When Marvel Studios released its superhero film *Black Panther* in 2018, kids across the continent of Africa began to salute one another Wakanda-style. They crossed their arms (in a gesture like the pharaohs of ancient Egypt, who were laid to rest with their arms on their chests) and would end the greeting with the words 'Wakanda forever'.

Wakanda, of course, is a fictional country. It was created, so the story goes, when a massive meteorite made up of an equally fictional metal, vibranium, crashed into a location somewhere in East Africa. Understanding the value of vibranium, the leaders of Wakanda concealed this rare and valuable energy-giving resource. Many of the best scholars of Wakanda were sent to study abroad and, on their return, their work turned Wakanda into one of the world's most technologically advanced countries. Although Wakanda appears from the outside to be a poor, developing country, it is actually prosperous beyond belief.

We want to believe the story of Wakanda because it is so different from the reality of many African countries. All ten of the poorest countries on earth are in sub-Saharan Africa. According to the World Bank, sub-Saharan Africa has an average annual income of one-seventh of the world average.

This book is about understanding why this is so. We want to know why because we want to see things improve. We want to see all Africans thrive, much like the Wakandans in their technologically advanced city. We want to understand what the roots of Africa's prosperity will be, and what policies could help to achieve that.

How will we do that? In our search for answers, we turn to the study of global economic history. The logic is simple: we can learn from other places and from other times to help us understand why Africa has lagged behind these regions – and what can be done to accelerate Africa's fortunes.

Economic history is, as the name suggests, a combination of economics and history.[1] Economics is not just about money or wealth or fortunes: it is about how humans behave and interact with one another. Much as natural scientists develop theories about how the natural environment works, and medical scientists about how the human body works, so economists construct theories about how society works. History is our laboratory. History provides the raw data that allow us to test our theories; it is the evidence upon which our theories are accepted and survive or are refuted.

But humans are complicated beings. We do not all behave in the same way. We have different preferences, beliefs and biases. That is why, like the natural or the medical scientists, we cannot always find answers that are easily replicable. It is also why we need to continually test our theories in different settings and time periods. Our 'cures' for society are contingent on time and place, and so the same problem won't always have the same solution. It is the job of the economic historian to understand what solutions worked in the past, and why.

The good news is that many economic historians are now beginning to study African economic history to find ways to solve the continent's challenges. The rest of this book will review some of this exciting new work, but first it is important to understand where research in African economic history started. The present renaissance in African economic history builds on previous generations of scholars, each of whom developed their own theories to explain Africa's fluctuating fortunes. Anthony Hopkins, one of the leading scholars of African economic history, has identified six schools of thought that characterise the field since its establishment in the 1950s.[2] Let us briefly review how each of these schools understood African development.

African economic history only became a serious field of study after most African countries had gained independence from colonial rule. The first school of thought, modernisation theory, assumed a sharp distinction between 'traditional' and 'modern' societies. Adherents of this approach proposed that if 'successful' policies that had been implemented in the West were simply transferred to or replicated in the newly independent African societies, they would inevitably lead to development and prosperity. The actual transfer of policies took place, however, without consideration of the history and context particular to each region. When, by the early 1970s, many African economies had not transformed sufficiently or, in some cases, had stagnated, modernisation theory was found wanting.

The dependency school replaced modernisation theory. The two stand in diametric opposition to each other. The new school maintained that the solutions to Africa's underdevelopment were not to be found in the West – indeed, the West was to blame for Africa's condition. The arguments in Walter Rodney's seminal book *How Europe Underdeveloped Africa* were attractive to many African scholars.[3] Since it suggested that foreign capitalism had created underdevelopment, the policy response was to sever ties with the West. The dependency school allowed African governments to craft their own solutions without learning from other places in the world. Yet despite their contrasting views, dependency theory ultimately fell into the same trap as modernisation theory. Hopkins remarks that 'the emphasis on external influences obliged adherents to adopt the position that indigenous societies had only a limited ability to shape their own history'.[4] In other words, because Africa's malaise was entirely the fault of the West, it suggested that Africans were not (or, worse, could not be) the agents of their own destiny.

Marxism, the third school, rightly shifted the focus to Africans and their own modes of production. Marxist historians, by the 1970s, were ploughing their way through African archives in search of evidence that would show the pre-colonial roots of class conflict. They then tried to fit the evidence into a preconceived Marxist framework. They soon ran into difficulties, though, as the complexity of African societies that they were uncovering in the archives was at odds with their preconceived ideas. African history simply did not square well with the class structure that Marxism required.

The good thing about the Marxist school was that it shifted the attention to those on the margin of society or, put differently, to a history from below – a history of ordinary people. By the 1980s the

Annales school, associated with the style of an earlier generation of French historians, attracted interest too. Its approach was to focus on long-term social history that included groups usually excluded from conventional history, such as women and children. It also incorporated unconventional topics such as demography, climate and disease. Yet, even though the Annalistes wrote *about* the oppressed, they did not necessarily write *for* them; whereas Rodney's book was a call to political action, the Annalistes were more 'concerned to understand the world rather than change it'.[5]

This lack of political ambition meant that the Annalistes were soon displaced by the postmodernists, the fifth school. But the focus with postmodernism was different: instead of material reality, attention turned to cultural history. As Hopkins explains: 'Unlike its predecessors, postmodernism made no contribution to economic history. Its focus on textual images, its scepticism about the concept of reality, and its limited interest in causality provided methodological grounds for avoiding some of the central preoccupations of historical enquiry.'[6]

By the early 2000s, then, with African economies on the rise, there was a renewed interest in understanding Africa's fluctuating fortunes. Two interwoven branches emerged within the quantitative school, both of which we will encounter in this book. Since its inception the descriptive approach has been interested in using quantitative sources – trade statistics, tax records, military attestation forms – to provide new empirical facts about Africa's economic past. On the other hand, the cliometricians, led by economists using new statistical tools, are most interested in understanding the persistent impact of historical events on contemporary outcomes.[7] Both groups are responsible for a revival in the study of African economic history.[8]

One concern, and one additional reason for writing this book, is that much of this renaissance has been the work of scholars based outside Africa.[9] While their initiative is commendable, the risk is that the lessons learned from this new wave of scholarship are not internalised on the continent, either in research or in policy.

What are these lessons? There are many, and this book hopes to cover most of them. One of the first lessons from studying economic history is that the answers we look for depend very much on the questions we ask. Just as citizens in sub-Saharan Africa are, on average, poorer than those in the rest of the world, there are also large income differences within Africa. Even within cities and towns, neighbourhoods and families, we find large differences in income. The most popular question is to ask why it is that people are poor. That is a good question for certain situations, but, as I hope to persuade you in this book, perhaps it is not the most historically appropriate question. Only five hundred years ago, around 1500, the world was a very different place. Almost everyone was what we would today consider to be impoverished. Even the emperors of China or the caesars of Rome or the pharaohs of ancient Egypt generally lived short, unhealthy lives. The ones we remember were the exceptions.

Throughout history, humans have always been poor. Poverty is the historical norm. Put differently, wealth and high living standards are historical outliers. It is incredibly difficult to create and sustain a prosperous society. If you build a house but then neglect to maintain it, it will, within a few years, become dilapidated and, ultimately, crumble and collapse; entropy, a gradual move towards chaos, is the natural order of things.

So, it is instead more historically accurate to ask: why is it that people are rich? And what are the causes of prosperity, of economic growth, of high living standards? When we switch the question in this way, our focus turns to the mechanisms of economic development. Once we understand the mechanisms, we can begin to ask how we can use them to power African development.

The world has seen significant increases in living standards over the last two centuries. We have already discussed the massive improvements in our prosperity, health and well-being. Another way to summarise this, as Figure 1.1 illustrates, is to show the remarkable decline in absolute levels of extreme poverty, especially in the last three decades. Because it is so deceptively simple, look carefully at this graph. According to the numbers on the axis, the share of people living below the extreme poverty line ($1.90 per day) has fallen from 44% in 1980 to less than 10%. That may seem like just another statistic. But think of it this way: a newspaper editor could have printed the following headline every day between 1990 and 2020, and it would have been true: 'The number of people in extreme poverty fell by 128,000 since yesterday.' It is a fact so outrageous that it is almost impossible to believe.[10]

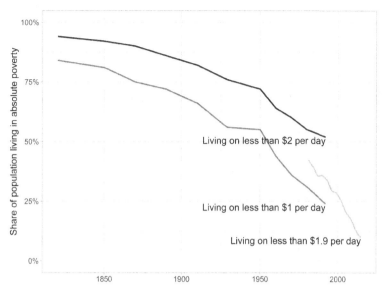

Figure 1.1 Share of the world population living in absolute poverty, 1820–2015

And yet we never see this headline in newspapers. That is because good news tends to occur over years, while bad news tends to occur suddenly. As humans, we have evolved to be risk-averse, which means we are attracted to bad news that might threaten our survival. This book wants to restore balance.[11] It wants us to pay attention to the good news too and learn from it by asking: how have we grown so remarkably affluent? How can we sustain this incredible newspaper headline into the future?

Figure 1.1 helps us to dream about a world – and a continent – where poverty is a thing of the past. If we learn from history, that world is indeed possible. But it depends on the stories we tell ourselves and the next generation. The real architect of Wakanda, the production designer Hannah Beachler, remarked in an interview with the magazine *FastCompany*: 'World history is essential to produce an authentic story.'[12]

I hope the next generation of African economic historians will tell authentic stories of our continent's remarkable history – stories in service of our quest for a prosperous future.

2 What Happened at Blombos in 70,000 BCE?

The Out-of-Africa Hypothesis and the Peopling of the World

About 300 kilometres from Cape Town on the south-west coast of South Africa is a cave that overlooks the Indian Ocean. Archaeologists have been digging at Blombos Cave since 1991. What they have found has changed our view of human evolution.

Anatomically modern humans evolved in Africa. *Homo sapiens* is a species of the hominid family, the great apes. Genetic evidence suggests that apes diverged from other mammals around 85 million years ago; the earliest fossils we have of apes are from around 55 million years ago.

There are two things that make humans unique from other apes: bipedalism and language. Bipedalism, our ability to walk on two legs, also resulted in other skeletal changes, to the pelvis, the vertebral column, feet and ankles, and the skull, including an increase in the size and structure of the brain. These evolutionary changes to our brain made social learning and language acquisition in children possible, two traits which we developed about 2 million years ago.

The reason we evolved to walk on two feet, scientists suggest, was to take advantage of environmental change in Africa. As the climate changed, the jungle (a natural habitat for our ape-like ancestors) gave way to the open savannah. It meant that we had to find alternative sources of food, and as a result new technologies such as speech and making fire were developed. These new technologies affected human evolution: because cooking doubles the energy we can extract from our food, our command of fire allowed our ancestors' teeth, stomach and gut to shrink and the brain to grow bigger.

None of this was a linear process ending with *Homo sapiens*, as the well-known caricature would have it. Human evolution should rather be seen as a web. New research shows that humans interbred with other hominid species. For example, there is evidence that almost all humans share genetic material with Neanderthals, a species that roamed Eurasia from 400,000 to around 40,000 years ago. Those with sub-Saharan and Western European heritage tend to have the lowest levels of shared genetic material, while Indigenous Americans, Asians and Aboriginal Australians and Papuans tend to have substantially more.[1] Scientists are still unravelling the mysteries of when and where this exchange (or exchanges) of genetics happened.

What we do know is that at some stage in our more recent history, humans migrated out of Africa. Again, the evidence is not clear-cut. There are different theories about when and how humans migrated, and scientists are continually updating these theories on the basis of new genetic or archaeological evidence. What the latest genetic evidence shows is that there was a single migration from Africa between 50,000 and 65,000 years ago, a very short period of time on the evolutionary timeline. All non-African humans are thus descended from these migrants. A second theory is that there were two migrations. One early wave of humans exited Africa around 75,000 years ago from the Horn of Africa (modern-day Somalia) when sea levels were much lower, populating the Indian subcontinent and Asia, and a second wave migrated across the Persian Gulf, populating the Middle East and Europe.

Regardless of which theory is true, humans evolved in Africa. Africa today is thus home to the greatest variation in human DNA anywhere on the planet. Humans would, over thousands of years, trek to all places on earth, reaching South America around 15,000 BCE and the island of New Zealand around 1300 CE. The people who reached these far-off places at the end of this millennia-long journey had relatively low genetic diversity.

A few years ago the economists Quamrul Ashraf and Oded Galor posited that this variation in genetic diversity in different parts of the world explains something about the distribution of income today.[2] Their theory has been called the Out-of-Africa hypothesis.

According to this theory, in places with a lot of human genetic diversity there will be many new and competing ideas, which is good for innovation and economic growth. In places with low human genetic diversity there will be very few new ideas, which is bad for growth. But they also argue that in places with high human genetic diversity coordination and trust will be low, which is bad for economic growth. By contrast, places with low human genetic diversity will have high levels of coordination and trust. This results in a goldilocks effect: you want some human genetic diversity but not too much.

The two economists then took the distance from Addis Ababa, the capital of Ethiopia, as a proxy for how much human genetic diversity each present-day country has, and plotted this against the income levels of those countries. What they found is an inverted-U curve as in Figure 2.1, which is exactly what their hypothesis predicted. This, they argue, supports the claim that distant events – such as the human migration out of Africa – still affect living standards today.

Their paper has come under severe criticism. One excellent critique, published in *Current Anthropology*, notes the many errors

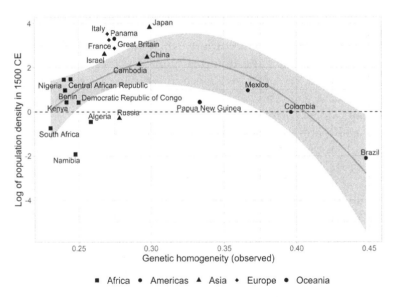

Figure 2.1 Observed genetic diversity and population density, 1500 CE

their research makes.[3] These include misattributing genetic diversity to migratory distance, misconstruing the link between genetic diversity and diversity of ideas, selecting and reporting factually inaccurate data, and making simplistic assumptions about the nature of human behaviour. The authors of the critique warn economists and other social scientists about the dangers of working with genetic data: 'It is crucial to remember that nonexperts broadcasting bold claims on the basis of weak data and methods can have profoundly detrimental social and political effects.'[4]

What Ashraf and Galor's 'Out-of-Africa' research, and the critiques that followed, show is that the scientific process, although sometimes slow and frustrating, does move our understanding of the world forward. Ashraf and Galor had an idea that they tested against the evidence. Other scientists judged their evidence to be insufficient to support their hypothesis. Very few economists or other social scientists now believe that wealth and poverty differences today are the result of migratory patterns that occurred 50,000 years ago. And even fewer, if any, would suggest policies to create an 'optimal level' of genetic diversity in a society. We will meet many old and new theories in the rest of this book. It is the job of natural and social scientists to identify which are the ones with merit and which are the ones, like Ashraf and Galor's Out-of-Africa hypothesis, that do not stand up to the evidence.

Let us return to Blombos Cave. What did the archaeologists find there that overturned our previous ideas about human evolution? For a long time scientists believed that the early humans who exited Africa (whether in one or in two waves) were very limited in their speech and other cultural attributes. One indicator of modern human cognition and behaviour is the ability to produce abstract or descriptive artworks. Before the discovery of Blombos, the earliest human paintings known to archaeologists were located in caves in southern France, produced around 40,000 BCE. This would mean that the artwork in France was produced only after the emigration from Africa. However, the archaeologists who excavated Blombos Cave found 'a cross-hatched pattern drawn with an ochre crayon on a ground silcrete flake recovered from approximately 73,000-year-old Middle Stone Age levels'.[5] It means that this art pre-dates any other known artwork in the world by more than 30,000 years. The implication is that the humans who inhabited Africa before the migration from the continent had all the features of human cognition and behaviour that we associate with humans today.

Humans evolved in Africa and spread across the globe. They settled in all parts of the world, adjusting to the diverse environments they would come to inhabit. But there is no plausible evidence that such human genetic diversity as exists leads to different economic outcomes today. Genetics does not explain why some societies are rich, and others poor. We need to continue our search for other explanations.

3 Why Are the Danes So Individualistic?
The Neolithic Revolution and the Rise of Civilisations

In his bestselling book *Sapiens*, Yuval Noah Harari writes: 'We did not domesticate wheat. It domesticated us.'[1] This statement captures a fundamental truth about the Neolithic Revolution, sometimes also called the Agricultural Revolution, which began about 10,000 BCE. This was a period in history when humans transitioned from a lifestyle of hunting and gathering to one of farming and settlement.

For most of our history, humans have lived nomadic lives. We would cluster into small bands of between 30 and 150 people – and roam the countryside looking for animals to hunt, and seeds, berries and fruits to gather. We know something about this lifestyle of our nomadic ancestors by observing the few groups of people that still live in this way. In southern Africa we are most familiar with the San, although most San people today have now switched to a sedentary lifestyle.

Life as hunter-gatherers was tough. In periods when food was plentiful there was ample time for leisure and procreation. But because hunter-gatherers are nomadic, there were limited opportunities to save and accumulate for the proverbial rainy day. When resources were scarce, this could quickly lead to famine and conflict. A large proportion of men in hunter-gatherer societies died violently.

One might think that the transition to agriculture made humans better off, but there is enough evidence now to suggest that the first farmers did not live materially better lives than their hunter-gatherer counterparts.[2] This is a paradox. Why did hunter-gatherers then switch to crop farming if their lives did not improve? The answer is that many of them may have been forced to because of climate change: access to the animals they were hunting or the fruits they were gathering had dwindled. The timing of this shift – in the Levant and Fertile Crescent, a region that today comprises the countries of Iraq, Syria, Israel, Palestine, Jordan, and parts of Turkey and Iran – correlates with the end of the last Ice Age. It is likely that as sea levels rose because of a warmer climate, certain plant species, such as wheat and barley, began to thrive in these areas, leading to larger populations and reducing the 'wild' food available for hunting and gathering. In order to survive, people had to find an alternative source of sustenance.

Once farming became the primary source of food, life changed considerably. For one thing, farmers are more productive than hunter-gatherers. This allows them to produce a surplus beyond their daily needs. Farming also forces one to settle down in order to care for crops, to move from a nomadic to a sedentary lifestyle. The combination of surplus production and sedentary living enabled these early farmers to begin to accumulate 'capital'. They could start to build houses to live in and storerooms to preserve their surpluses for longer. It also allowed them to 'invest' their surpluses. Instead of searching for food (or, when food was plentiful, using their time for leisure), they could now allocate part of their time to constructing things such as irrigation systems that would make them even more productive, allowing for even larger surpluses and even more investment and capital accumulation.

One reason that farming was not immediately attractive was that the varied diet hunter-gatherers found in their environment was replaced by the monotonous diet of starches farmers produced. But because farmers were producing a surplus, they could trade away their surplus for other food types or household goods. Farmers could, for example, specialise in harvesting wheat or breeding sheep, produce more than they needed for themselves and their immediate families, and trade their surplus with a specialist in another field, such as a fisherman or a potter or a blacksmith. This allowed them to obtain products that they could not produce themselves. The blacksmith, for his part, could now specialise in making knives or spears and trade with the farmers to obtain food. Specialisation and trade are key components of how societies become prosperous.

Specialisation also led to urbanisation. Blacksmiths, potters and other specialists had no reason to stay far away from each other. In fact, it was more useful for them to be in close proximity, so that when the farmers brought their surplus production to market, they could trade with all the specialists in one place. This meant that villages developed in those areas where farmers would gather, typically a place that was easy to access and close to a source of water. This, in a very stylised way, is how towns and cities were established in the ancient world.

We have, of course, neglected one important component that characterises large civilisations: rulers. The surpluses these farmers produced also had to be protected, either from animals or, more commonly, from other humans. This necessitated a system of defence and, consequently, the emergence of another specialist: the soldier. Armies required leadership, which gave rise to more complicated forms of social organisation. Instead of the egalitarian structure of the hunter-gatherer societies, agricultural societies typically had strong social hierarchies. Inequality was thus born.

The surpluses farmers produced ensured another important advantage over hunter-gatherers: a higher fertility rate. Farming not only allowed specialisation between households but also within the household. Because of the physical strength required, men were more likely to be engaged in arable farming, whereas women could 'specialise' in having and raising children. This, combined with the greater quantity (if lower variety) of food, meant that more stomachs could be fed sufficiently for agricultural societies to grow much faster than hunter-gatherer groups. Over time, as farmer numbers grew, they would encroach on the territories of hunter-gatherers, and either displaced them or incorporated them into their new communities.

This process of agricultural expansion explains, according to the economic historians Ola Olsson and Christopher Paik, why northern Europeans are today more likely to be individualistic than their southern European counterparts.[3] They begin by defining collectivist norms as the preference to conform, to value duty, honour, tradition and leadership. People who adhere to more collectivist norms consider it important for children to be obedient to their parents and are more willing to accept hierarchies and social structures. By contrast, individualism is associated with independence, openness to new ideas and egalitarianism.

So, what does agriculture have to do with collectivist norms? The argument goes like this. The people living in places where agriculture emerged were the first to develop highly collectivist norms. This happens because, as we have just seen, agriculture requires a far more complex social hierarchy than that of hunter-gatherer societies. Within such social hierarchies, the traits associated with collective norms – such as honour, tradition, leadership and obedience – would be likely to culturally evolve.

Around 10,000 BCE these early farming societies first emerged in the Fertile Crescent. From there agriculture spread, over several millennia, across southern Europe and then into northern Europe. How it spread is important for our story.

Imagine a society with a range of people, some having very collectivist norms and others more individualistic norms. It is very likely that the individualistic ones would move away because they do not tolerate the strong norms of the other members of their group. Once they moved, they would establish a new farming community. After several generations this new community would again contain some members with more collectivist norms and others with more individualistic norms, and once again the more individualistic ones would pack their belongings and leave in order to establish a new society. The same process would be repeated until ultimately northern Europe was reached – where only the most individualistic would end up. The process is demonstrated in Figure 3.1. That is what Olsson and Paik think happened in Europe several thousand years ago.

How do we know if this is true? The two authors argue that these norms persist until today. We should thus expect that northern Europeans are more individualistic in comparison with southern Europeans, who should have more collectivist norms. And that is exactly what the authors find when they use contemporary survey data. The Danes are more individualistic, it seems, because they acquired agriculture much later than the Greeks or the Italians or the Spanish.

In a 2020 paper these two authors go one step further.[4] They argue that the timing of the Neolithic Revolution not only affects modern-day norms but could also explain contemporary political

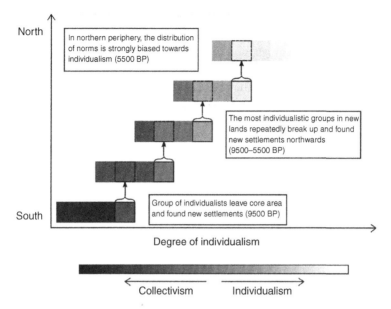

Figure 3.1 How individualised norms spread through migration

systems and income levels. For most of human history, agriculture was the dominant sector of production. As we have seen, collectivist norms flourish in such systems. But such norms lead to more autocratic regimes and discourage innovation. It explains why, until around 1500, the Middle East and the southern part of Europe were more affluent than the north.

But because individualistic norms reward creativity and risk-taking, these norms became more beneficial, the authors argue, once market economies arose. Individualistic norms are also more likely to favour democratic institutions. There thus occurred a reversal of fortunes in Europe after around 1500, with the north growing richer than the south. Using an updated map of all Neolithic sites in Europe and the Middle East and correlating that with income levels today, the authors find a robust negative relationship between the number of years since the transition to agriculture and income levels both across and within countries today. Whereas the ancient (agricultural) civilizations of the Assyrians, Babylonians, Egyptians, Greeks and Romans were all located in the Middle East and southern Europe, today the wealthiest countries are in northern Europe. The

Danes are not only more individualistic, but it seems they are also wealthier and more democratic as a result.

Just how much our distant transition from hunting and gathering to agriculture still affects us today remains a subject of contention – and surely the focus of future research. What we do know is that these new farming communities transformed not only their mode of food production, but the entire structure of their societies. A planet that was inhabited by small groups of hunter-gatherers had become, from around 10,000 BCE, a place with far greater numbers of farmers producing a surplus and supporting specialists in villages and towns. Soon the first civilisations would emerge. Wheat not only domesticated us; it made us the demigods of this planet.

4 Why Does isiXhosa Have Clicks?
The Bantu Migration

Long-haul tourists visiting South Africa are always fascinated by the clicks of isiXhosa. Foreign to their ears, the eighteen click consonants can be grouped into three types: the 'c' is a dental click made by the tongue at the back of the mouth, the lateral 'x' is made by the tongue at the sides of the mouth, and the alveolar 'q' is made by the tip of the tongue on the roof of the mouth.

IsiXhosa is part of the Nguni language group, which also includes Zulu and southern and northern Ndebele. Yet few of these or the other South African vernacular languages have clicks, and those that do have them use them far less. How is it that isiXhosa came to use clicks so commonly?

One clue comes from the other languages of southern Africa that also make use of clicks – and there are lots of them. Although they are not well known, the Ju|'hoan language, spoken by an estimated 10,000 people in Botswana and Namibia, has 48 clicks, and the Taa language, spoken by only 4,000 speakers in Botswana, has 83. The implication is that those Nguni speakers who acquired clicks – what later became isiXhosa – must have been in close contact with the people who spoke click-heavy languages. As we will see, this integration of people at the southern tip of Africa came right at the end of what has become known as the Bantu migration (or the Bantu expansion). It is the largest-known human migration and it transformed the demography and economy of central, eastern and southern Africa over the last five millennia.

As we've seen from Chapter 2, humans evolved in Africa and then spread across the globe. Africa has thus always had remarkable human diversity. To tell a coherent story, we will simplify this diversity into five major human groups that inhabited the continent before the Bantu migration. These were what we would now know as Bantu-speaking Africans, Berbers, Central African foragers ('Pygmies'), Khoesan and Asians.

Now let us imagine Africa around 3000 BCE.[1] The northern coastal zone next to the Mediterranean Sea was inhabited by Berbers, the ancestors of modern-day Egyptians, Libyans and Moroccans who are not descended from the Arab conquests of the eighth century. The Sahel (the savannah region below the Sahara Desert), as well as the tropical regions of West Africa, was inhabited by Bantu-speaking Africans. The Central African tropics were inhabited by foragers, also known as African Pygmies, a hunter-gathering people of short stature. All of eastern and southern Africa was inhabited by the Khoesan, a combination of pastoral Khoe and hunter-gatherer San people. We will learn more about them in Chapter 13. Finally, the island of Madagascar, 400 kilometres off the eastern coast of Africa, was entirely devoid of humans in 3000 BCE. It is believed that the island was only settled by humans – Asians who had migrated from the island of Borneo several thousand kilometres to the east – between 200 BCE and 500 CE.

Around 3000 BCE something happened in West Africa that would change African history forever: the domestication of African yams, a plant that grows large tubers which look a bit like sweet potatoes. Why this happened is not entirely clear, but the latest evidence from plant genetics shows that Bantu-speaking farmers located in present-day southern Nigeria or northern Cameroon acquired this new 'technology'. Yams allowed the farmers to produce larger surpluses and increase their population size, giving them an advantage over their hunter-gatherer neighbours.

This productivity advantage set off a migration in two directions. As shown in Figure 4.1, one group migrated south, through the tropics, down the west coast of Central Africa. Another group migrated east, around the Central African tropics, to the east coast and then south, through the Great Lakes region and into southern Africa. Somewhere along the way, probably in the Great Lakes region as they came into contact with traders along the Nile, they

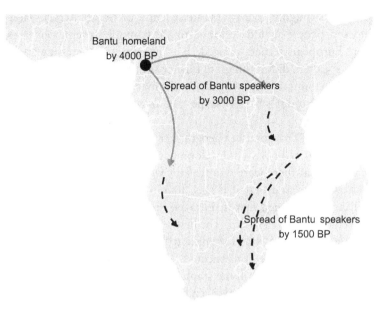

Figure 4.1 Map of migration of Bantu speakers in Africa

obtained another technology: ironworking. Agriculture and ironworking allowed them to speed up their colonisation of southern
Africa. Archaeological evidence shows that they crossed the
Limpopo River, the northern border of modern-day South Africa,
around 300 CE. The final outcome of this massive migration was
that almost all of central, eastern and southern Africa became the
home of Bantu speakers.

What happened to the people who had lived there before? It
seems that most of them were displaced, either being subjugated or
pushed into environments where farming was not viable, such as the
forests or the deserts. Central African foragers moved deeper into the
forests. Today there are very few of them remaining. Their own
languages are gone; each forager band adopted the language of the
neighbouring Bantu-speaking farmers. The same is largely true for
the Khoesan. Most were displaced by the incoming Bantu-speaking
farmers. Those who remained moved into the deserts (of Namibia,
South Africa or Botswana), with one exception.

The one place where Bantu speakers did not settle was the
region with a Mediterranean climate at the southern tip of the

continent, roughly today's Western Cape of South Africa. Here Khoesan people would continue to thrive until, several centuries later, European settlers arrived. It is interesting to consider why Bantu speakers did not migrate further south and west, all the way to Table Mountain, and why their slow march halted roughly at the Fish River in today's Eastern Cape. The answer requires us to look at geography.

Jared Diamond is a geographer who has written one of the most influential books on development. In *Guns, Germs and Steel* he argues that there were two reasons why Eurasians were lucky in their location, and that it is this 'luck' that helps to explain why civilisations emerged first in Eurasia, despite the fact that humans evolved originally in Africa. The first reason is that Eurasia, notably the Fertile Crescent, was fortunate to have many of the plants and animals that could be domesticated. These included wild wheat and pulse species that are still the staple diet of most people around the world, such as wheat, barley, chickpeas and lentils. These are all winter-rainfall crops. By contrast, sub-Saharan Africa had far fewer domesticable plants. Sorghum and pearl millet were probably domesticated in the summer-rainfall Sahel region, and yams, palm oil and kola nuts in the wet tropics of West Africa. Yet none of these crops would be as nutrient-rich as wheat, barley, rye and oats, or rice (in China) and maize or corn (in the Americas), the most common staples in the rest of the world.

Why did wheat not travel to Africa? The answer links to the second reason why Africa was 'unlucky'. Africa is a 'vertical' continent, longer than it is wide, while Eurasia is 'horizontal', wider than it is long. This is important because climatic zones vary a lot longitudinally (vertically) but not latitudinally (horizontally). For example, a crop domesticated in the Fertile Crescent could easily be transported west to southern Europe or east to the Indian subcontinent or even further to southern China, because all these regions fall roughly in the same climatic zone. Wheat was grown in Egypt, of course, because that country also had a Mediterranean climate, but it could not travel the long journey south through the Sahara Desert, the summer-rainfall savannah of the Sahel, the tropics of Central Africa, the (summer-rainfall) highlands and savannah of eastern and southern Africa, and finally to where it could adapt – the winter-rainfall Mediterranean climatic region along the southern tip of the continent. It was only after 1650, when Europeans settled, that wheat would be grown in the Cape.[2]

The same was true of animals. To domesticate a wild animal, says Diamond, it must be sufficiently docile, submissive to humans, cheap to feed, immune to diseases, able to grow rapidly, and breed well in captivity. Although Africa is the continent of big mammals, none of these large beasts could be domesticated, as not one fulfilled all the criteria Diamond mentioned. An elephant can be tamed, yes, but its offspring will be genetically similar to an elephant that roams in the wild. Even today, with all our modern technology, we still cannot domesticate any of Africa's large mammals. The only two animals to be domesticated south of the Sahara are the guinea fowl (around 0 CE) and the hedgehog (in the 1980s).[3]

Those living in the Fertile Crescent and elsewhere in Eurasia had a very different experience with their animals. Cattle, horses and sheep were used for a variety of purposes – as a source of food and clothing, for transport, and for pulling ploughs. Even though the Egyptians and other North Africans acquired these animals quite early, tropical African diseases, notably the tsetse fly, delayed the spread of livestock further south. The low yields of yams compared with wheat, barley, rice and corn, and the delayed access to large, domesticated mammals, are two of the most important reasons why Africans south of the Equator never produced the large civilisations that Eurasia did.

The Khoesan, who lived south of the tropics, were simply unlucky not to live in a region with many domesticable plants and animals. Once Bantu speakers had domesticated yams in western Africa they were enabled to move east and, in a second wave, south after they acquired new crops (like sorghum), domesticated animals (like cattle) and new technologies (like ironworking). These new crops, animals and technologies had come from North Africa and Western Asia. The advantages of these technologies allowed them to displace or, in a few cases, absorb the existing Khoesan people.

And that is why isiXhosa has clicks in it. The Bantu-speaking migrants, with their ironworking tools and summer-rainfall crops, moved all the way south until they reached the borders of a region that had a Mediterranean, winter-rainfall climate. Here their crops could not grow, and they could not displace the Khoesan entirely. Over hundreds of years they instead integrated with eastern

Khoesan clans, adopting (some of the) clicks into their language. The fact that the Bantu migration came to a halt roughly at the Fish River in the Eastern Cape allowed the various Khoesan clans to remain in the small, winter-rainfall region at the south-western tip of the continent, trading, marrying and sometimes warring with their more technologically advanced Bantu-speaking neighbours to their north-east. This is the situation European explorers found when they first sailed round the Cape of Good Hope, in approximately 1500 CE. The guns, germs and steel that the European explorers brought with them had nothing to do, as Diamond notes, 'with differences between European and African peoples themselves'. Rather, they were due to 'accidents of geography and biogeography'.[4] The luck of geography helps to explain part of the global income distribution today.

5 How Did Joseph and His Eleven Brothers Solve the Three Economic Problems?
Custom and Command in the Ancient World

Throughout human history, societies have had to solve three economic problems. The first is to ensure that enough goods are produced. The second is that enough of the right goods are produced. The third is that these things are distributed fairly to everyone. The first two are problems of production and the third is a problem of distribution.

How did societies in the distant past solve the problems of production and distribution? John Hicks, in *A Theory of Economic History*, proposes three ways humans have done so. The first is through custom (sometimes also known as tradition). Imagine a San hunter-gatherer or Nguni farmer: the decision about what to produce and how to distribute that production was almost entirely determined by beliefs or customs that had been handed down from generation to generation. Tasks and occupations, titles and hierarchies were inherited. If you were a Batswana *kgosi* (chief), it was very likely you were also the son of a *kgosi*. The same was true of distribution: there were set customs according to which a successful gemsbok kill by a San hunter would be distributed among the rest of the family and clan.[1] The tributes that a Batswana herder would have to pay the chief were shared in a similar fashion. Even today elements of the custom approach live on in almost all societies: the children of doctors, for example, often follow in their parents' footsteps.

The custom approach means that production and distribution are organised in the same way they always have been. For most of human history this was how we organised our societies: we did just the same things that our elders did, and they did just the same thing their elders had done, and so on. It was a static solution to the two economic problems of production and distribution, but it ensured our survival for a long time.

Yet the custom approach came with a heavy cost: there was almost no progress. If we believed the same thing our elders did and we followed the same routines they did, then there was no reason to innovate and improve things. Parents were happy if their children survived into adulthood and could achieve the same standard of living as they themselves had. There was no sense of building a better life for one's children.

To change things required another solution to the three problems: command. As we have seen from Chapter 2, at some stage societies became sufficiently complex to justify a steep hierarchy of power and position. Imagine the pharaohs of ancient Egypt: they had the power to command their people to build great monuments such as pyramids. This was surely not tradition at work; it was, rather, a ruler who gave orders to produce and distribute things in a new way.

The great advantage of the command approach is its ability to force economic change. Later in this book we will discuss at least two modern societies that have explicitly opted to solve the problems of production and distribution in this way (in Chapter 22 we will encounter Stalinist Russia; and in Chapter 24, Mao's China). But these societies are not unique: almost any modern economy has some element of command, such as a monarchy or parliament that makes decisions about how tax revenues must be spent. Command is especially useful in times of crisis – such as when natural disasters, wars or pandemics occur – to ensure that production and distribution are maintained.

The command approach may be attractive to spur change, but it has one major weakness: it removes personal freedom. Once a pharaoh dictated that a pyramid should be built, the workers – in the ancient world, they were most often slaves – had no choice in the matter. In the Soviet Union, as we will see, the Politburo's decisions forced citizens to produce and consume things that others decided for them. What work you do, what you earn, where you live, and often even what you read and who you are allowed to socialise with are not up to you. Command comes at the great cost of personal economic freedom.

The third way to solve the problems of production and distribution is the market approach. Here, everyone does as he or she pleases – there is no custom or command that dictates what one must do. The production and distribution processes are, instead, entirely determined by the consumers in society, who in turn react to and determine the movement of prices. As winter approaches and more umbrellas are needed, it is not up to the king or custom to produce more umbrellas; it is producers who react to the price mechanism. The more consumers who want umbrellas, the greater the demand. And the greater the demand, the higher the price. And the higher the price, the greater the incentive for producers to make more umbrellas. Voila!

It sounds extraordinarily simple, but the market approach hinges on a fundamental truth. It requires that the fibres of society be strong: a market system can only succeed where there is trust. The fact that I can walk into a shop and purchase an umbrella from a stranger with little pieces of paper (or, nowadays, an electronic card or even a few clicks on my mobile phone) is only possible because of our trust in the system. Today, most societies solve many of their production and distribution problems through the market approach.

The study of economics is mostly concerned with why the market approach has been so successful in solving the three economic problems. Yet it is only recently that the market approach has become the preferred solution. For most of human history, custom and command were largely the ways in which the problems of production and distribution were solved. In hunter-gatherer groups or Neolithic farming communities, custom was the preferred approach. And in the more complex ancient civilisations of the Sumerians, Egyptians, Chinese, Indians, Greeks, Mesoamericans, Romans and many more, the command approach was central to production and distribution, despite the fact that all of these societies also used prices to exchange goods.

In fact, it is best not to see these three approaches as absolutes. They are more like the corners of a triangle. Sometimes societies are more likely to be in the custom corner, with little command or market activity. At other times, when a powerful leader emerges, these societies might gravitate towards the command approach. And at other times again, perhaps when there is a new technological or institutional innovation, that same society might move more towards the market approach.

What determines these gravitational pulls in one or the other direction? The historian Steven Marks provides a fascinating answer: it is access to information.[2] In *The Information Nexus*, Marks explains that the profit motive has existed since ancient times. But the ability of farmers to trade had always been limited by their poor access to information. There simply were no quick and reliable communication and transport networks that would allow them to get their produce to market, or allow traders the opportunity for arbitrage – buying low in one place to sell high in another. But as technology improved – the wheel, the printing press, the computer – so did our access to information, and our ability to interact and exchange. Sometimes information was monopolised by the government, which meant greater command and control. But in other times, at least over the last several hundred years, new systems, institutions and technologies have democratised information, pushing us towards the market approach.

The Hebrew Bible is a somewhat surprising way to illustrate how the lack of information constrained a market approach. Genesis 37 tells the story of Joseph and his eleven brothers. Joseph was born around 1562 BCE, the eleventh son of Jacob, who lived in Canaan, or what is roughly modern-day Israel. He was especially loved by his father, and his brothers became jealous of him. While they were herding sheep one day, they sold Joseph for twenty pieces of silver to a caravan of Ishmaelite traders. The traders took Joseph to Egypt, where he was sold to Potiphar, the captain of the pharaoh's guard. Potiphar's wife, however, tried to seduce Joseph and he was then put in prison.

There he correctly interpreted the dreams of the pharaoh's butler and baker, and two years later, after the pharaoh had strange dreams himself, he was summoned to interpret those too. He predicted seven years of abundance and seven years of famine. The pharaoh believed him and put him in charge of gathering and storing all the surplus grain from across Egypt during the first seven years, in anticipation of the years of famine. When the seven years of famine came, just as Joseph had predicted, Egypt was the only place that had food.

Joseph's remarkable story reveals much of the economy of the ancient world. Clearly, there were long-distance traders – evidence of some market activity. But the rest of Joseph's story is full of custom and command. All his brothers were farmers, just like their father. The pharaoh commanded him to build storage facilities; it was certainly not a forward-thinking, profit-maximising investor that did so.

Canaan and Egypt, much like all the other ancient civilisations, were predominantly agricultural societies ruled by autocrats – societies that relied predominantly on a combination of custom and command. Trade in the market was, at best, a peripheral activity. This would only begin to change after new innovations and institutions in towns and cities lowered the costs of information and incentivised market-oriented solutions to the three economic problems. Why agriculture remained such an important part of the economy for so long will be the subject of the next chapter.

6 What Do Charlemagne and King Zwelithini Have in Common?
Feudalism

On Christmas Day in the year 800 CE, Charlemagne, the king of the Franks and the Lombards, and father of at least eighteen children, was crowned 'Emperor of the Romans' by Pope Leo III at Old St Peter's Basilica in Rome. Charlemagne thereby united most of Western Europe under his rule, a vast area home to between 10 and 20 million people.[1] Almost all of these people lived in the countryside.

The reason for this was that, after the fall of the Roman Empire in the fifth century CE, Western Europe was characterised by conflict, population decline and de-urbanisation (the movement of people from the cities to rural areas). The Romans, of course, were known for their prosperous cities. A visitor to Rome today can still see the impressive ancient architecture of the Palatine Hill, the Forum, the Colosseum, and the Pantheon. But there were many other even more impressive architectural wonders built across the Roman Empire, which suggest an empire of opulent cities: the Library of Celsus in Ephesus (Selçuk), Turkey, the Aqueduct of Segovia in Spain, the Temple of Baalbek in Lebanon, Diocletian's Palace in Croatia, and the Arena of Nîmes in France.

But these ancient Roman cities were unlike those we know today in an important aspect. Most cities in the ancient world had one purpose: to benefit a small elite. Power was attained not through producing things, but through politics and warfare. No one remembers the famous innovators or entrepreneurs of ancient Rome, but we all know the famous emperors and generals – people like Julius Caesar and Mark Antony.

This meant that the cities of the ancient world maintained a parasitic relationship with farmers; they extracted the surplus from the farms but gave little in return. That is why most farm workers were slaves, usually people captured through conquest, even in 'democratic' Greece. The Roman economy depended, to a large extent, on acquiring new territories that would supply food or slave and bonded labour to sustain its affluent cities and large armies. The wealth of a few depended on the unfreedom of many.

Why the Roman Empire collapsed remains the subject of much debate. It was the historian William McNeill, in his 1976 book *Plagues and Peoples*, who suggested that one important factor could be the Plague of Cyprian around 250 CE. This plague killed about half the population of the Roman Empire.[2] Pandemics like these, McNeill argues, left the empire with a population too small to support its large military and state bureaucracy. The parasitic nature of the cities had become too heavy a burden on the dwindling population of farmers and slaves in the countryside.

The fall of Rome marks the start of the Middle Ages, which lasted from about the fifth to the fifteenth centuries.[3] In Europe this period was characterised by feudalism, a system structured around the relationship between land and labour. The economic historian Marc Bloch identified two types of relationship in the context of feudalism.[4] The first was between the lord and the vassal. Charlemagne, as king, had many vassals who managed his vast lands. In exchange for the land (also known as a fief) they were required to serve as knights in his armies. The second relationship was between the vassals (knights) and their serfs. The serfs worked the land of the vassal in exchange for physical protection.

What should be clear is that the feudal economy was almost entirely based on agriculture. The reason is quite simple: farming then was far less productive than it is today. In the ancient and feudal world, two families in agriculture could, if things went well, support one family in non-agriculture. That meant that about 70 per cent of all people who worked had to do so in agriculture to sustain those who did not, such as soldiers or craftsmen. Things today are very different. Let's take the largest economy in our time and also the largest exporter of food: the United States. Although around 2.6 million Americans work in agriculture, this accounts for only

1.3 per cent of the total employed US population. Farmers are vastly more productive today than they were in the past.[5]

One reason for this low level of agricultural productivity was that the serfs of feudal Europe had almost no incentive to produce large surpluses or invent new techniques that would allow them to do so. Any surplus would simply be extracted by the vassal or his king. And even if there was an incentive to produce more, there were limited means to do so: because they did not own the land they worked on, they could not use it as collateral to obtain loans to reinvest in capital equipment such as irrigation or acquire more land to achieve economies of scale.

It is true that not all production was limited to the country-side in feudal Europe. Villages and towns, especially after the twelfth century, did produce an increasing array of manufactured goods. These producers were often organised into guilds. A guild was an association of skilled artisans that specialised in the production of a specific good, such as weavers, jewellers and blacksmiths. Sometimes guilds in a number of towns would form a long-distance trading association. The most famous of these was the Hanseatic League, which at its height in the fourteenth century stretched from the Netherlands in the west to Russia in the east and achieved a monopoly over maritime trade in the Baltic Sea.

The wonderfully preserved Market Square of Brussels gives us a glimpse today into the assortment of guilds at the time: walk along its western side, and you will pass the House of the Corporation of Bakers, the House of the Corporation of Greasers, the House of the Corporation of Carpenters, the House of the Oath of Archers, the House of the Corporation of Boatmen and the House of the Corporation of Haberdashers.[6] But despite the rich decorations of their houses, guilds were based on poor economics. Guilds would limit new entrants into the market, thus reducing competition and ensuring high prices for their goods. Apprentices often had to spend years learning from a master craftsman. The reason for this, the guilds maintained, was to ensure a high-quality product, but it came, much as in agriculture, at the cost of new innovations.[7]

We might think that this feudal world is far removed from our own setting, but for a third of South Africans it would sound very familiar. That is because these South Africans still live in areas that have very similar feudal institutions. The Charlemagne of our era is the king of the Zulu, an ethnic group of between 10 and 12 million people.

The Zulu monarch – Misuzulu Zulu, appointed on 7 May 2021 after the death of his father, Goodwill Zwelithini, who reigned from 1971 to 2021 – is the sole trustee of the Ingonyama Trust, a corporate entity which owns 30 per cent of the land in KwaZulu-Natal, one of South Africa's nine provinces. Much as in the time of Charlemagne, the Zulu king has vassals – traditional leaders or chiefs – who lease land to Zulu household heads, many of whom are subsistence farmers. Although there are strong customary laws that protect the rights of these Zulu households, these are usage and not ownership rights, which means that the land cannot be used as collateral for loans. The economic outcomes in Zululand are thus not very different from those in feudal Europe: farmers have little incentive to expand production, acquire neighbouring farms or invest in capital equipment that can make them more productive.

Feudalism is a system that discourages innovation and improvement. Western Europeans during the Middle Ages would only see a sustained improvement in their living standards when they adopted a new attitude towards economic life.

7 Why Do Indians Have Dowry and Africans Lobola?
Pre-Colonial African Economic Systems

Africa is a massive continent. One could fit all of Western and Eastern Europe (including the UK), India, Japan and China, and the United States into the continent, and still have space left. Africa, of course, has far fewer people. In 2021 an estimated 1.4 billion people lived on the African continent. The combined number for those other countries was a startling 3.7 billion people.

This makes Africa a land-abundant continent. In other words, Africa has a low labour-to-land ratio – there are about 46 people for every square kilometre in Africa as compared to 150 people, on average, in those other regions. The numbers for China (153), Western Europe (174) and India (464) are much higher.[1]

This high land–labour ratio is not a new phenomenon. Africa has historically also had an abundance of land relative to the number of people who can work it. As we will see in this chapter, it has shaped the types of production systems and institutions that developed on the continent.

Our story begins around 1000 CE. This is roughly when the Bantu migration had reached the Eastern Cape of South Africa and when Islam had spread to most of North Africa. Although there were some societies, notably in West Africa, that specialised in mining and light manufacturing, notably textiles, most African societies were predominantly agricultural. There are three main reasons for this. The first we have already encountered in Chapter 4: Africans were unlucky that they did not have access to domesticable plants and animals, as Eurasians did, which meant that the agricultural surpluses that could sustain large towns and cities were absent.

The second reason is the high land–labour ratio.[2] It is this ratio that also explains the type of farming most prevalent: most Africans practised extensive agriculture; that is, they did not use a lot of inputs to keep the land fertile. Once the soil became depleted, they picked up their things and moved on. There was thus little incentive to invest in capital goods such as irrigation or storage and transport infrastructure. The third reason is the harsh environment. Many parts of Africa are not only characterised by poor soil conditions but also have high disease burdens. These include the tsetse fly, malaria and sleeping sickness.

Of course, these are broad generalisations. It helps to be more specific, and to do that, we follow the economic historian Erik Green and divide the continent into five ecological zones. These are the tropical rainforest, the savannah, the highlands, the deserts and the temperate zones.[3] Figure 7.1 shows the location of these zones.

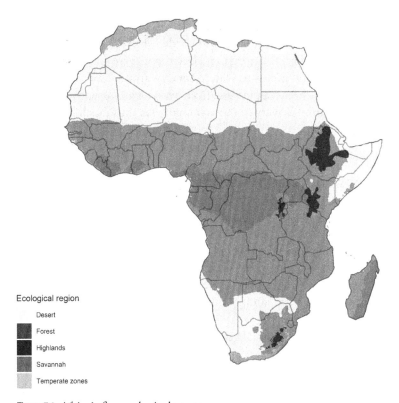

Figure 7.1 Africa's five ecological zones

Because most Africans traditionally lived in only three of these – the rainforests, savannah and highlands – we will continue to discuss the economic systems of only those three.

The forests of West and Central Africa were both a blessing and a curse. Yams, palm oil and plantains (a type of banana) were the most popular crops, not only because they produced high yields in the fertile soil, but also because they did not require a lot of labour. The curse of the forests was disease. Malaria affected – and still affects – many people, and the tsetse fly, unique to Africa, killed animals, making cattle breeding almost impossible. Research by the economist Marcella Alsan shows that ethnic groups that lived in tsetse-fly areas were less likely to use domesticated animals and the plough and, as a consequence, had lower population density.[4] Those who inhabited the rainforests thus had to balance the benefits of the labour-saving, high-yield crops with the costs of debilitating diseases that affected the productivity of humans and animals.

The savannah was usually less fertile than the forests but had the benefit of a lower disease burden. Here the most common crops were millet and sorghum, but these were limited to those places with good access to water, notably around lakes and rivers. The areas of the savannah far from water were usually uninhabited. Population density in the savannah was thus much lower than in the forests.

The highlands, found in northern Tanzania, central Kenya and Ethiopia, were the only regions where Africans developed intensive agriculture. It is useful to pause for a moment here to understand why that is so. The highlands were not only very fertile, they were also free from most of the diseases that plagued the forests and the savannahs. This allowed African farmers to invest in irrigation and other ways of preserving the land, such as terracing or manuring. In some cases, such as the highlands of Ethiopia, the plough was introduced, which further boosted agricultural productivity. Fertile land, combined with capital investment, produced larger surpluses, greater population density and more complex political systems. It is thus not entirely surprising that Ethiopia was one of the few African countries never to be colonised by Europeans.

The geography of Africa affected not only its production systems, but also the social, political and cultural institutions that developed alongside them. The shortage of labour and abundance of land meant that the most valuable commodity was never land, as in Western Europe and India, for example. It was people. Warring neighbours had little incentive to steal land from each another – that was the abundant resource. Instead, they stole people. The high land–labour ratio gave rise to indigenous African slavery long before the emergence of the Atlantic slave trade.

Labour shortages also meant that family members were often the only source of labour. Social status was therefore closely associated with the number of children in a household. Men thus competed intensively for women, which gave rise to the social institution of bride price, the practice by which a husband's family paid compensation to the family of the bride for the loss of her labour and company. Polygamy, the practice of having more than one wife, was another social institution that emerged as a consequence of the labour shortage.

Similar institutions would not emerge in parts of the world with low land–labour ratios. India, for example, has the practice of dowry payments, in which there is a transfer of money or gifts from the wife's family to the husband's upon marriage. In Africa, with its high land–labour ratio, institutions such as lobola, as bride price is known in South Africa, became commonplace.

All of this may give the impression of a very unchanging pre-colonial economy and society. But it would be a mistake to come to that conclusion. Pre-colonial African economic systems were diverse and dynamic. The diversity can be attributed to the varied ecological environments we have described above. The dynamism was largely a consequence of the availability of new technologies. We have already seen, in Chapter 4, how Iron Age tools allowed Bantu-speaking migrants to displace Stone Age Khoesan. But the most important 'technology' of the pre-colonial era was new crop types. One, in particular, stands out. Maize (corn or 'mealies') was introduced into Africa around 1600 CE. It was first domesticated in the Americas and then found its way across the Atlantic aboard Portuguese ships. It was quickly adopted by African farmers because of its high energy yield, its low labour requirements, and its short growing season.

The adoption of maize had long-term consequences. We have already seen how the internal African slave trade was an institutional response to the high land–labour ratio on the continent. What maize did was to boost population growth significantly. Two economists, Jevan Cherniwchan and Juan Moreno-Cruz, show that in places that were suitable for maize agriculture, notably West Africa, population growth increased after the introduction of maize.[5] They then show that it was also here that slave shipments to the Americas increased most rapidly.

Maize had one important detrimental quality: it was not very resistant to drought. This meant that production could vary enormously depending on the weather. In good years the surplus was large, but bad years could lead to famine. As a result, African farmers had to diversify their production across a variety of crops. Erik Green summarises this best:

> From what we know about the forest and savannah regions, it seems likely that hunger was common, and famines occurred quite regularly. Diversification rather than special-isation was the most important strategy for coping with hunger crises and famines. People grew a variety of crops and tried, as far as possible, to exploit a variety of environments. Cultivation of drought resistant crops like cassava continued to be an important strategy despite the spread of maize, and people invested in livestock even where there was a shortage of grazing land.[6]

Africans were unlucky to live on a continent with low-yielding crops and a harsh environment. This meant that they had to diversify their production, which in turn reduced their surpluses and kept population sizes small, leading to a high land–labour ratio. This gave rise to institutions that entrenched property rights in people rather than in land. Elements of both institutions – slavery and bride price – persist into the present.

8 Who Was the Richest Man Ever to Live?
The Spread of Islam in Africa and the Crusades

Around 1300 CE, so the legend goes, the king of the Malian empire in West Africa hatched a plan. He believed that the earth was round and wanted to prove it, so he equipped 200 boats full of men and another 200 full of gold, water and victuals, and sent them west. After a long time only one boat returned, reporting that 'we have navigated for a long time, until we saw in the midst of the ocean as if a big river was flowing violently'.[1] Not happy with the answer of the only boat to escape the danger, the king doubled down, and equipped 2,000 boats for a second voyage. This time he travelled with them. Just before he left he put his deputy in charge. The king and his fleet never returned. In 1312 this deputy became the tenth ruler of the Mali empire. His name was Mansa Musa.

In 2015 the online magazine *Money* compiled a list of the ten richest men in history. Mansa Musa was ranked first. Although it is a somewhat silly exercise given the difficulty of comparing wealth across regions and time periods, there is no doubt that Musa was indescribably affluent. As the story about his predecessor already demonstrates, the source of the Malian empire's wealth was its rich gold and salt mines, whose contents were exported across the Sahara to North Africa and Europe. But Musa was not content to rely on the natural resources of his empire. He embarked on a large construction programme, building mosques and madrasas (centres of learning) in Timbuktu and Gao, including the famous University of Sankoré in the former city, which had one of the largest libraries in the world.

He also expanded the Mali empire substantially, adding at least twenty-four cities and their territories. By the end of his rule the Malian empire would include most of modern-day Mali, Senegal, The Gambia, Guinea, Niger, Nigeria, Chad and Mauritania.

Musa was a devout Muslim, and is best remembered for the journey he took in 1324 to Mecca for his hajj pilgrimage. His procession reportedly consisted of 60,000 men, including 12,000 slaves. Thousands of horses and camels carried gold bars and bags of gold dust, silk and other gifts, which he generously donated to the cities and the poor on his way east. Yet his generosity would soon have consequences: because of the influx of gold, the prices of goods and wares became greatly inflated. This was the only time in recorded history that one man directly controlled the price of gold in the Mediterranean.

By the time Musa became king, Islam was well established in Africa, arriving soon after the death of the Prophet Muhammad in 632 CE. It first spread rapidly to Egypt (642 CE) and Libya (647 CE), which were then under Byzantine rule. In 698 CE Muslim Arabs conquered Carthage, in what is now Tunisia, expanding the Umayyad caliphate to all of North Africa. In the first two decades of the next century the caliphate would also occupy most of Iberia, modern-day Spain and Portugal, so that its empire extended from the Atlantic coast in the west to Pakistan and Uzbekistan in the east, an area including approximately 33 million people, making it one of the largest empires in history.

The caliphate ruled over a multi-ethnic population. Christians, who were still the majority of the population, and Jews were allowed to continue practising their faiths, but had to pay a poll tax from which Muslims were exempt. This, as economic historian Mohamed Saleh shows, helps us to understand income differences between Christians and Muslims in Egypt today.[2]

Saleh asks why it is that Copts (Egyptian Christians) were far more affluent in the nineteenth century than Egyptian Muslims; 33 per cent of Copts, for example, worked in white-collar jobs, compared to only 14 per cent of Muslims. That Copts were so much more affluent than Muslims is all the more surprising because before the Arab conquest of Egypt in 642 almost everyone was Christian, and there has been little in- and out-migration since then. Saleh argues that the Copts' relative affluence can be ascribed to the head tax imposed after the conquest. It worked like this: because the poll tax was a regressive tax – in other words, it affected the poor more than the rich – it incentivised poorer Egyptians to convert from Christianity to Islam. Because this happened over more than 1,200 years, by the end almost all the Copts who remained were rich compared with the much larger but poorer Muslim population. There was thus nothing inherently different between Christians and Muslims in nineteenth-century Egypt; the reason why Copts were wealthier was religious self-selection over more than a millennium.

Islam travelled across the Sahara and into West Africa with Arabic traders. The first to convert, by the middle of the tenth century, were the inhabitants of the Sahara, the Berbers. Thereafter it spread into the Senegambia region, Mali, Chad and, later, Hausaland in northern Nigeria. Although some African kings tried to resist its influence, Islam spread rapidly for at least four reasons: it accepted many of the African customs (such as polygamy); it provided access to formal education and scientific knowledge; it was often used as justification for war (jihad); and it advanced long-distance trade by reducing transaction costs between peoples of different ethnicities.[3]

At the same time that Islam began to expand throughout West Africa, Christians in Western Europe were joining the Crusades in an attempt to reclaim the Holy Land from Islam. Figure 8.1 shows the various empires that ruled over Jerusalem from 2000 BCE to 2000 CE. Note the turn to Islam from the seventh century. The Crusades were a series of religious wars between Christians and Muslims from the eleventh to the fifteenth centuries that had some initial successes for the former. But the Crusades did not only comprise Church-sanctioned wars against Muslims. Several Crusades involved campaigns against pagans and heretics, or simply opportunistic attempts to gain political or territorial advantage. One branch of the Crusades was aimed at conquering the Iberian Peninsula (present-day Spain and Portugal) from the Muslims. Some 780 years after the Umayyad conquest of Iberia, the Nasrid kingdom of Granada – one of the longest-ruling Muslim dynasties in the region and the builders of the still awe-inspiring Alhambra palace complex – finally fell in 1492 to the expanding Christian Spanish kingdoms of Castile and Aragon.

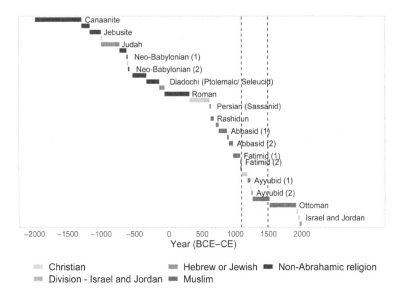

Figure 8.1 Timeline of Jerusalem's history, showing the start and end of the Crusades

Economic historians Lisa Blaydes and Christopher Paik argue that the Crusades may help us to understand why it was that Western Europe, a relatively poor and backward region by 1000 CE, began to discard the feudal institutions that we discussed in Chapter 6.[4] They first identify the geographical origins of each of the crusading forces in the Holy Land. They then show that, after taking into account underlying levels of religiosity and economic development, regions where large numbers of crusaders were recruited experienced increased political stability, a higher probability of establishing parliamentary institutions, higher downstream levels of tax revenue, as well as greater urbanisation after their return. The reason for these developments, according to Blaydes and Paik, is that the Crusades impelled Europeans to abandon the personal relationships that characterised feudalism and move towards the creation of increasingly impersonal and consolidated states. 'European monarchs began to enjoy greater political power over what had previously been a loose network of decentralised local elites.'[5] This is important for two reasons. First, economic historians have always dated the emergence of representative political institutions in Europe to events after 1500; the research of Blaydes and Paik shows that events that occurred much earlier were also important in the process. Second, their study demonstrates that Europe did not create these institutions in isolation: developments in the Islamic world, much of it in North and West Africa, are critical to understanding the evolution of European political institutions.

9 How Did 168 Spanish Conquistadores Capture an Empire?
Europeans in the New World

In 1532 a motley band of 168 Spanish soldiers arrived on the outskirts of Cajamarca, the capital of the mighty Incan empire in present-day Peru. Already on his third expedition to the New World, Francisco Pizarro had one aim: to find gold and claim it for the Spanish king. He first sent his trusted captain, Hernando de Soto, to meet with the Incan emperor – Atahualpa – and invite him to a meeting. De Soto rode out on his horse. It was the first time Atahualpa had ever seen such an animal. Impressed with his strange visitor, he agreed to meet Pizarro the next day.

Pizarro, however, had different plans. He prepared an ambush and, when Atahualpa arrived with 6,000 unarmed men, he attacked with 106 soldiers on foot and 62 on horses. The Incas were completely caught off guard; about 2,000 Inca died in the volleys of gunfire that ensued. In what is now known as the Battle of Cajamarca on 16 November 1532, Atahualpa was captured and used to extract a massive ransom from the Incas over the next few months: enough gold to fill a room and silver that could fill two. Once Pizarro believed there was not much more that could be extracted, he asked that Atahualpa be baptised and then executed. Atahualpa's last words reflected his continuing disbelief at what had happened: 'What have I done, or my children, that I should meet such a fate? And from your hands, too, you who have met with friendship and kindness from my people, with whom I have shared my treasures, who have received nothing but benefits from my hands!' After Atahualpa's death the Spanish would continue to use force against the inhabitants of the area until the last Inca monarch was murdered in 1572, four decades after Pizarro's arrival.

But was the conquest really so easy? Were the Incas so impotent as to be unable to protect themselves against 168 Spanish soldiers? Of course not. It helps to know a bit of what happened before Pizarro's arrival. Atahualpa had just concluded a civil war with his half-brother, Huáscar. In fact, the news of the final victory arrived on the same day that Pizarro and his troops arrived in the town of Cajamarca. Atahualpa's strongest armies and smartest generals were far away from Cajamarca. Pizarro and his men not only faced a much-weakened enemy, but they had three things that counted in their favour. First, the Inca empire was already suffering from smallpox and other diseases that Europeans had brought with them on previous trips. Second, Pizarro had, on his way to Cajamarca, made alliances with smaller indigenous groups that were upset with Atahualpa. Third, Pizarro was quick and ruthless. He used the surprise of his guns and horses on people who had never seen these technologies before, to stunning effect.

Atahualpa's story is perhaps the most dramatic in the colonisation of the Americas, but it is not unfamiliar. Wherever Europeans arrived, indigenous 'Americans' suffered, either through direct conflict, such as in the case of Atahualpa, or, most often, through disease and loss of resources. It is very difficult to know exactly how many people died; numbers are, at best, fragmentary, even for those regions with prolonged European contact. Our best guesstimate is that 37 million people lived in Mexico and Central and South America in 1492, the year Christopher Columbus reached the Americas. That would imply a death rate from disease of about 80 per cent by 1650, when only 9 million people remained. It would only be by the late nineteenth century that Latin America's population numbers again reached the same level as in 1500.

The arrival of Europeans brought not only demographic upheaval but also economic disruption. Europeans set up colonies all across the Americas, from modern-day Canada in the north through Central America and the Caribbean to Argentina in the south. Their experiences were not the same. The places most sought after by the Europeans were those in the tropical climates. This was because farming there was incredibly profitable; European settlers could produce and sell commodities such as sugar and tobacco to the 'Old World' and so attain remarkably high standards of living. In 1700, for example, inhabitants of the British colonies in North America had incomes similar to European settlers living in Mexico. European inhabitants of Barbados and Cuba, by contrast, had incomes that were at least 50 per cent higher. Even in 1800, on a per capita basis, Haiti was probably the richest country in the world, and the Caribbean was still more affluent than the territories that would become the United States.

Today we know things are very different. The United States is one of the richest countries in the world (with GDP per capita in 2018 of $55,335), while Haiti is one of the poorest ($1,729).[1] To put it another way, the average person in the United States is thirty-two times more affluent than the average person in Haiti. How can we explain this reversal of fortunes?

One feature of the Caribbean colonies, as well as other tropical regions, was a high marginal product of labour – in other words, they attained more output from employing additional labour. Crops such as sugar, coffee, rice, cotton and tobacco flourished. These crops demanded a large labour force. When there were not enough European labourers settling in the area – or not enough of them who could survive malaria and other tropical diseases – a substitute was found. Millions of Africans were shipped to the Americas as slaves to work on these plantations.[2] This gave rise to a specific production system: large landholdings (owned by European settlers or absentee European landlords) with large numbers of African slaves working in the fields. This system was naturally characterised by high levels of inequality.

This system was not found everywhere in the Americas. In the more temperate zones of the northern United States, Canada and Argentina, a different production system arose. It was not profitable to employ slaves on these farms because of the comparably low marginal product of labour (the value of output each additional worker could produce). Instead, most European households farmed by themselves, usually with grains or hays, perhaps employing a few recent European immigrants as wage labourers during the harvest season. These new immigrants would only work until they had enough saved up to purchase their own (small) farms. In these temperate zones, a far more equal distribution of income existed.

The economic historians Stanley Engerman and Kenneth Sokoloff help us to understand how these early conditions would affect the development paths of these regions.[3] In the tropics, the small elite (the landowners) that emerged because of the system of production began to adopt institutions that protected their privileges. They first ensured that only they had political rights, and thus had a controlling say over the laws and other institutions of the country. This enabled them to impose land policies that benefited themselves, often through measures that discriminated on the basis of race. It also enabled them to restrict education to their own children. In addition, they closed off the country to other European immigrants, which meant they did not have to share their privileges with more people. In short, they ensured that only a small group of European settlers and their descendants had access to the things that make economic freedom possible. The rest of society, the indigenous populations and the enslaved Africans, obtained none of these freedoms.

Almost the exact opposite happened in the temperate zones. There, farms were smaller, often equal in size and owned by those who worked the land. Although there was a degree of inequality – some people had arrived earlier and thus had more time to develop their farms – an elite that could prevent immigrants from obtaining the political and economic rights they needed to prosper never emerged. This meant that these regions were more democratic in their political systems (although women and freed slaves were often still excluded) and education was more widely accessible than in tropical regions. Immigration was also rarely inhibited, so that throughout the seventeenth to the early twentieth centuries there was a constant stream of new migrants from Europe (and, later, from elsewhere in the world).

Engerman and Sokoloff argue that these institutions explain the reversal of fortunes that the different regions of the Americas experienced between the eighteenth and twentieth centuries. Severely unequal societies developed institutions that protected the privileges of a few. While this made them initially quite wealthy, it came 'at the cost of society not realising the full economic potential of disadvantaged groups'.[4] More equal societies shared their economic and political freedoms, giving everyone a chance to live the 'American dream'. The consequence was that, once modern economic growth began in the nineteenth century, it would be the societies with better education, greater political rights and a more equal distribution of property and income that would benefit most. The roots of America's prosperity and Haiti's poverty, according to Engerman and Sokoloff, lie in the institutions set up by the early European settlers on their arrival in the New World.

10 Why Was a Giraffe the Perfect Gift for the Chinese Emperor?
The Indian Ocean Trade and European Imperialism

On the east coast of Tanzania, south of Dar es Salaam, lies the tiny island of Kilwa Kisiwani. From the thirteenth to the fifteenth centuries the port city of Kilwa was the centre of trade for the entire Swahili coast, integrated in a trading network that stretched as far as Arabia, India and even China. The inhabitants of this beautiful city were ethnically mixed – including Persians, Arabs and Bantu-speaking Africans – and, over time, they developed a distinctive East African culture and language – Swahili, which literally means 'coast dwellers'. This cultural influence stretched all along the East African coast, from Inhambane and Sofala in the south (modern-day Mozambique) to Mombasa and Malindi (Kenya) and Mogadishu (Somalia) in the north.

The trade network along the East African coast had ancient roots. Some Chinese records suggest trade connections between Africans and Chinese as far back as the Han dynasty in China (206 BCE–220 CE). But much of our evidence come from archaeologists who have excavated and analysed glass beads in East Africa.[1] What their studies reveal is an intricate pattern of trade in places like Zanzibar dating back to between the eighth and tenth centuries. Two different types of networks seem to have existed. The first was trade with southern Africa (beads were found as far as Tsodilo Hills in modern-day Botswana), which seems to have been limited to the Persian Gulf, whereas in the second network, the East African cities of Zanzibar and Kilwa had direct connections with South Asia (India and Sri Lanka) and perhaps even China.

We do know that a Chinese ship visited the Swahili coast in 1417. When Zhu Di became emperor in 1402, he announced that a new capital would be built for China, in Beijing. He appointed his favourite commander, Zheng He, to lead massive expeditions to all the known parts of the world, including Africa, and conduct tributary missions. On his fifth voyage Commander Zheng arrived on the African coast to collect as many exotic goods as possible, including a giraffe. Why was he looking for a giraffe specifically?

A few years earlier the Chinese emperor had received a giraffe as a gift from the sultan of Bengal, who, in turn, had received it as a gift from an emissary of Malindi – in what looks like a medieval version of regifting! The giraffe caused a stir in China because it was thought to be similar to a mythical creature in Chinese folklore, a qilin, whose appearance was said to presage the imminent arrival of a great ruler. The arrival of a giraffe in China thus gave Emperor Zhu Di and his project of a new capital – with the Forbidden City at its centre – spiritual legitimacy.

The Chinese expansion and their trade voyages would not last long. China would turn inward, abandoning its foreign trade and refocusing its efforts on keeping the Mongols out of the new capital, Beijing, which was close to the Mongol border. These efforts would include building the Great Wall of China. While China was fighting the Mongols, a new oceanic power would soon arrive in the Indian Ocean, adding to the Chinese empire's need for defence: Western Europeans in search of spices.

By the end of the fifteenth century European monarchs began to send expeditions west and south in search of new routes to the East Indies. Spices were in high demand across Western Europe because of its importance in food preparation and medicine. Silk was in high demand too and was often used in church ceremonies and decorations. These commodities traditionally followed an intricate overland trade route to Europe from the spice islands in present-day eastern Indonesia, where nutmeg, mace and cloves were exclusively found, or from China, where silk was produced. The Venetians had long held a monopoly in the Mediterranean silk and spice trade with the Byzantine Empire in the Middle East, with both the Venetians and the Byzantines imposing hefty trade tariffs and making these goods prohibitively expensive. This gave an incentive for competing Western European powers to find alternative routes.

Knowledge of a possible route around Africa reached the Portuguese, probably from the Chinese, who must have known about the southern tip of Africa. The prospect of sailing around Africa directly to the source of the spice trade was incredibly appealing and the reason that, by the early fifteenth century, the Age of European Discovery began with several exploratory voyages along the African coast. The young Prince Henry the Navigator could see the profit-making opportunities for Portugal, and generously supported these ventures. Although the Portuguese made many discoveries during his lifetime, including the Atlantic islands of Madeira and Azores, it was only after the death of Henry in 1460 that Portuguese navigators started making significant progress in their search for a sea route to the spice-producing regions in the East. In 1488 the Portuguese explorer Bartolomeu Dias rounded the Cape of Storms, sailing as far as the Fish River before his crew forced him to turn back to Portugal. Ten years later, on 20 May 1498, Vasco da Gama finally reached Calicut in India, after stopping in Mozambique, Mombasa and Malindi on the East African coast. He returned to Lisbon on 10 July 1499, more than two years after departing. While the trip had come at a high cost – two ships were lost and more than half the crew had died – it showed that the spice trade around Africa could be a success. In the next century the Portuguese would continue their voyages into the Indian Ocean, establishing trading ports as far as Goa (in modern-day India), Malacca (Malaysia), Macau (China) and Nagasaki (Japan). Because of its convenient location on the east coast of Africa, Mozambique would later become a Portuguese colony.

The Portuguese voyages were quickly followed by those undertaken by other Western European countries. In the late sixteenth century the Dutch were at war with Spain. Because Portugal and Spain were allies, the Portuguese trade ships became an appropriate target for the Dutch navy – and, of course, the lucrative profits were attractive to Dutch merchants. But it was only with the establishment of the Dutch East India Company (VOC) in 1602 that Dutch shipping traffic around the southern tip of Africa really took off. The VOC was a chartered company with a formal monopoly from the Dutch government over the lucrative Asia trade. The Dutch trade, and later that of the British and French, would ultimately supplant most of the Indian Ocean trade networks of the Portuguese.

The arrival of more European traders in the Indian Ocean reduced the incredibly high profits enjoyed by those first voyages. Economic historian Jan de Vries explains why: '[The] European companies conducting trade with Asia via the Cape route faced a long-term deterioration of their profitability *as trading operations*. Their gross margins were under long-term pressure while transaction costs as a whole were stubbornly resistant to reduction.'[2] These companies had two options. They could either increase profitability by reducing transaction costs or they could extract political rents. For most of the seventeenth century they followed the former strategy. They did this by expanding their intra-Asian trade and improving the efficiency of their ships. But once this trade was blocked (for example, when Japan barred trade), the companies resorted to political rent extraction. By using their superior military power, they could gain direct control over Asian territories and force their new subjects to pay tolls and taxes. Although these types of income had never accounted for more than a small percentage of the VOC's Asian revenue in the seventeenth century, it reached 44 per cent by the 1760s.

But conquering territory was a fatal strategy. Despite the VOC's increased revenue from tolls and taxes, the costs of protecting and administering the territories were always greater. Although the British East India Company did slightly better from these revenue streams – notably because of the capture, in 1757 at the Battle of Plassey, of the lucrative Indian market and the Chinese opium trade – it would also come under frequent financial strain, and the company was dissolved by the mid-nineteenth century.[3]

What is clear is that, as de Vries notes, these trading companies 'were transformed into colonial rulers and/or replaced by their national states. What began as an age of globalisation – soft and limited, but real – ended as an age of colonialism, something completely different.'[4] The reason for this was the economic and political institutions of the time. Because they were national monopolies, the trading companies could count on the financial and military support of their national governments. Whereas a free market would have encouraged innovation, rent seeking was the preferred choice for these monopolistic merchant companies.

This change in strategy not only reduced the profits of the European shareholders but had devastating consequences for the millions of people in the newly conquered African and Asian territories. The European companies became colonial rulers. The Portuguese acquired Mozambique and Angola, the Dutch Indonesia and the English India. In many places, European traders displaced the local traders and rulers. This happened on the East African Swahili coast too. By the nineteenth century, after several invasions and occupation by the French, Kilwa Kisiwani was abandoned. There is little that remains today of this once majestic trade city. The story of Kilwa provides an early lesson in how monopoly companies can shape government policies to the detriment of ordinary consumers.

11 Who Visited Gorée Island on 27 June 2013?
The Atlantic Slave Trade and Africa's Long-Run Development

Gorée is a small island off the coast of Dakar, Senegal. Enjoying an exquisitely grilled filet de saint pierre in one of the harbour restaurants as the sun sets, it is easy to imagine the place as a summer resort for the West African rich and famous. But below its serene exterior lies a dark history.

On 27 June 2013 one of the descendants of the people who suffered under this dark history recounted her visit:

> We saw the dark, cramped cells where dozens of people were packed together for months on end, with heavy chains around their necks and arms. We saw the courtyard where they were forced to stand naked while buyers examined them, negotiated a price, and bought them as if they were nothing but property. And we saw what is known as 'The Door of No Return', a small stone doorway through which these men, women and children passed on their way to massive wooden ships that carried them across the ocean to a life of slavery in the United States and elsewhere – a brutal journey known as the 'Middle Passage'.[1]

Michelle Obama, the former First Lady of the United States, is a descendant of Africans who were shipped to the Americas to be sold as slaves. In total, about 13 million people were forcibly shipped across the Atlantic from Africa between the sixteenth and nineteenth centuries. An estimated 1.5 million of them died en route.

How did such a cruel system arise? As we've seen in Chapter 7, Africa has always had a high land–labour ratio. Because of the high demand for labour, women's ability to reproduce and men's ability to work the land were reflected in the cultural institutions that prevailed, such as bride price and slavery. Warfare in Africa was constantly a fight for labour, not land. Slavery was thus endemic to the continent, but, as economic historian Patrick Manning reminds us, it was small in scale.[2] Slavery can only exist if the captors have substantial resources and incentives to motivate their system of oppression. And it can only expand where there is significant demand for labour. Various factors can give rise to it, such as the presence of strong rulers with the ability to use force, the existence of markets for slave-produced goods, or the efforts of purchasers to transport captives some distance to where these conditions are met.

Although long-distance slave routes out of Africa had existed for centuries – such as the trans-Saharan route, the Red Sea route into Arabia, or the Indian Ocean route – all three conditions were only met after the Columbian Exchange – the transfer of products, people, plants and parasites across the Atlantic – had been established in the fifteenth century. By then, European traders had connected the fertile lands of the Americas with European demand for products such as sugar and coffee. To produce these commodities in the New World, the European conquerors needed labour – and Africa's existing institutions of slavery provided the answer.[3] European slave traders did not have to create completely new institutions. With the assistance of African slave traders, often in exchange for guns that further facilitated the capture of people deeper into the interior – what some scholars have called a vicious 'gun–slave cycle' – Africans were walked to the coast, to the slave ports where European slave ships would dock, waiting for their next shipment.[4] It was under these harrowing conditions in the sixteenth century that the largest and most violent slave trade in human history was born. It would continue until deep into the nineteenth century, for a period of more than 300 years.

The Atlantic slave trade, as Chapter 9 explains, shaped the development trajectory of the Americas in profound ways, giving rise to severe inequality in Latin America as well as institutions of exclusion that remain today. Far fewer Africans ended up in the United

States – as demonstrated by Figure 11.1, which maps the ten largest slave Atlantic slave routes. But even in the USA the legacies of the slave trade persist into the present. In 1870 the income of African Americans was 25 per cent of that of white Americans; by 2015 the number was higher, but still a distant 65 per cent.[5]

It is useful to ask to what extent slavery contributed to US development. As can be imagined, this is a fraught, and highly politicised, debate. On the one side, slavery is understood to have underpinned American prosperity. As historian Sven Beckett explains, slave labour was the largest input in cotton production, and raw cotton was the most important input into textiles, the leading sector of the Industrial Revolution.[6] The cheap, uncompensated labour of enslaved Africans, he argues, not only made slaveholders wealthy, but was the catalyst for American (and global) industrial take-off.

There are two concerns with Beckett's hypothesis. First, as the economic historians Alan Olmstead and Paul Rhode note, one should not equate unfree labour with cheap labour.[7] Just like the African continent, the USA was a land-abundant and labour-scarce country: 'just because slaves did not capture the benefits of their scarce labour does not mean that they were cheap'.[8] This means that America's comparative advantage in cotton production was not the result of cheap labour, but was rather the result of a succession of new cotton varieties that made cotton farming more productive than elsewhere in the world.[9] Biological innovation rather than labour expropriation seems to best explain cotton's success.

Second, economic historian Gavin Wright notes that although cheap cotton was undoubtedly important for the growth of textiles and for its contribution to the Industrial Revolution, cheap cotton did not require slavery.[10] How do we know this? Consider that after five years of civil war in the USA, which culminated in the abolition of slavery, cotton prices returned to their pre-war levels. Output increased after the Reconstruction. Coercion was not a necessary input into the production process.

A different interpretation of the contribution of slavery to American prosperity, then, is that the institution of slavery, with its unfathomable hardships and injustice, retarded the South's economic dynamism. Southern farmers grew prosperous not because

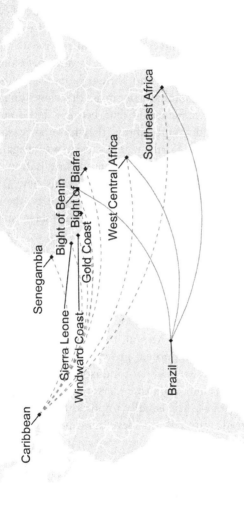

Figure 11.1 The top ten slave routes, with number of known voyages, 1650s–1860s

of access to cheap labour, or because of more sophisticated techniques of repression, as some have argued, but because of access to fertile land, high cotton prices and new crop types.[11] But once cotton varieties had improved and all available land had been settled, labour productivity stagnated. This was because the institution of slavery did not incentivise labour-displacing innovation. The famous Scottish philosopher who is widely regarded as the father of economics, Adam Smith, already noted this in his 1776 *Wealth of Nations*: 'slaves ... are very seldom inventive; and all the most important improvements, either in machinery or in the arrangement and distribution of work which facilitate and abridge labour, have been the discoveries of freemen'.[12] Smith did not mean that slaves do not have the ability to be inventive. He meant that, because they do not own the returns from their ideas and labour, they have no reason to be inventive. It would be the North, where slavery was illegal, rather than the South, that would lead America's industrialisation.

A more comparative approach supports this view. If slavery was indeed the driving force of American prosperity, then surely other countries that received large numbers of slave shipments would also have prospered. Brazil, as we have seen, was the largest recipient of enslaved Africans, and therefore provides a good comparison. Slaves constituted one-third of the Brazilian population in 1822, when the country became independent from Portugal. Yet Brazil was a poor country, and remained largely agricultural until the twentieth century. A recent study confirms that slavery was detrimental to rather than helpful for Brazilian development: 'Rather than promoting economic growth and development, the evidence shows that slavery held back industrialisation in Brazil.'[13]

Although it is important to understand the consequences of slavery in the Americas, it is equally important to know how the Atlantic slave trade affected the development trajectory of the Africans who remained behind on the continent. Manning has estimated that Africa's population would have been twice as big as it was by 1850 had it not been for the slave trade.[14] That is clearly a large shock, but just how these demographic changes affected Africa's present-day fortunes remained difficult to measure until economist Nathan Nunn used a novel approach to do so. Nunn asked whether African countries that suffered greater population losses because of the slave trade are also poorer today.[15] The novelty of his research lies in the causal claim. By using a novel instrument – the distance from Africa to the American slave markets – Nunn not only showed a correlation between high slave export regions and underdevelopment today, but also demonstrated that the slave trade *caused* the underdevelopment.[16]

Saying that slavery caused underdevelopment does not answer the question why. Nunn addresses that in two follow-up papers. The first, written with economist Diego Puga, argues that land ruggedness may be an important explanation.[17] To protect themselves from the slave trade, Africans preferred to live far from the trade routes that were easily accessible from the coast. This meant that many lived in rugged and inhospitable areas. While this may have protected them against the slave trade, it also meant that they could not easily trade the surpluses that they were producing. As we have seen several times in this book, specialisation, surplus production and trade are essential to a thriving economy. Africans, through the very sensible decision to hide from slave traders, were constrained by geography, even after the slave trade ended.

The second explanation for the persistent effects of the slave trade on Africa's development is trust. Africa's own slave trade was unique in that, unlike that in other places and time periods, individuals of the same or similar ethnicities would often enslave one another. Nunn and Leonard Wantchekon use contemporary survey data to show that people whose ancestors were most affected by the slave trade in the past have lower levels of trust today, several hundred years later.[18] This includes trusting relatives, neighbours, people of the same ethnicity and even local government. Such a lack of trust has costs: in Chapter 5 we discussed how important trust is to the process of solving the economic problems of production and distribution through the market system. Without trust between Africans there could be little trade and investment. Nunn and Wantchekon argue that the slave trade created these antagonistic cultural values and beliefs, which were passed on from one generation to the next, with detrimental consequences for Africa's long-run development.

Although Nunn's work has inspired others to investigate the consequences of the slave trade in Africa – with evidence emerging that it has caused political fragmentation and reduced access to credit for households and firms[19] – Nunn's work is not without its critics. One important concern is the 'compression of history', the idea that there is simply too much history between what happened five centuries ago and today to assign any meaningful causal effect to slavery.[20] One example will suffice: although Nunn finds that the slave trade caused lower levels of development in the year 2000, when the analysis is repeated for the year 1950, the correlation disappears. Why the effect of the slave trades would become larger across time is unclear. Perhaps there is simply too much history to consider.[21]

Even if the exact causal mechanism between the past and the present remains murky, there is little doubt that the Atlantic slave trade radically altered Africa's development trajectory. Reflecting on her experience of visiting Gorée, Michelle Obama wrote: 'People who came through this island could never have imagined how history would unfold. And they certainly could never have imagined that someone like me – a descendant of slaves – would come here with her own family and look out through that door of no return.'[22] The Atlantic slave trade not only shaped the futures of the New World countries that the enslaved would later come to call home, but also irrevocably hurt the economic prospects of the continent they left behind.

12 What Is an Incunabulum?
Book Printing and the Reformation

On 31 October 1517 a thirty-three-year-old priest in the small German town of Wittenberg wrote a letter that would change the course of history. Addressed to the bishop of his parish, Martin Luther's letter complained about the Roman Catholic Church's selling of indulgences, the practice by which the Pope would grant remission from the punishment of sin. The more Luther read the Bible, the more he became convinced that it was not by performing good deeds that one obtained salvation, but by faith alone through God's grace. It was wrong to claim, he argued in the Ninety-Five Theses contained in the letter, that indulgences could absolve buyers from eternal punishment and grant them salvation.

These indulgences were, of course, a valuable source of income for the Church, especially at a time when Pope Leo X planned to rebuild St Peter's Basilica in Rome. For this reason Luther's letter upset the Pope, especially those parts, such as thesis 86, that challenged him directly: 'Why does the Pope, whose wealth today is greater than the wealth of the richest Crassus, build the basilica of St Peter with the money of poor believers rather than with his own money?'[1]

After several public debates, Luther was excommunicated in 1521 and forced into hiding. During this time he translated the New Testament into German and wrote many other books and pamphlets that further developed this new doctrine, spreading what became known as the Protestant Reformation.

Of course, there had been others who had come before Luther with similarly radical ideas. There was the Waldensian movement of the twelfth and thirteenth centuries, John Wyclif in the fourteenth century, and the Prague preacher Jan Hus, who led the Hussite movement in the early fifteenth century. But none of these movements gained the traction that Martin Luther did in the early sixteenth century. Why?

This is where economics can help.[2] Think of the Catholic Church as having a monopoly on religion in Western Europe before the Reformation. Monopolies that command incontestable markets, as we know from economic theory (and as we saw in Chapter 10), are prone to rent seeking and poor performance. Clerical neglect and corruption certainly characterised the Catholic Church when Luther voiced his concerns, creating demand for a new religious movement.

Another reason for the quick spread of the Reformation may have been the political competition within north-western Europe, where Protestantism took root. Think of the interplay between a ruler and a religion. A ruler can benefit from the legitimacy that a church provides: if the church anoints or sanctions a leader, his subjects could believe that his regime is divinely ordained. In exchange, the church might want to extract certain privileges from a ruler, such as tax exemptions or commercial monopolies or, as was often the case, the grant of feudal land. Where there exists a strong political leader and a monopoly religion, the two strengthen each other, and it is difficult for anyone new to enter and compete. However, where there is political competition, as was the case in north-western Europe with its many principalities, duchies and small kingdoms, the door is open for competing religions, because rulers may prefer the religion that offers them the most legitimacy at the lowest cost. The privileges that the Catholic Church demanded of rulers may have been one reason why several German states quickly switched to the new religion once it had gained a foothold.

Although these are useful explanations for understanding *why* the Reformation happened, they struggle to explain why it happened *when* it did. These same conditions were also true before, when earlier attempts at reformation failed. To help us understand the timing, we need to turn away from demand-side reasons (why people wanted a new religion) to supply-side reasons (what allowed the new religion to spread easily).

Technology is the most obvious candidate here. And the story begins with Johannes Gutenberg, who introduced the printing press to Europe. Gutenberg was trained as a goldsmith, and it remains unclear how he discovered the idea of mechanical movable type. The Chinese had, of course, discovered the printing press several centuries earlier. What we do know is that in 1455 Gutenberg printed 180 copies of his forty-two-line Bible in his workshop in Mainz, Germany. The Gutenberg Bible is an example of an incunabulum, the Latin word for a book printed before 1501. There are about 30,000 distinct incunabula known today, and they are very valuable. This is even more true of the Gutenberg Bible, of which only twenty-one complete copies survive. The last sale of a complete copy took place in 1978. Eight leaves of the book of Esther from an original copy were sold by Sotheby's in June 2015 for $970,000.

Although Gutenberg was a poor businessman and lost his workshop to his creditor and business partner, his creation sparked a transformation in how information was disseminated. The printing press spread to more than two hundred cities in Europe within a few decades, and the number of printed book volumes rose from about 20 million in the first fifty years of its existence to almost 200 million in the next century. Figure 12.1 shows the growth in numbers of books by region until 1800.[3]

The printing press made the Reformation possible. Even Luther admitted the role the printing press played in spreading his message, calling it 'God's highest and ultimate gift of grace by which He would have His Gospel carried forward'.[4] The economist Jared Rubin wanted to know whether this was true: did the printing press really aid the spread of Protestantism?[5] Much like Nathan Nunn in Chapter 11, Rubin employed an instrument to identify the causal relationship. A good instrument should be correlated with the spread of the printing press but should have no reason to be correlated with the spread of the Reformation. Rubin used the distance from Mainz, the town in which Gutenberg first printed his Bible, as his instrument, and showed that a city with a printing press in 1500 was 29 percentage points more likely to adopt Protestantism by 1600 than one that did not have one.

The cities that adopted Protestantism also became more affluent than the cities that remained Catholic. The reason for this, according to the German sociologist Max Weber, was that the states

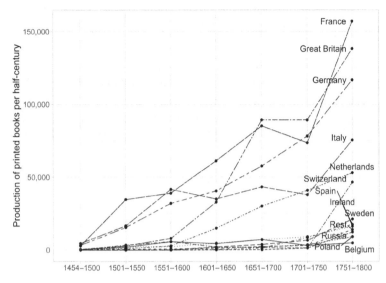

Figure 12.1 Growth in the production of printed books per half-century (in thousands of books), 1454–1800

that accepted Protestantism also adopted a new work ethic, what he called the Protestant ethic. The beliefs of Protestantism – especially in its Calvinist form – encouraged hard and honest work. It was sinful to be seen as lazy or, worse, unemployed. Work brought one closer to God, the Protestants believed. This meant that they were more likely than their Catholic counterparts, according to Weber, to accumulate money and build wealth.

Calvinists also believed in predestination, the doctrine that holds that only a select few would go to heaven. One way to discern who these fortunate ones were, of course, was to observe how people lived. Wasting one's hard-earned money and purchasing luxuries was considered sinful. Donating money to the poor was discouraged because it promoted begging. Poverty was the result of laziness; only work could glorify God. Hard work and frugality were thus two qualities that many of the Reformed aspired to.

Weber's Protestant ethic has attracted much attention as an explanation for the emergence of capitalism. But its causal claims remain tenuous. Was it Protestantism that caused capitalism or capitalism that caused people to adopt Protestantism? Or was it some other factor that caused both capitalism and Protestantism? If only we had a laboratory where we could assign some the Protestant faith and others the Catholic faith, and see what happens over time!

Actually, we can. But because we cannot test our theories in a laboratory, we turn to history to find real-life experiments – what in the economic history literature are called 'natural experiments'. Our first 'natural experiment' comes from South America. By the seventeenth century, following the exploits of the conquistadores, whom we encountered in Chapter 9, European missionaries were arriving in South America to win souls for the Catholic Church. The Jesuit order was one of the first to set up mission stations in the forests of what are today the countries of Argentina, Brazil and Paraguay. The economic historian Felipe Valencia Caicedo set out to test whether the Jesuit mission stations, established among the Guaraní from 1609 until 1767 (when the missionaries were expelled), had any long-run effects.[6] (*The Mission*, a 1986 film starring Robert De Niro and Jeremy Irons, is set in the final Jesuit mission years. The soundtrack is one of the most recognisable movie scores in film history.) The Jesuit missionaries built schools and introduced formal education to their followers. After they were expelled, many of these stations were abandoned. Yet Valencia Caicedo found that, despite the absence of mission activity in the two centuries after the missionaries were expelled, districts with a former Jesuit presence within the Guaraní region have 10–15 per cent higher educational levels today, and about 10 per cent higher incomes, than places where there were no mission stations. Somehow, the norms and knowledge the Jesuit missionaries had brought to the Guaraní were transmitted from generation to generation, even after the mission stations were abandoned. It is a remarkable story of educational and income persistence.

But that is a story only of Catholic missions. What about the Protestants? For them, we turn to Africa. By the nineteenth century, European missionaries were establishing mission stations across the African continent. Some of these were Protestant and others were Catholic. By looking at the difference between these mission stations today, we can get a sense of whether Protestant beliefs promoted better outcomes. The answer seems to be both yes and no. Some scholars find that regions with larger numbers of Protestant missions are today more educated than regions with Catholic mission stations.[7] The reason, though, is not the Protestant ethic, as Weber proposed, but rather competition. In places where Catholic missions competed with Protestant missions, the former had similar outcomes to the latter. Many Catholic regions, however, did not allow Protestant missions in their territories. In those places, Catholic stations performed significantly worse in educating their followers.

Several scholars, however, caution against an overly optimistic view of missionaries. There are three concerns. First, converting to Christianity and learning to read uprooted many of the traditional systems and beliefs, and not always for the better; today, for example, those living closer to mission stations have a higher likelihood of HIV infection and have lower levels of interpersonal trust.[8] Second, while the positive effects are often attributed to European missionaries, much of the work at mission stations was performed by African converts. Many Africans also set up their own mission stations, settlements that are usually excluded from the mission atlases used in these types of analysis.[9] Finally, some have more fundamental concerns about the nature of these 'natural experiments': upon their arrival in Africa, European missionaries did not just settle randomly. They settled in healthier, safer, more accessible, and more developed regions.[10] This would suggest that the large effects we attribute to missionaries might actually be a consequence of some other omitted factor.

What we do know is that the missionaries did not only convert souls but also bolstered formal education. It is this education that is key to understanding the consequences of the Reformation, in Europe and elsewhere. The printing press and Protestantism – the belief that one must read and study the Bible on one's own without the mediation of the Church – were the main reasons that literacy and education spread rapidly across north-western Europe and then, in the footsteps of the missionaries, to the entire world. And it would be literacy and education that proved instrumental in the emergence of the Age of Enlightenment, the Scientific Revolution and, in turn, the Industrial Revolution, a topic we turn to in Chapter 16.

13 Who Was Autshumao's Niece?
The Arrival of Europeans in South Africa and the Demise of the Khoesan

At least two decades before the arrival of the first European colonists at the southern tip of Africa, Autshumao, the chief of the Gorinhaikonas, settled in Table Bay. Although Europeans had sailed past the Cape in 1488, the volume of ships only increased after the establishment of the VOC in 1602 and the expansion of the spice trade between Europe and the East Indies. For many a ship's captain Table Bay offered a place of refuge and replenishment, where they could find fresh water, wood for fuel, and meat purchased from the Gorinhaikonas, the Khoesan clan who lived in and around the bay. But communication for the purpose of trade proved difficult and so, in 1630, Autshumao was taken aboard a Dutch ship to Bantam in present-day Indonesia, where he learned Dutch and English. Two years later he opened a trading post on Robben Island, delivering letters for European ships, before moving back to the mainland in 1640.

When officials from the VOC arrived in Table Bay on 6 April 1652 to establish a permanent settlement that would help to replenish the company's ships, Autshumao was well placed to serve as interpreter and trader. To facilitate this process, he took his twelve-year-old niece to work for the commander of the fort, Jan van Riebeeck. Her name was !Goro|gôas or, in the Dutch pronunciation, Krotoa. At the fort she was christened Eva.

Autshumao would soon fall out of favour with the Dutch. When the fort could not produce enough food to eat, van Riebeeck released nine company servants, in 1657, to become settlers: they would farm for themselves but sell their surplus to the company. But they struggled to farm in the windswept Cape Peninsula and, just one year after they set up on their own, they stole cattle from the Gorinhaikonas. War broke out, and Autshumao was captured and sent to Robben Island, the first person to be imprisoned there. After escaping on a rowing boat and with the war ended, Autshumao again applied for and received permission to work as interpreter for the Dutch. He died in 1663, one year before Krotoa married Pieter van Meerhof, a Danish surgeon, becoming the first Khoe to marry according to Christian custom.

But such a marriage was the exception rather than the rule. After another series of conflicts between the settlers and the much stronger Khoesan group, the Cochoqua, in the 1670s, the Dutch settlement expanded rapidly into the fertile valleys west of the mountain ranges that surround the Cape Peninsula. The Khoe who survived the conflicts either had to flee or join the colonial economy as farm labourers. Their numbers further collapsed in 1713 after a severe smallpox epidemic ravaged the colony. Just as European settlement would devastate indigenous populations in the Americas and Australia, European guns and germs left large tracts of Cape land available for further European settlement.

As European settlers entered these lands, first north and then east along the mountains that hugged the south coast, the colony's borders rapidly expanded. Settler numbers were boosted when about 180 Huguenots joined after fleeing persecution in France. But it was the settlers' high fertility rates – in the order of seven surviving children per woman – that mostly boosted their colonisation of the interior. The first Fourie to settle in the colony, for example, had twenty-one children and ninety-nine grandchildren.[1]

Historians have long subscribed to the idea that although these settlers were productive in the bedroom, they were not very productive farmers. Some have described the colony as 'more of a static than a progressing community' which 'advanced with almost extreme slowness'. It was especially the settlers who migrated deeper into the interior who lived 'for the most part in isolated homesteads' and 'gained a scanty subsistence by the pastoral industry and hunting'.[2]

This view was predominantly informed by letters of com-
plaint that the settlers had written to the VOC shareholders in
Amsterdam. Because the company had founded the Cape, it was
ruled not by a colonial government but by shareholders half
a world away. These shareholders had little interest in the welfare
of the settlers or, for that matter, the other inhabitants of the
colony; they cared only about profits. Their decisions were thus
shaped by what was best for the company – not the colony. This
resulted in a string of strange economic institutions. Although the
settlers were 'free' to farm what they wanted, they were only
allowed to sell their produce to the company, and at fixed prices.
They were not allowed to sell manufactured goods – and only
a few, those who purchased the monopoly concessions from the
company, were allowed to bake bread or brew beer. Most importantly, they were not allowed to trade with the passing ships or
with the Khoesan. It was an economy devoid of any economic
freedom.

To compensate them for these restrictive institutions, the
company gave them cheap loans to purchase agricultural inputs and,
most importantly, allowed them to participate in the slave trade to
obtain labour. The Cape was thus a slave economy. In Chapter 14 we
return to this aspect of the colonial economy.

Despite these concessions, Cape farmers complained frequently and vehemently to the company shareholders, asking for
the relaxation of several onerous restrictions, but to no avail.
European visitors who travelled into the interior would often repeat
the farmers' complaints in their accounts, noting the poverty they
sometimes observed.

There is no doubt that some of these farmers were indeed
very poor, but the confidence placed by historians in the observations
of a few angry farmers and potentially prejudiced travellers seems
misplaced. And so, when I was a graduate student in the late 2000s,
I came across an obscure paper from 1987 that piqued my interest. In
it, the historians Robert Ross and Pieter van Duin, after assembling
a lot of statistics concerning eighteenth-century Cape agricultural
output, remarked: 'While signs of dynamism in the nineteenth century Cape have been recognised by those few authors who have
worked on the period, the backwardness of the colony at the end
of the eighteenth century has yet to be fully challenged, or indeed

fully investigated.'[3] Here was a challenge for an eager student. And I accepted it.

My PhD thesis, completed in 2012, asks the simple question: how affluent were these settler farmers?[4] It turns out that the Cape settlers were some of the wealthiest humans on the planet at the time. How do I know this? For my analysis I used more than two thousand eighteenth-century Orphan Chamber probate inventories (lists of possessions the settlers owned when they died). Households at the Cape owned, I found, on average 54 cattle, 6 horses and 350 sheep, and about 3 buckets, 10 chairs and 5 paintings.[5] A poor household living just above subsistence level could not have had so much wealth. In fact, I showed that the numbers of buckets, chairs, books and paintings, to name just a few household items, were higher than those owned by the average household in England or the Netherlands, the two richest countries at the time. In later work with economic historian Frank Garmon, I used tax censuses collected by company officials to show that Cape settlers were also more affluent than American settlers in Maine, Massachusetts and Virginia.[6]

But if settlers at the southern tip of Africa were more affluent than their counterparts in Europe and America at the end of the eighteenth century, when did Europe (and its offshoots) become the affluent place it is today? This is a big question in economic history, one that has become known as the Great Divergence debate. In 2000 the historian Kenneth Pomeranz wrote a seminal book – *The Great Divergence* – in which he argued that differences in income between Europeans and Asians only arose in the nineteenth century rather than, as many scholars believed at the time, a few centuries earlier. Although China under the Song dynasty (960–1279) is widely acknowledged to have had the highest standard of living in the world, most scholars had thought that the Chinese lost their advantage in the fifteenth century after their inward turn. Pomeranz questioned this assumption. Using scattered data that covered only parts of the economy, he argued that some regions of China maintained their higher standards of living over Europe until after the industrial take-off in Europe.

Economic historians have, however, developed a rich set of tools to test this hypothesis. Our most important tool is historical reconstructions of GDP. Pioneered by economic historian Angus

Maddison, historical GDP estimates require painstaking data collection and calculation to allow comparisons across time and space.[7] Probably the most reliable comparison comes from economic historians Stephen Broadberry, Hanhui Guan and David Li.[8] In order to test Pomeranz's Great Divergence hypothesis, they calculate GDP per capita in the Yangzi Delta (the wealthiest part of China) and compare it with that of the Netherlands and England (what they call the European frontier). They show that the gap opens at the beginning of the eighteenth century, not as late as Pomeranz argues but also not as early as the Eurocentric writers of an earlier generation believed.

It is this same GDP per capita that confirms that the Cape was affluent. With the economic historian (and my former supervisor) Jan Luiten van Zanden, I show that GDP per capita at the Cape was above that of England, the Netherlands and the early American Republic.[9] Figure 13.1 plots the upper estimates of GDP per capita for the Yangzi region in China, the European frontier (the Netherlands until the 1790s and England to the 1860s) and the Cape Colony. For the Cape, one GDP per capita estimate includes the

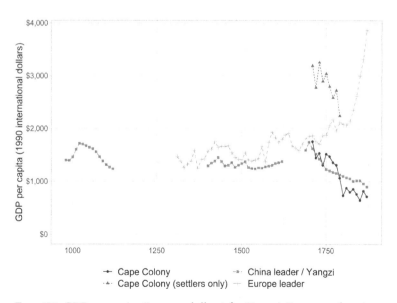

Figure 13.1 GDP per capita (in 1990 dollars) for Yangzi, European frontier and Cape Colony, 1400–1860

enslaved and Khoesan. A second only shows the GDP per capita for the European settlers.

How could Cape settlers become so wealthy given the constraints the Dutch East India Company imposed on them? Let's first think of the demand side: thousands of soldiers and sailors arrived at the Cape every year in need of fresh food and, in particular, wine and brandy. This created a ready market for the Cape's agricultural output, a market with no competitor.[10] On the supply side, there were at least three reasons for the settlers' wealth. I have already mentioned the relatively inexpensive land that, once the threat of the Khoesan had been reduced, allowed farmers to practise extensive mixed farming, producing wheat and wine close to Cape Town and raising livestock beyond the mountains. Cheap labour helped too. Khoesan men and women who did not flee from the advancing settlers were ultimately incorporated, sometimes violently, into the farming economy. It was especially in the pastoral districts on the frontier, several months' travel from Cape Town, that Khoesan labour was an essential input in the production process. Closer to Cape Town, slaves acquired from the Indian Ocean slave trade were the dominant source of labour. Although slave labour did not come cheap, it offered other advantages to the settlers, as we shall see in the next chapter. A third reason was the skills the settlers brought from Europe, notably in wine making.[11]

Why did this wealthy eighteenth-century society not experience an industrial revolution like its counterpart in north-western Europe?[12] To answer this, we again turn to institutions. In Chapter 9 we examined the Engerman–Sokoloff hypothesis, which attributed the differences in income between North and South America today to the high levels of inequality and the concomitant institutions that were established during colonial times. The Cape, much like Latin America, was a highly unequal society, with institutions that evolved to protect the elite. These institutions removed the freedoms – such as access to private property, education and representative government – that are so essential to broad-based economic development. Instead, the institution of slavery (and indentureship of the Khoesan, a system very similar to slavery) prevailed at the Cape. And as we explained in Chapter 11, once the institution of slavery is embedded in a society, the incentives for innovation and capital investment in the technologies that raise productivity disappear.

The Cape economy was thus rich but unable to grow further; because of its institutions of unfreedom, it had reached a plateau. The only opportunities lay in expanding the frontier eastwards until, by the end of the eighteenth century, the settlers would enter the lands of the Xhosa, a Bantu-speaking group that was more technologically advanced than the Khoesan. This encounter would ignite a series of wars that lasted a century.

What of the Khoesan? Their numbers declined significantly after the arrival of Europeans.[13] While some maintained their independence by moving away or settling in small villages protected by missionaries, others became part of the colonial economy, working on settler farms. Krotoa's fortunes would mirror that of her people. After marrying Pieter van Meerhof in 1664 she had three children, but when her husband was murdered in Madagascar, she suffered a personal decline and was banished to Robben Island, where she died in 1673.

That is not the end of her legacy, though. Her daughter, Pieternella van de Kaap, went on to marry the VOC vegetable gardener Daniel Zaaijman and have eight children. Today, all South Africans with the surname Saayman/Zaaiman can trace their roots to Krotoa.[14]

14 What Did Thomson, Watson & Co. Purchase?
The Emancipation of the Enslaved

It rained on the first day of December in 1838. This was a day to remember. Across the Cape Colony the yoke of forced labour had been lifted from the almost 40,000 inhabitants who had formerly been classified as slaves. They were now free.

It had been a long road to freedom. When the Dutch first settled the Cape in the mid-seventeenth century the Atlantic slave trade was expanding. As we discussed in Chapter 11, hundreds of thousands of Africans were being shipped across the Atlantic by Portuguese, British, French and Dutch traders and sold to settlers in the New World. Because of the profitability of the trade, the rivalry between these slave-trading nations was intense. It would be this rivalry that would bring the first shipment of Angolan slaves to the Cape.

On 23 January 1658 the Dutch ship *Amersfoort* sighted a Portuguese slaver off the coast of Angola with about 500 slaves on board.[1] After a twenty-four-hour chase the ship was captured and about 250 people were taken to the Cape. When the ship anchored in Table Bay two months later, only about 174 of those slaves were still alive. One of those who survived was a young boy given the name of Anthonij.

At the Cape, Anthonij of Angola was sold to Nathaniel West and then, a few months later, to Christiaan Jansz. Anthonij would move from one owner to the next until, some time in the late 1670s, he gained his freedom. Just how this happened is not clear, but by 1680 he was concluding contracts as a free man and by 1683 he had bought a farm with his business partner (and former slave), Manuel of Angola. The farm, which he appropriately called Angola, was situated in the beautiful Jonkershoek valley, probably close to the present-day luxury wine farm of Lanzerac in Stellenbosch. One year later Anthonij would acquire his own slave, Sijmon Ham. When Anthonij died in 1696, Susanna of Mombasa, his common-law wife (they could not legally marry because of her slave status), and her two children were manumitted.

Anthonij's story provides a glimpse into the complex lives of slaves during the early years of the Cape Colony. Like Anthonij, some earned their freedom and became part of settler society. Angela of Bengale, a slave from India, married the settler Arnoldus Basson and would become a wealthy widow who lived until the age of seventy. Her daughter, Anna de Koning, who arrived with her mother as a slave girl, married Olof Bergh, a rich Swedish settler, and became the mistress of one of the most prosperous farms at the Cape, Groot Constantia.[2] Not only did de Koning and Bergh have twelve children, but at the time of her death, in 1734, she owned twenty-seven slaves, one of whom came from Bengal, in India, the place where she had been born.

But the stories of Anthonij and Angela were exceptions. For most of those captured and sold as slaves, life was miserable. As their names indicate, they came from far-flung places – between 1652 and 1808 about 63,000 slaves were taken to the Cape from Indonesia (23%), India (26%), Madagascar (25%) and the African east coast, mostly Mozambique (26%).[3] The company retained many of them to work on its own fortifications and in its trading activities. By 1770 the Slave Lodge in Cape Town – today the Iziko Slave Museum – housed more than a thousand slaves. At the Cape, in contrast to other parts of the world, slavery was thus, at least initially, an urban phenomenon.[4] The lives of those in the lodge were probably better than those on the farms. Company slaves were fed and clothed, all were baptised and many, on reaching their twenty-fifth birthdays, were manumitted. There was even a slave school; we know of letters that were sent from formerly enslaved men to their friends in the lodge. But despite these concessions, slavery was still a system of unfreedom and exploitation. Slaves would be punished for any misdemeanour in the most horrifying ways. Their many attempts to escape, few of which were successful, suggest that slave life, even in the lodge, was bleak.

Most slaves who arrived in Cape Town were sold to farmers. They were an important source of labour. The company had banned the enslavement of Khoesan. This was probably more a strategic than a moral choice: Khoesan men and women could escape easily in the countryside, which made their supervision costly. And because they were important trading partners with the Dutch, it was important to keep relations between them amicable. The trouble was that few free men were willing to work as wage labourers while there was ample land available to farm. In fact, when in 1717 a commission of inquiry was set up to investigate whether slaves should be the primary source of farm labour or if the immigration of free labourers from Europe should be encouraged, six of the seven commissioners agreed that slave labour was preferable. Their reason was simple: slaves could be more easily coerced than free labourers. The commissioners argued that if European immigration were to be encouraged, the new arrivals would not wish to work on the farms of other settlers but would rather want farms of their own. The only way to ensure enough workers for the wheat and especially the wine farms was to obtain a steady supply of slave labour. Their argument would mirror the hypothesis of two scholars, H. J. Nieboer and Evsey Domar, two centuries later: that when land is abundant and labour in short supply, the only way to ensure a reliable source of labour is to coerce someone.[5] Slavery is the extreme form of labour coercion. In fact, we have already discussed a version of the Nieboer–Domar hypothesis in Chapter 7, relating it to Africa's high land–labour ratio and endemic slavery.[6]

Until recently, the labour that slaves performed was seen by historians as their main economic contribution – and the reason that slaves, for much of the eighteenth century, outnumbered settlers at the Cape. But new research reveals that slaves also inadvertently contributed to the economy by being an important store of value: in the parlance of the time, slaves were property that belonged to an owner. Owners could sell their 'property' to someone else, but they could also use it as collateral on a mortgage. In a setting where there were no formal banks, slave capital, rather than land (which is not a very liquid asset), was used to lubricate a dense informal financial network between settlers.

This provides an additional clue as to why such an abhorrent institution was so pervasive at the Cape and why it survived for so long. Slave owners may have justified their actions in racist language, but their motives were economic. Even after Britain took control of the Cape in 1806 and abolished the slave trade in 1807, the practice continued. In fact, the end of the slave trade brought greater coercion against the Khoesan – again, a predictable consequence when land is freely available and in the absence of representative institutions.

But the global economy was changing at that time. As we will discuss in Chapter 16, England was then at the start of its Industrial Revolution. New ideologies, such as free trade, were rapidly gaining ascendancy in the British parliament, reflecting the interests of the new business elite rather than the landed gentry. People like William Wilberforce led moral campaigns against the injustices of slavery. The end of slavery in the British Empire drew near.

Yet it took until 1833 before the Slave Emancipation Act was finally signed, and only after a negotiated settlement. In what seems a remarkably unjust outcome to us today, it was agreed that slave owners across the British Empire would be compensated for the loss of their 'property'. The compensation would consist of indentureship – another four to six years of uncompensated labour for the former masters – and cash. The total cash amount paid to slaveholders was £20 million, or 40 per cent of the British budget. Britain had to borrow the money; and British taxpayers finally repaid all the instalments on its loans in 2015.

At the Cape, commissioners went round to all farms to 'value' each of the almost 39,000 slaves. The total amount exceeded £3 million, but the Cape was allocated only £1,247,401 by the British government. On top of this, slave owners had to go to London to claim the money, a long and expensive trip. This is where entrepreneurial British merchants such as John Thomson and Harrison Watson stepped in. Thomson, Watson & Company and a few other merchant companies began to buy up slave owners' compensation claims. They then sent them to their agents in London and took a percentage of the returns. These companies would, by the end of the emancipation process, invest their profits in the new colonial banks and insurance companies, a shift away from the informal capital markets of the countryside towards a more formalised commercial capitalism.[7]

In the US South, slavery would only end three decades after slaves had been emancipated in the British Empire. It took a brutal civil war to do so. And it would be another two decades – only in 1888 – before slavery would finally be abolished in Brazil, the largest destination for Africans shipped during the Atlantic slave trade. Using an innovative methodology, economic historians Richard Hornbeck and Trevon Logan calculate that the aggregate productivity gains of emancipating enslaved Americans was equivalent to 41 per cent of US GDP.[8]

But despite these large economic gains, emancipation was not welcomed by the former slaveholders, even those who received compensation. At the Cape, most slaveholders received a fraction of what they expected to receive and considered the entire process a major injustice. Because slaves were frequently used as collateral, many slaveholders defaulted on their loans and faced bankruptcy. Some of them, as we will see in Chapter 15, chose to move deeper into the South African interior.

And what of the former slaves? Despite almost two centuries of enslavement, they received no compensation or any other form of support.[9] After that rainy day on 1 December 1838, when freedom finally came, many moved to Cape Town to build new lives as masons or carpenters or seamstresses.[10] Others moved to the mission stations that dotted the countryside where they could gain perhaps small plots of land to farm for themselves. And others stayed on the farms of their former masters, having to negotiate a new wage dispensation. The freedom from coercion was a first, if tentative, step in their long walk to economic freedom.

15 What Do an Indonesian Volcano, Frankenstein and Shaka Zulu Have in Common?
The Mfecane and the Great Trek

In April 1816 eighteen-year-old Mary Godwin travelled to Geneva with her lover, the poet Percy Shelley. (They had eloped and were to marry later in the year.) They stayed in Geneva for the summer with her half-sister, Claire, and another of England's great poets, Lord Byron. But the weather was terrible. Instead of rowing on a calm and pleasant Lake Geneva, Mary wrote of a 'wet, ungenial summer, and incessant rain [that] often confined us for days to the house'. It was during one such dark and stormy evening that a member of the travelling party suggested a game: each should write a ghost story. After several days of toying with different ideas, Mary Shelley conjured up the story of Victor Frankenstein, who creates a monster in a scientific experiment. Published in 1818, *Frankenstein* changed literary history and is today considered one of the first science fiction books. It still sells approximately 40,000 copies per year.

But 1816 was not all fun and games. The 'year without a summer', as 1816 would come to be known, caused mass starvation across Europe. Lord Byron put this most succinctly in the poem 'Darkness':

> Of famine fed upon all entrails – men
> Died, and their bones were tombless as their flesh ...

Baron Karl Drais was witnessing the same devastation in Mannheim, not too far from Lord Byron and Mary Shelley's holiday home. One thing that struck him was the deaths of thousands of horses. The rivers were in flood. Transportation, which then relied on horses and boats, came to a halt. Drais, a mathematician and inventor, had an idea: what if one could substitute human power for horsepower? Although his initial idea was to invent a four-wheel carriage, he soon realised that this would be too heavy. He refocused, ultimately designing his *Laufmaschine* ('running machine'). Today we know it as the bicycle.

It was not just in Europe that the weather was unusual. From Asia to the Americas, reports came of strange weather conditions, although no one could identify the cause.[1] In southern Africa, too, we have evidence of dramatic weather changes. Our sources are different. Because we do not have written accounts from those who must have experienced this, we instead use oral histories and even evidence from tree rings. All of these sources reveal the same thing: a prolonged drought early in the nineteenth century, around 1815.[2] The Nguni remember this time as *madlathule*, literally 'let one eat what he can and say nothing'. Reconstructed rainfall data show a significant decline during the period. Tree-ring evidence in Zimbabwe confirms that tree growth was slower, suggesting a severe drought.

The drought had major implications. As Chapter 7 mentioned, maize was introduced into Africa around 1600. By 1800 it had spread all the way to the south coast of the continent, where Bantu-speaking farmers, in present-day KwaZulu-Natal, preferred its higher yields to those of sorghum and millet. Yet, as mentioned before, maize has one major disadvantage: it is not drought resistant. When a severe drought hit the region at the beginning of the century, disaster ensued.

The lack of food led to famine and war. The two most powerful polities during this time were the Ndwandwe and the Mthethwa. Under the leadership of King Zwide, the Ndwandwe defeated the Mthethwa and murdered their leader, Dingiswayo. One year earlier, in 1816, the leader of one of the Mthethwa's minor clans, Chief Senzangakhona of the Zulu, had died. He was replaced by his illegitimate son, a young but ambitious soldier, in a relatively bloodless coup. When Zwide defeated Dingiswayo, this young soldier swore revenge against the man who had defeated his king. Only two years later, after strategically bringing all the defeated forces together and by using innovative military tactics,

Shaka, king of the Zulu, defeated the mighty Ndwandwe in a series of battles.

These battles were the beginning of the Mfecane, a period of chaos and suffering in much of southern Africa. After their defeat the Ndwandwe split up and moved, some into Eswatini (formerly Swaziland), others into Mozambique (to establish the Gaza empire) and others much further north into Zambia and Malawi. Wherever they went, they caused turmoil as they uprooted other groups. The arrival of the Ndwandwe in Mozambique, for example, pushed some Tsonga across the Lebombo mountains into Mpumalanga and Limpopo, provinces in present-day South Africa.

The loose alliances within the Zulu kingdom could also not endure the devastation. The Khumalo clan under Mzilikazi split off from the Zulu but, after defeat in several clashes, Mzilikazi chose to move away in the direction of present-day Pretoria, where he set up the Ndebele state. The Ndebele would later be pushed further north and ultimately settle in Matabeleland in what is now Zimbabwe.

The conflicts also sparked migrations in the west. The Kololo group under Sebitwane moved from present-day Lesotho, plundering Tswana settlements on their way through Botswana, before settling in present-day Barotseland in Zambia, where they conquered the Lozi people. Along the coast, refugees from the Zulu wars, known as Mfengu, moved into the lands of the Xhosa. Such migrations had a domino effect, further exacerbating the effects of drought and warfare. It was indeed a scattering, a *mfecane*, of people all across southern Africa.

While most fled the Zulu, one notable exception involved the Sotho under Moshoeshoe I. He gathered several smaller clans together, strategically used the rugged terrain of the Drakensberg mountains and fought off several attacks, ultimately establishing the kingdom of Lesotho.

One of the defining characteristics of the twenty years between 1815 and 1835 was the way it changed the spatial distribution of people. Not only did famine, war and migration reduce population numbers substantially, but they also caused more people to live in rugged areas – places, like Lesotho, the most rugged country on earth, where they could protect themselves more easily. Here it is perhaps useful to reflect on a paper discussed in Chapter 11. Nathan Nunn and Diego Puga suggested that many Africans, in an attempt to escape the ravages of the slave trade, settled in rugged areas far from the coast or in inhospitable mountainous terrain. The same could be applied to the Mfecane. The only places that remained densely settled were the rugged areas in the Eastern Cape, Zululand, Eswatini and Lesotho. While this strategy was a great way to protect oneself against conflict, it had detrimental economic consequences: ruggedness increases trade costs, and this in turn reduces the incentive to produce a surplus and trade.

But there was an even bigger consequence of the migrations into rugged areas. By the 1830s many of the regions once densely inhabited by Bantu-speaking groups had become desolate. Vast tracts of land in the interior of southern Africa were now only sparsely populated, both because of an absolute decline in population numbers and because of a shift towards rugged areas. This was an opportunity for bands of settlers – frontier farmers in the Cape Colony – to move in and occupy the land. It was a migration that would become known as the Great Trek.

Why these frontier farmers left the colony is a subject of much debate. After the British takeover in 1806 the institutions set up by the Dutch East India Company in the eighteenth century began to change slowly. English became the new language of government. From the 1810s onwards new political systems, labour laws and property-rights regimes were introduced, the most important of which, as we saw in Chapter 14, was the emancipation of slaves. In 1820 the British government sent about four thousand British subjects to the Cape and settled them in between the Dutch farmers and the Xhosa to stabilise the frontier region. It achieved exactly the opposite.

Although the exact reasons for the Great Trek of frontier farmers are still up for debate, what we do know is that by the 1830s frontier farmers were already exploring the area beyond the Orange River – a region that would later become known as the Orange Free State. Hunters had returned to the Cape Colony, noting the devastation of the Mfecane and the possibilities of settlement across the Orange. By 1836 several hundred settler families had left their farms and trekked in ox-wagons into what they considered unclaimed land. These were not the most prosperous farmers. In fact, one of the ringleaders, Piet Retief, was clearly trying to escape debts he owed in the colony. Some would have been motivated by notions of political freedom and independence, frustrated by the changes British rule had brought (including emancipation of the slaves). But it is equally likely that some Voortrekkers (literally, 'those trekking first') were motivated by financial gain, opportunistically hoping to claim land that could be sold to the next wave of trekkers.

The consequence of this outward migration of settlers from the Cape Colony into the southern Africa interior would be – after several skirmishes against, notably, the Zulu of Dingane and the Ndebele of Mzilikazi – the establishment of two Boer republics: the South African Republic (1852) and the Orange Free State (1854). Within forty years, from 1815 to 1855, the South African economic and political landscape had been transformed entirely. It went from a settler colony at the southern tip of Africa, with densely settled Bantu-speaking groups inhabiting the summer-rainfall interior, to a largely depopulated interior settled by scattered Boer migrants on large, pastoral farms with densely settled Bantu speakers mostly limited to the lush but rugged regions of the country. This pattern of settlement established by the 1850s would, largely, persist into the present.[3]

The drought that began all the conflict in 1815 was not just a normal one – and it was not unrelated to the changing weather conditions in Europe, Asia or the Americas. It would be only in the 1890s that researchers studying these disparate events drew links to another event that happened in 1815: the eruption of Mount Tambora in Indonesia on 10 April. It was the largest volcanic eruption in recorded human history. It was so large that the explosion was heard 2,600 kilometres away, with ash deposits found as far as 1,300 kilometres from the volcano. An estimated 100 cubic kilometres of ash were ejected – reducing the height of the mountain by 1,500 metres – much of which stayed in the atmosphere for months and which was blown by longitudinal winds around the globe. That is why global weather patterns changed, not only causing a 'year without a summer' and the birth of the bicycle and Frankenstein's monster in Europe, but also igniting a series of conflicts in southern Africa that would have enormous repercussions for the region's future.

16 Why Was the Spinning Jenny Not Invented in India?
Science, Technology and the Industrial Revolution

There was nothing special about James Hargreaves. Born in 1721 near Blackburn in Lancashire, he never learned to read. As he grew to adulthood his only job prospect was that open to other Blackburn men of his standing: he became a hand-loom weaver who turned yarn into fabric to make a living. From his meagre salary he supported his wife and thirteen children.

Eighteenth-century England was an important textile producer. To produce fabric from wool or cotton requires three steps: carding, spinning and then weaving. At the time, it usually took three carders to provide the roving for one spinner, and three spinners to provide the yarn for one weaver. To increase the amount of fabric, one needed to speed up the process early in the chain of production. And so, in 1764, the story goes, Hargreaves was working with a one-thread spinning wheel when it accidentally fell over. As it was lying on the floor, an idea struck him: if he placed a number of spindles upright and next to each other, he could spin several threads at once, producing far more yarn with the same number of workers. The machine that Hargreaves ultimately invented – the spinning jenny – held eight spindles, allowing a single spinner to be far more productive.

Although Hargreaves initially kept his invention a secret, he built a few more machines that he sold to friends. Word got out, and so the amount of yarn that was spun increased rapidly, which had the obvious consequence that its price fell. Given their already poor incomes, many spinners were not happy, and some of them broke into Hargreaves's house and forced him to leave the place of his birth.

The lesson: technology disrupts. As economic historian Joel Mokyr remarks: 'Every invention is an act of rebellion against time-honoured beliefs and deeply entrenched customs.'[1] Later, a whole movement – the Luddites – would organise protest action to destroy textile machines in an attempt to save jobs.

But Hargreaves was not the only one inventing new machines in eighteenth-century England. Richard Arkwright not only improved on Hargreaves's invention with the spinning frame, but also invented a carding engine. John Kay had invented the flying shuttle a few years earlier, improving the process by which yarn becomes fabric. These inventions were not just limited to textiles. Early in the century Thomas Newcomen invented the first commercially successful steam engine, which was further improved by James Watt, and later used by Richard Trevithick and George Stephenson in building the steam locomotive.

Why were all these new machines invented in eighteenth-century England? This is probably the most debated question in economic history – because the answer helps us understand the origins of our prosperity. Knowing what caused these men to invent new things would explain why it was England, in the eighteenth century, that experienced an industrial revolution of a nature and on a scale that no other society had experienced before. Although we call it a revolution, it was very different from political revolutions such as the French Revolution of 1789. This was more like an evolution, a slow shift in productivity over several centuries that ultimately lifted the living standards of everyone. Consider Figure 16.1. Per-capita gross domestic product in England was flat for much of the period before 1700. Then, slowly, we see an increase, which accelerates in the nineteenth century and, despite two world wars in the twentieth, rises to levels that would have been unbeliev-able to even the most optimistic person just a few centuries earlier.

Why had there not been an increase before the eighteenth century? In 1798 the English cleric Thomas Malthus proposed a theory as to why higher wages had never before resulted in a sustained increase in living standards.[2] It was a rather pessimistic view of humanity. Whenever there is a good harvest, Malthus explained, wages will increase. Higher wages will lead to higher

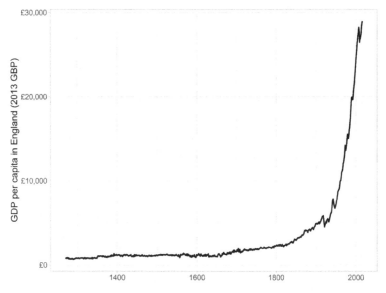

Figure 16.1 GDP per capita in England, 1270–2016

fertility rates which, within a few years, will lead to an increase in the supply of labour. More labourers will suppress wages to below subsistence level, and famine or conflict will inevitably follow. In short, 'the power of population is indefinitely greater than the power in the earth to produce subsistence for man'.[3]

But, ironically, just as Malthus was writing his influential treatise about why living standards will always fluctuate around subsistence levels, England was exiting this Malthusian trap. Average wages were increasing without a concomitant increase in fertility. Why? To answer that, we have to ask another question: What enabled Hargreaves and friends to invent these new technologies that made English manufacturing more productive than any other in history?

There are at least two plausible theories. The economic historian Robert Allen believes it was because it made financial sense for them to do so.[4] He shows that wages were exceptionally high in England relative to the price of capital. This made it profitable to use the jenny in England but not elsewhere. And since it was profitable to use in England, it was the only place where it was worth incurring the costs of developing it. To put this in economic terms: the reasons these technologies were not invented in France or India was that the rate of return to inventing it was too low there. There was no demand for these technologies outside England. We know this because even after they were invented in England, they were not adopted immediately elsewhere. Despite many supply-side differences between England and the rest of the world that can be used to explain England's exceptionalism, Allen argues it was the favourable relative factor prices in England (the price of labour over the price of capital) that gave British inventors an incentive to invent technologies that replaced expensive labour with cheap capital.

But why did England have a higher relative wage? Allen argues that it was England's higher rates of urbanisation, larger factories and abundance of coal that raised the demand for labour in manufacturing, thereby boosting wages. While this makes sense, it just shifts the question to why England had a higher urbanisation rate and larger factories and could benefit from its supply of coal, and others not. Factor prices that created a demand for labour-saving innovations, although useful in explaining the proximate causes of new technologies, do not seem to tell the entire story.

Joel Mokyr thinks so too. He argues, instead, that the real reason for the Industrial Revolution was the development of a scientific culture. By the eighteenth century, men and women in England began to understand that not only could new innovations such as the spinning jenny make them more productive workers, but that this higher productivity could translate into higher living standards for everyone.[5] In other words, scientific advancement was the catalyst to building a prosperous society. It was, fundamentally, the widespread adoption of this idea – this cultural belief, as Mokyr calls it – that made the modern world possible.

How do economists think about something as fuzzy as cultural beliefs? Let us digress for a moment. Economic historians see formal institutions as the rules and laws of society while informal institutions are the social norms and customs.[6] Culture is the information that guides this behaviour, the part of our behaviour that is not hard-wired by our genes but is learned through experiences and acquired from others. Or think of it this way: formal institutions are our hardware, informal institutions our software, and cultural beliefs are the updates we download every week.

Back to the Industrial Revolution. Mokyr argues that its origins lie in the radical confidence in the benefits of science, promoted by cultural entrepreneurs such as Francis Bacon and Isaac Newton, and the circulation of these ideas within universities and also the newly established scientific societies and coffee houses where people would gather to discuss the latest inventions. The Republic of Letters that developed was a long-distance intellectual community (in Europe and the United States) that shared ideas about new scientific experiments and progress freely (what we today would call open source). This community of scientists and experimenters could emerge because no European monarch was able to silence them; if they tried to, the learned men would simply move to another country. These communities were especially strong in places like Amsterdam, Paris and London where scientists were offered the most freedom to pursue their endeavours. And, of course, their work was made easier by the invention of the printing press (as we discussed in Chapter 12), which allowed scientific ideas to reach new audiences through books, journals and pamphlets. Coalescing in what came to be known as the European Enlightenment, this intellectual movement had two profound ideas: that a better understanding of nature can and should be used to improve the material conditions of humanity; and that this knowledge should not be limited to the rich and powerful, but extended to society at large.

For most of human history it was the rich and powerful who had controlled and even stifled new ideas or extracted their proceeds. The institutions this political elite set up were designed to ensure they maintained their privileged position. Innovation often threatened these privileges. But such notions of maintaining privilege were changing in Europe during the seventeenth and eighteenth centuries, and in England in particular. The political changes that led to the Glorious Revolution of 1688 moved England away from an absolute monarchy and towards a more representative government that respected basic civil rights. The bourgeoisie – the urban middle class – gained new freedoms, including the freedom to innovate and experiment. The image of the noble soldier was replaced by that of the thrifty entrepreneur.[7]

Of course, this change in beliefs did not happen overnight. Mokyr notes that 'the rise of the Enlightenment in the late seventeenth century was the culmination of a centuries-long process of intellectual change among the European literate elite'.[8] But although these new beliefs spread predominantly among the intellectual elite, it was not limited to them. As the case of the illiterate James Hargreaves illustrates, once the shift to a scientific and entrepreneurial culture had been embedded in English society, everyone could participate.

How sure are we that it was this scientific culture that made all the difference, and not other factors, such as the slave trade or the expanding British Empire? As we discussed in Chapters 11 and 14, there is little doubt that the slave system benefited slave owners in Britain. Colonial officials also profited from territorial expansion and extraction. We also know that the English working classes had to endure terrible working conditions in the mines and the factories of Manchester and Liverpool. But there are at least three reasons why these explanations fail to account for the transformation in eighteenth-century England. First, timing: both the slave trade and England's imperial expansion had begun much earlier than the Industrial Revolution. In fact, slavery was abolished just as the Industrial Revolution was taking off. Second, comparisons: Britain was not the only – or even the largest – slave-trading nation in the Atlantic. Slavery was also an ancient enterprise, yet no previous slave economy had experienced an industrial revolution. The same was true for territorial expansion; every ancient civilisation had expanded its borders but none had ever experienced an industrial revolution. Third, size: even if we add up all the labour and land extracted through slavery and colonisation, the amount would not come close to the remarkable wealth created since the early eighteenth century. Not only had the global population increased eightfold, but the income of the average *global* citizen – which includes the people in those regions that were colonised – had increased by a factor of 18. In fact, most economic historians would now agree that the extractive enterprises of enslavement and empire probably hurt the *average* British taxpayer more than it benefited them, delaying the process of industrialisation rather than buttressing or financing it. Remember from Chapter 14 how British taxpayers had to pay compensation to slave owners: the only ones to benefit from the rent seeking and exploitation of slavery and colonialism were the privileged few, to the detriment of many, both within and outside Britain. Economic and political unfreedoms suppress rather than foster development.

The Industrial Revolution originated in a culture of scientific inquiry and entrepreneurial enterprise – Mokyr calls it 'useful knowledge' – accompanied by the expanding freedoms of people across all walks of life, not just the rich and powerful, and enabling them to participate. Slowly but surely, over several centuries, England was transformed from a predominantly feudal society, ruled by a privileged class, into one where a spirit of innovation and enterprise filtered down to even the illiterate Hargreaves, a poor weaver from Blackburn. By the time he invented his spinning jenny a culture of science had given rise to high wages that encouraged more innovation in an attempt to replace expensive labour with cheap capital, making workers even more productive and further boosting their wages. It marked the dawn of a new age, one that would, within two centuries, touch every part of the globe.

17 Why Did Railways Hurt Basotho Farmers?
South Africa's Mineral Revolution

In March 1887 Robert Germond, a missionary in charge of a small mission station at Thabana Morena on the western border of present-day Lesotho, reported sad news. Basutoland, he wrote, 'produces less and finds no outlet for its products. Its normal markets, Kimberley and the Free State, purchase Australian and colonial wheat … Basutoland, we must admit, is a poor country … Last year's abundant harvest has found no outlet for, since the building of the railway, colonial and foreign wheat have competed disastrously with the local produce.'[1]

Thabana Morena is about 330 kilometres from Kimberley. Then part of the British protectorate of Basutoland, the region was the breadbasket of the South African interior. Basotho farmers produced grain for the rapidly growing local markets of Griqualand West, a division of the Cape Colony whose major town was Kimberley, and the Orange Free State, one of the two Boer republics set up in the 1850s after the Great Trek. For much of the first two decades of its establishment, the Boers of the Free State were more interested in war with the Basotho than trade. The period of conflict eventually ended in 1869 when the British government intervened. The parts of Basutoland that were not lost in the conflict became a British protectorate, similar to Bechuanaland (Botswana) and Swaziland (Eswatini), which is the reason why these territories are not part of South Africa today.

The year 1869 was an opportune time for peace. Two years earlier, in 1867, a fifteen-year-old boy, Erasmus Jacobs, had picked up a pebble on a farm close to Hopetown, on the banks of the Orange River. He showed the stone to a neighbour, who believed that it might be valuable. It was sent – by post in a normal paper envelope – to the Cape Colony's foremost mineralogist in Grahamstown, William Atherstone. The stone turned out to be a 21.25-carat diamond and was immediately christened Eureka. The discovery of the Eureka diamond, together with the colossal 83.5-carat Star of South Africa discovered two years later, started what has become known as South Africa's mineral revolution, a revolution that would transform the South African interior into the economic powerhouse that it remains to this day.

The Eureka and Star discoveries made big news not only locally, but especially in Europe – a replica of the Eureka was even displayed at the 1867 Paris Exhibition. Soon thousands of hopeful locals and foreigners rushed to the South African interior in search of riches. One spot, a hill known as Colesberg Kopje, seemed especially promising. It would eventually become the Big Hole of Kimberley. What was at first just a hill dotted with small claims was, within five years, the second-biggest city in the colony. And it was a modern and sophisticated place: on 2 September 1882 Kimberley became the first city in the southern hemisphere to install electric lights – beating even London to it.

This wealth in and around Kimberley also attracted migrants from other African regions hundreds of kilometres away. Most were men hoping to earn high wages within a short space of time, purchase guns and ammunition, important for both hunting and warfare, and then return to their villages. Some became property owners, buying up claims in the contested Griqualand West area. But white diggers, who held the political power in the Orange Free State and, after the region was annexed by the Cape Colony, in the Cape parliament, did not want to compete with black proprietors. By 1874 they had imposed a policy that limited black ownership, and black migrants had little recourse but to find employment as temporary diggers. A migratory labour system developed to accommodate these temporary workers, a system that suited the mine owners very well, because it meant that they did not have to pay wages high enough to allow the workers to purchase permanent accommodation or support their families. Black workers could, instead, be housed in cheap compounds. This system was quickly institutionalised, and became a feature of the diamond mines and, later, the gold mines on the Witwatersrand.

To mine successfully, though, mine owners needed more than cheap labour. As the mines deepened in search of diamonds, so the need intensified to pump water from them, and the need for capital to finance the machines that would do the pumping. Onto the scene stepped a young Englishman named Cecil John Rhodes. Only eighteen years old when he arrived in Kimberley in 1871, Rhodes, with the support of Rothschild & Sons, began renting out water pumps to miners. The profits from this operation were reinvested in buying up the claims of small mining operators. By 1888 Rhodes had created De Beers Consolidated Mines by merging his companies with those of Barney Barnato, a move which ensured a monopoly on the production and sale of diamonds in the country.

It is worth considering whom this monopolist exploited. Certainly, by the time Rhodes formed De Beers, black workers on the mines were earning wages below those of whites, staying in compounds temporarily and suffering from all the racial prejudice that was common at the time (including poorer public services). The monopoly that Rhodes created would not have helped these mine workers or improved their conditions. But a monopolist still has to pay wages in a competitive market – workers could, for example, find work on farms or on the newly built railways – whereas it sells its products in an uncompetitive one. What Rhodes thus managed to do was to exploit the diamond *consumer*. In a more competitive market, consumers would have had a choice in whom they might buy from, giving them the opportunity to bargain prices down. But as the only producer of diamonds, Rhodes could reduce supply and raise prices, extracting consumer surpluses. It was a lucrative venture which made the shareholders of De Beers, Rhodes especially, incredibly wealthy.

But Rhodes's ambition was not limited to making money. At the same time as he was building his mining empire, he joined the Cape parliament in 1881 and, two years after he founded De Beers, he became the prime minister of the Cape Colony. There were many benefits to being an elected member of parliament. One of them was that you could influence government's spending priorities. And the most expensive spending category – by far – was something in which Rhodes had a special interest: railways.

The Kimberley diamond rush created a massive demand for food and fuel in the dry and barren interior. At first this demand was supplied by transport riders, who would journey from places such as Basutoland to provide the mining town with wheat, meat and wood. Transport costs, however, were excessive – and the prices of food-stuffs in Kimberley were often substantially above those elsewhere in the colony. This meant that the owners of the mines, people like Rhodes, had to pay both wages high enough to attract workers and exorbitant fuel prices to keep their machines running.

One way to reduce these high input costs was to find an alternative mode of transport. Although George Stephenson is credited with building the first commercially successful locomotive in England – the *Rocket* – in 1829, construction on the first Cape railway only began in 1859. Progress was initially slow, but once diamonds were discovered, construction accelerated rapidly. The plan was to first link the port cities of Cape Town, Port Elizabeth (today Gqeberha) and East London to Kimberley, and then build several branch lines that would link other important towns to these trunk lines. The connection between Cape Town and Kimberley was finally completed in 1885.

The railways lowered transport costs substantially, and this had a huge impact on the economy. In a paper I wrote with economic historian Alfonso Herranz, we calculate that the railways accounted for 22–25 per cent of the increase in GDP per capita in the Cape Colony in the period between 1873 and 1905. In other words, a quarter of the rise of all income in the colony can be ascribed to the railways. This, we conclude, is a 'very large share for a single investment and a clear indicator of the transformative power of the railway'.[2]

The Cape was not the only colony where railways transformed commerce. In colonial India (modern-day India, Pakistan and Bangladesh) a massive 67,247-kilometre railway network was built by the British colonial government – then known as the Raj – between 1853 and 1930, connecting isolated inland districts with coastal markets. In a seminal contribution to the literature, the economist Dave Donaldson calculates that, on average, whenever a new district was connected to the network, agricultural income in that district rose by 16 per cent.[3] The main reason for this was the reduction in trade costs, allowing inland districts to specialise in those goods they were relatively good at, and exchange the surpluses for things they were not so good at. Across the globe, from Algeria to Japan, Thailand to Uruguay, Ghana to Sweden, railways facilitated trade, buttressed industrialisation and boosted incomes.[4]

At the Cape, however, not everyone benefited from the coming of the railways. The missionary Germond's report quoted at the start of this chapter suggests that Basotho farmers certainly did not. This was because, for political reasons, the railway lines circumvented the grain-producing districts of Basutoland. Once the trunk line between Cape Town and Kimberley was completed, it was cheaper to transport wheat produced in the region around Cape Town by rail to the mines – a distance of 1,000 kilometres – than over the 330 kilometres from Lesotho to Kimberley with transport riders and their carts. In fact, as Germond further notes, it was cheaper to import Australian and American wheat and send it to Kimberley than purchase Basutoland grain. Transport costs matter, a lot.

Building the railways, however, was not cheap. As I show in a paper with economic historian Abel Gwaindepi, the railways put the Cape's public finances in a precarious position.[5] Cecil Rhodes was largely to blame. Even though the mine owners, spearheaded by Rhodes, extracted much of the benefit of the reduced transport costs that the Cape Town–Kimberley rail connection brought, they did not pay any major taxes to help government fund this expenditure. The railways were, in fact, mostly financed through debt or, to put it differently, they were funded by future taxpayers. This can be clearly seen from the exorbitantly high debt-to-GDP ratio in the colony, shown in Figure 17.1.

Some members of parliament noticed how Rhodes and his allies used public funds to support their own interests. The MP John X. Merriman asserted as much in a budget debate of 1902 in response to a very optimistic speech by another member: 'But regarding the state of the prosperity of this country, my honourable friend is living in a fool's paradise ... the success alluded to by the honourable member was perhaps only in the Cape Peninsula and not in the rest of the country.'[6]

The discovery of diamonds was only the beginning of the mineral revolution. In 1886 gold would be discovered further north, in the South African Republic (ZAR), another Boer republic. The

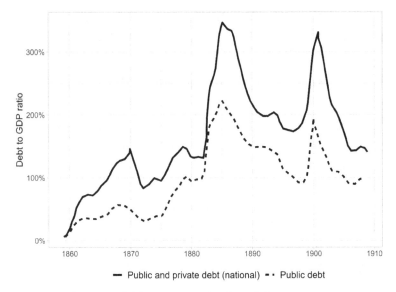

Figure 17.1 The ratio of debt to GDP in the Cape Colony, 1860–1910

discovery of gold dwarfed that of diamonds. Johannesburg, the city that was to grow up around the first goldfields, became the major financial capital of Africa in the space of just two decades. It remains the financial hub of Africa today.

There was one major difference between diamonds and gold. While Kimberley was part of the Cape Colony, and therefore the British Empire, the Witwatersrand was not. Rhodes's imperial ambitions and his vision of British rule from the Cape to Cairo could only be met if the South African Republic joined the British Empire. Railways again played an important part in this story. The ZAR identified an alternative port – Lourenço Marques, today Maputo – in Mozambique through which to export its gold. This meant that the British-controlled ports in Durban and the Cape Colony could not earn any import taxes on the goods proceeding to the large new market that arose around the gold mines. Once the Johannesburg–Lourenço Marques line was completed, and the Cape Colony lost an important source of import tax revenue, the colony's financial problems became particularly acute. There was one alternative that could both eradicate the high levels of debt and achieve Rhodes's imperial ambitions: to acquire the rich goldfields of the ZAR. But there was a problem: the ZAR was fiercely independent and did not want to lose its autonomy. The only outcome was war.

In 1899 the area we today call South Africa entered the largest and most expensive colonial war ever fought, with the two Boer republics on one side and the British Empire (including the Cape Colony and Natal) on the other. When peace was finally signed, on 31 May 1902, the ZAR and Orange Free State formally became British colonies and, in 1910, were combined with the Cape and Natal into the Union of South Africa. South Africa had become one country, although one with very unequal rights, as the next chapter will explain.

18 What Did Sol Plaatje Find on His Journey through South Africa?
Property Rights and Labour Coercion

'Awaking on Friday morning, June 20, 1913, the South African Native found himself, not actually a slave, but a pariah in the land of his birth.'[1] So begins Sol Plaatje's *Native Life in South Africa*, a book in which he appeals against one of the most consequential pieces of legislation passed by the new Union of South Africa after its establishment in 1910. The Natives Land Act of 1913 restricted ownership of land by black South Africans to a small fraction of the available agricultural land of the country. It decreed that whites and blacks were not allowed to buy land from each other. And although the Act did not have an immediate impact, as many, including Plaatje, had thought it would, it began a process of legislative segregation that would ultimately culminate in Grand Apartheid – the division of South Africa into white and black territories or 'homelands' – half a century later.[2]

Plaatje was devastated by the new Act. Together with other prominent black leaders, he travelled to England to appeal to the British government. Britain could overturn legislation regarding 'native affairs' passed by the South African parliament, but the pleas from the delegation fell on deaf ears: war was about to break out in Europe, and the British government, despite its liberal convictions, feared that any attempt to overturn the legislation would create a backlash among white South Africans and jeopardise their support for Britain. While the delegation returned empty-handed, Plaatje stayed on in England, writing and teaching. It was in London, in 1916, in the midst of the First World War, that *Native Life* was first published.

Until this moment Plaatje's life had been one of upward mobility. Born on the lands of the Tswana people south of Mafeking (today Mahikeng) in 1876, Solomon Tshekisho Plaatje moved with his parents to a mission station when he was young. There he entered a mission school, and quickly excelled in the class-room. When he was fifteen he became a pupil learner, teaching some of the younger students. In 1894, when he was eighteen, he moved to Kimberley, where he found work as a telegraph messenger and wrote the Cape Colony's civil service examination. He passed with the highest grades in Dutch and typing in the entire colony.

He quickly made a name for himself. He founded several Tswana newspapers in Kimberley and Mafeking and was an influen-tial voice as an editor and journalist. The Cape Colony had a liberal franchise, meaning that any literate man who owned or rented property and earned an income above a certain threshold could vote. Plaatje, like many other black intellectuals of the time, was eager to see these rights extended to the other regions of South Africa. The Cape liberal franchise, however, was under threat. During the previous two decades legislation had been introduced in an attempt to disenfranchise many black voters; the income thresh-old for voter qualification, for example, had been raised and the property qualification was restricted to freehold rights, thus exclud-ing the forms of communal tenure under which most black people lived. But this legislation was only partially successful.[3] By 1909 there were still thousands of black voters on the Cape Colony voters' rolls.

Plans to extend these rights to the rest of the country during negotiations for the unification of the South African colonies were, however, met with fierce resistance by more conservative voters in the former Boer republics. To secure peace between English- and Dutch-speaking whites after a long colonial war – a war, it should be added, that had also included black soldiers and servicemen on both sides – the British government acceded to these demands, and accepted a franchise restricted to white voters in all parts of South Africa except for the Cape. In opposition, black leaders united around a new organ-isation, the South African Native National Congress, established in 1912. Plaatje became its first secretary-general; ten years later it was renamed the African National Congress. But because only whites could be elected to parliament, this new organisation had limited political influence. Instead, parliament only reflected the interests of a quarter of South Africans, an important reason why the Natives Land Bill would be tabled in 1913.

It is perhaps best to let Plaatje explain what happened in his own words:

> It is moreover true that, numerically, the Act was passed by the consent of a majority of both Houses of Parliament, but it is equally true that it was steam-rolled into the statute book against the bitterest opposition of the best brains of both Houses. A most curious aspect of this singular law is that even the Minister, since deceased, who introduced it, subsequently declared himself against it, adding that he only forced it through in order to stave off something worse.
>
> Indeed, it is correct to say that Mr. Sauer [the minister of native affairs], who introduced the Bill, spoke against it repeatedly in the House; he deleted the milder provisions, inserted more drastic amendments, spoke repeatedly against his own amendments, then in conclusion he would combat his own arguments by calling the ministerial steam-roller to support the Government and vote for the drastic amendments. The only explanation of the puzzle constituted as such by these 'hot-and-cold' methods is that Mr. Sauer was legislating for an electorate, at the expense of another section of the population which was without direct representation in Parliament.[4]

In these excerpts Plaatje refers to some dissenting voices among white parliamentarians who spoke against the Act. To understand this political dynamic, it is useful to ask what the motive for the Act was – or, put differently, in whose interests it was introduced. This has long been the subject of debate. Three reasons are often listed: segregation, labour and capital. Let's discuss each in turn.

First, there was wide agreement among whites (and even some black intellectuals) that South Africans could only be at peace if there was segregation between black and white. J. B. M. Hertzog, the most populist of the new Afrikaner politicians, even believed that there should be total separation of English- and Dutch-speaking whites, as he considered the descendants of the British and Dutch settlers two different 'races'. The Land Act, in distinguishing the areas where whites and blacks could own land, can thus be seen as one of the first policies of the Union government that would ultimately lead to segregation and, later, apartheid.

Other historians claim that white farmers' need for land and labour is key to understanding the motive for the Act. Many black farmers were sharecroppers on white farms and produced large surpluses of maize or owned sizeable herds of cattle. Some even rented out the oxen that ploughed the fields of white farmers. This interrelationship was, however, not seen as a good thing by all white farmers. While some clearly benefited from it, others were concerned that sharecropping reduced the available pool of labour. The same could be said for the mine owners, who were concerned that a prosperous class of black farmers would reduce the supply of labour to the mines. What is clear is that there was not a uniform 'white' position: some whites had an interest in preserving the existing system, while others would benefit from a policy such as the Land Act.

So why was the Act passed? The answer is, simply, politics. While almost all parliamentarians supported some form of segregation, many were against the harsh clauses of the Act. However, a small but zealous minority – mostly Orange Free State farmers, led by Hertzog – threatened that they would split off from the incumbent South African Party if the Act was not introduced. To keep the peace and unity within the party, most parliamentarians, including the new minister of native affairs, J. W. Sauer, an old Cape liberal, relinquished their ideological positions and accepted the extreme measures of the Act.

The lesson is clear: unless all voices are reflected in parliament, a tiny minority can easily sway policy to the detriment of those excluded. The irony is that the Act did not prevent a split in the ruling party. In January 1914 the politicians who had pushed hard for the Act created a new political party, the National Party. More than three decades later, after the South African Party and National Party had merged into the United Party, another radical breakaway minority, now called the Purified National Party, would come to power in

1948 and introduce an even more extreme version of segregation: apartheid.

South Africa, of course, was not the only country where labour demand shaped land ownership. Just as the Witwatersrand gold mines were in desperate need of cheap, unskilled labour, a topic we return to in Chapter 28, so too the world's largest silver mine, Potosí in Peru, depended on a steady supply of mine workers. One way to ensure such a supply was, of course, to pay high wages in a competitive labour market. But this is usually not the desired outcome for mine owners. Instead, they often find it easier to lobby government for legislation that forces workers off land – either through legislation such as the Native Land Act or through labour taxes. One of the most famous examples of such a tax was the mining *mita*, a forced labour system instituted by the Spanish government in Peru and Bolivia in 1573 and abolished in 1812. The *mita* required all families on one side of a boundary to send one-seventh of their adult male population to work on the Potosí silver or Huancavelica mercury mines. Those on the other side of this (largely random) boundary were exempt from this labour tax. In one of the most cited recent studies in economic history, economist Melissa Dell uses an innovative technique to show the persistent effects of the *mita*: even though the tax was abolished more than two centuries ago, families living in former *mita* areas are today 25 per cent poorer compared with families living just across the artificial boundary.[5] This is because, Dell finds, the Spanish colonial government did not allow private ownership of land in the *mita* areas. While large farms – known as *haciendas* – could be developed outside the *mita* areas, and roads and schools could be built that would benefit later generations, those in the *mita* areas were stuck in a cycle of poverty. Land policies have long-term consequences.

Let us return to Sol Plaatje. After the Land Act became law, Plaatje toured parts of South Africa to witness its consequences. He was appalled. One anecdote sums it up. On his travels he met a Boer policeman from the Transvaal. Plaatje asked him about the effects that the Act had had on black farmers. The policeman responded by explaining that he 'knew [them] to be fairly comfortable, if not rich, and they enjoyed the possession of their stock, living in many instances just like the Dutchmen'. Then he added: 'Many of these [black farmers] are now being forced to leave their homes. Cycling along this road you will meet several of them in search of new homes, and if ever there was a fool's errand, it is that of a [black man] trying to find a new home for his stock and family just now.'[6] *Native Life* is filled with many such anecdotes.

Economic historians are not satisfied with anecdotes, however. We would like to know what the aggregate effect of the Act was on black living standards during this time. The challenge is that wages, incomes and other measures of living standards were often not recorded for a representative sample of the population. It is thus not easy to measure the effects of the Land Act or other such discriminatory policies.

This is where economic historians have to be creative. One possibility comes from measuring heights – basically, how tall people were. Although this might sound strange, there is ample evidence to show that babies that are undernourished during infancy grow to be shorter than their peers. So, this means that while roughly 80 per cent of an individual's height is determined by genetics, 20 per cent is determined by environment. There is very little genetic change within two or three generations. If heights across a population vary significantly over time, it must be because of a change in their environment.

With economic historians Bokang Mpeta and Kris Inwood, I investigated the heights of black men over the twentieth century.[7] And what we found, illustrated in Figure 18.1, supports the case that Plaatje made: living standards deteriorated significantly during the first three decades of the twentieth century. It was only in the 1930s, when gold mining expanded significantly, as I explain in Chapter 28, that babies were better nourished and there was an increase in their heights (measured when they were adults).

The dispossession of black farming land, which had begun during the nineteenth century, was institutionalised with the Land Act of 1913. Black sharecroppers on white farms were forced to give up their own stocks of cattle and become labourers or move into the overcrowded reserves. Sol Plaatje documented many of these tragic personal stories – and continued to fight for the rights of black South Africans until his death in 1932. Without political representation, however, this was an uphill battle, as black interests would always be trumped by those of white voters.

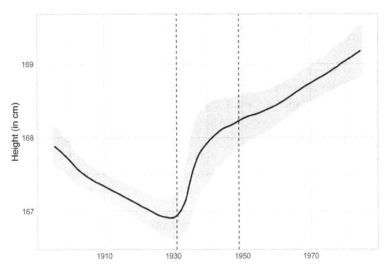

Conditional mean of black male heights and 95% confidence interval ━

Figure 18.1 Height of black South African men (older than eighteen), dated to their year of birth, 1900–1990

19 Why Can You Have Any Car as Long as It Is Black?
The Rise of American Industry

After one year, Henry Clay Frick quit the university he was attending and, with two cousins and a friend, founded the Frick Coke Company. The plan was simple. Using a beehive oven, they would turn coal into coke fuel. Coke is an important ingredient in making steel.

Henry's father had been a farmer and an unsuccessful businessman in Pennsylvania, and Henry vowed that his life would be different. Soon after establishing the Frick Coke Company, however, disaster struck – and it seemed that Henry would follow in his father's footsteps. A financial crisis in 1873 had reduced the price of coke to 90 cents per ton and Henry's business partners wanted out. But Henry chose to stay on, wrote a letter to an old family friend, Andrew Mellon, and received a loan of $10,000. For him, depressions were times of expansion; with his new loan he bought out his partners and acquired several coal mines from timid competitors at very low prices. And just as Henry had predicted, the panic did not last; within a few years the coke price had recovered to $4 per ton. By the time he was thirty, in 1879, Henry was a millionaire.

Two years later Henry married Adelaide Childs, and took her to New York for their honeymoon. It was not only for pleasure. In New York he met Andrew Carnegie, owner of vast steelworks in Pittsburgh and an important buyer of Frick's coke. Not long afterwards the two became partners in Carnegie Steel. Carnegie Steel would, in 1901, join forces with the Federal Steel Company and National Steel Company, in a deal financed by J. P. Morgan, to become the United States Steel Corporation, the world's first billion-dollar company.

Henry Frick's career overlaps with one of the most import-ant periods of American history. In 1860, when Henry was twelve, the United States was still mostly an agricultural society, with 43.2 per cent of all jobs in farming, fishing or forestry. By 1920, a year after Henry's death, that number had shrunk by almost half, being replaced by manufacturing and service-sector jobs.

What contributed to this transformation of the US economy in one lifetime? The Industrial Revolution, which began in England during the second half of the eighteenth century on the back of new scientific inventions (see Chapter 16), had spread to other parts of Western Europe and also, by the nineteenth century, to the United States. Just as in England, American manufacturing began with textiles: Samuel Slater, using secret information he brought from England, built the first cotton-spinning mill in 1790. But manufac-turing would only take off with the development of three important inputs: cheap energy, cheap transport and easy access to credit.

In 1836 steam power accounted for only 5 per cent of total power used in US manufacturing. Most power generation depended on water power. By 1900, however, steam had replaced water as the main source of power, with more than 80 per cent of all power used in manufacturing coming from steam. It was around this time, too, that steam reached its peak: a new technology – electricity – would rapidly expand during the early twentieth century.

What caused this large increase in steam power during the nineteenth century? The economic historians Nathan Rosenberg and Manuel Trajtenberg explain that as Americans moved westward after the Civil War of the 1860s, they moved into drier regions with fewer opportunities to generate water power.[1] This provided an incentive to improve steam power, and George Corliss responded by designing a machine that did two things: it was more energy efficient and it delivered a continuous, uniform flow of power. It was especially on account of its efficiency – reducing the cost of fuel by a third or more – that the 'Corliss' became the standard stationary steam engine in manufacturing. Its widespread adoption, of course, increased the need for coal, which is one reason Henry Frick's mines were always in demand. But the widespread adoption of the Corliss engine also meant that the geographical constraint of waterways was lifted. Factories could now be built anywhere, and not only next to rivers. This increased urbanisation and the growth of cities, something that would be augmented by the development of another important technology: railways.

Although horse-drawn barges on canals and paddle-wheel steamboats on rivers were in wide use during the early nineteenth century, the expansion of railways is often credited for the industrial rise of the United States. By 1840 there were as many miles of railways as there were of canals. A decade later the ratio had increased to two to one. By 1860 America had more railways than the rest of the world combined. This rapid expansion substantially lowered transportation costs, especially for those places without access to canals. This meant that the size of the market for many of those isolated in the interior expanded significantly. Just as was the case in India and elsewhere, the growth of railways in the USA expanded the market access of isolated towns in the American interior.[2] To calculate just how large this effect was, economists Dave Donaldson and Richard Hornbeck constructed a network database of railways and waterways and calculated the lowest cost for each freight route between various US districts. They concluded that 'railroads were critical to the agricultural sector in 1890: the absence of railroads would have decreased agricultural land values by 60%. Railroads' contributions to the agricultural sector were largely irreplaceable, either through extensions to the canal network or improvements in country roads.'[3]

The third factor that contributed to the rise of industry was banking and the credit it provided. Although the history of banking in the United States dates back to the 1780s, it was only in 1836 that an era of 'free banking' began, with mixed results. Although the number of banks expanded rapidly all across America, banks could issue their own currency with little or no security, which resulted not only in high transaction costs but also in frequent bank failures and financial crises. The National Banking Acts of 1863 and 1864 were introduced to curb the risky behaviour of these institutions. It granted state charters to establish new banks and incorporate them into a national banking system, thereby contributing to the development of a national currency backed by bank holdings of US Treasury bills.

One interesting feature was that the new Act required banks to hold twice the equity in towns with more than 6,000 people than they did in towns below that threshold. This made it more difficult to establish a bank in a town with just more than 6,000 people than in a town with just below 6,000. One study exploits this difference to show that banks in towns just below the threshold extended more credit and chose a higher leverage, leading to a local credit boom that was associated with an expansion in local manufacturing industry.[4] However, these same banks were also more likely to default during or after a financial crisis. Thus, places with less stringent regulations (and thus more bank competition) saw greater economic growth but also greater financial instability.

Innovations in energy, transportation and finance gave people like Henry Frick ample opportunity to make a fortune. But these innovations did not only benefit a small elite. The average American born in the 1840s, like Frick, would experience enormous changes in their lifetime. Their primary source of light changed from candles to kerosene lamps and then to electric light bulbs. Their mode of transport would change from walking and horses to steam-powered trains and electric trolley cars and, finally, by the beginning of the twentieth century, to gasoline-powered automobiles.

It was automobiles that would transform American cities anew, this time at the hands of another Henry. In 1903 Henry Ford established the Ford Motor Company and in 1908 produced the Model T, a car for the mass market that proved widely popular. Demand soon outstripped supply. In what was probably his most important invention, Ford realised that instead of using the same worker to manufacture an entire car, he could specialise the tasks for each worker, and thus produce far more cars in the same amount of time. The moving assembly line was thus born. To speed up production, all components were standardised and tasks were timed and reduced to a minimum. It is said that Ford one day noticed that black paint dried faster, and to cut down on production time he ordered that all cars be painted black. This explains his remark that 'a customer can have a car painted any colour that he wants so long as it is black'.

Not only did this new system allow the Ford company to produce more cars, it also earned them greater profits, which allowed them to pay their workers better: by 1914 Ford could increase the daily wage for an eight-hour day to $5 from a previous $2.34 for nine hours. Higher productivity translated into higher incomes, for rich and poor.

Higher incomes also meant more tax revenue for local governments, allowing them to invest in infrastructure that would further improve living standards. The best evidence of this comes from economists Marcella Alsan and Claudia Goldin's work on the impact of water and sewerage treatments built by municipalities around Boston between 1880 and 1920.[5] As we know from work in developing countries today, investments in water and sanitation infrastructure can yield large returns. Water infrastructure removes impurities, making water safe for consumption. Sanitation infrastructure removes excrement from drinking water, limiting exposure to gastro-intestinal diseases. In short: these unsexy investments can save millions of lives. And this is exactly what Alsan and Goldin found. Boston municipalities that built water and sewerage treatments with their additional tax revenue lowered infant mortality by almost 50 per cent; from roughly one in six children in 1896 to one in eleven by 1920.

In Henry Frick's lifetime, then, not only had the income of the average American soared from $3,713 to $10,450,[6] but life expectancy, despite a deadly flu pandemic in 1918, had increased from forty-two years for men at birth in the 1840s to fifty-six years by 1920. A country of horses had become a country of cars: by 1920 one in three American households owned one. Half of them were Model Ts. The agrarian America that Frick was born into had been transformed into an urbanised, industrial superpower.

20 What Does a Butterfly Collector Do in the Congo?
The Berlin Conference and the Colonisation of Africa

In October 1887 a veterinarian in Belfast was tinkering with his son's bicycle. Its metal wheels made the cycle slow, so to fix this, John Dunlop took some rubber that he used in his veterinary practice; he added the inflated tube of sheet rubber to a wooden wheel and rolled both the wooden and metal wheels across his yard in a game to see which could roll furthest. The inflated wooden wheel continued on long after the metal wheel had stopped rolling. The pneumatic tyre was born.

Dunlop's timing was impeccable. Two years earlier the Rover had first appeared on the market. In contrast to the penny-farthing, the Rover was a rear-wheel-drive, chain-driven 'safety bicycle' with two similar-sized wheels. It is the bicycle design still most common today. The two inventions – the new bicycle and the inflatable rubber tyre – transformed the bicycle industry. Although Dunlop retired in 1895 and his company was sold the following year, it was renamed Dunlop Rubber in the early twentieth century, just as Ford's first Model T, with its insatiable demand for rubber tyres, was rolling off the assembly line.

To satisfy this demand, new sources of wild rubber had to be found. Brazil had long been the only source, but the labour-intensive and generally unpleasant nature of harvesting rubber meant that production could not easily be scaled up. Central Africa offered the perfect solution. Here was a region richly endowed with wild rubber, with a large negative trade balance and a seemingly docile labour force. What could possibly go wrong?

It helps to start the story a bit earlier. In 1876 the king of the Belgians, Leopold II, hosted a geographical conference in Brussels to which he invited explorers. His aim was to stir up interest in the region around the Congo River, ostensibly as a civilising mission to 'improve' the local Congolese. After the conference, Henry Morton Stanley, an American explorer of Africa who is largely remembered for his quip 'Dr Livingstone, I presume' when meeting the famous Scottish explorer and missionary David Livingstone in 1871, was appointed by Leopold to explore the Congo River further and sign treaties with the local chiefs living on its banks.

But it was not only Leopold who was interested in Africa. One consequence of the Industrial Revolution in Britain and, by the end of the nineteenth century, also in the United States and Western Europe was a rise in the relative prices of commodities. Many of these commodities –such as ivory, groundnuts, palm oil, gum, sugar, rubber, cotton and various minerals – were found in Africa, and made the continent an attractive place for trade.[1] But imports could not keep up with demand – and, in any case, it required the cooperation of local entrepreneurs. Having to pay increasingly more for commodity imports from Africa, European rulers began to consider an alternative approach.

This became clear when Otto von Bismarck, chancellor of the German Empire, convened a conference of fourteen countries in November 1884 to discuss the principles that should guide European colonisation of African territories. Attended by Britain, France, the Ottoman Empire and the United States, among others, the conference opened in November 1884 and concluded in February 1885. The outcome – the General Act of the Berlin Conference – is generally considered to have formalised the Scramble for Africa by European powers, although it is perhaps best to see the Berlin Conference in a broader context, as one of many steps in the process of the European colonisation and occupation of Africa. Just as European trade in the Indian Ocean had morphed into colonisation, a topic we discussed in Chapter 10, so too trade over several decades turned into the European conquest and colonisation of Africa.

But the Berlin Conference was an important moment. The delegates around the table were perhaps unaware of (or uninterested in) the implications of their decisions, but in reality they were deciding the futures of nations. As Lord Salisbury, the British representative, noted: 'We have been engaged in drawing lines upon maps where no white man's feet have ever trod; we have been giving away mountains and rivers and lakes to each other, only hindered by the small impediment that we never knew exactly where the mountains and rivers and lakes were.'

In 2016 two economists, Stelios Michalopoulos and Elias Papaioannou, published a paper that investigated the consequences of this partitioning of Africa.[2] To do this they used George Murdock's Ethnolinguistic Map, which shows all the boundaries of African ethnic communities and kingdoms before colonisation and identifies those ethnic groups that were partitioned by the new colonial boundaries drawn up at the Berlin Conference. The point was to compare the outcomes today of those ethnic groups that were partitioned by the Conference delegates with those that were not. The outcome they were most interested in was violence, so they used a dataset of all acts of political violence that occurred on the continent between 1997 and 2013. These included conflicts between government forces, rebels and militias, and violence against civilians.

Their findings revealed the long-term consequences of the arbitrary partitioning of Africa. An ethnic group that was partitioned, they found, had an 8 per cent greater likelihood of some act of violence than an ethnic group that was not partitioned. The intensity of the conflicts was also 40 per cent worse for partitioned ethnicities. The largest effect was on conflict between governments and rebel groups; they found no effect, for example, of ethnic partitioning on riots and protests. This confirms what we know from history: partitioned ethnic groups that form minorities in a country are more likely to 'face discrimination from the national government' and therefore engage in rebellions, 'often with the support of their co-ethnics on the other side of the border'.[3]

The effects of partitioning are not only apparent in the likelihood of violence. Using a modern-day survey across twenty African countries, Michalopoulos and Papaioannou showed that the members of a partitioned ethnic group today have fewer household assets, poorer access to public utilities, and lower levels of education. This is not because the countries in which these partitioned groups reside are necessarily poorer; 'rather it is driven by the poorer economic circumstances of members of split ethnicities irrespective of their actual residence'.[4]

The Scramble for Africa began a haphazard process of European colonisation of the African continent that would formally end during the second half of the twentieth century. European occupation and rule was neither a uniform nor a linear process; the motives for the colonisation of Africa and the ways in which it was carried out varied considerably between colonial powers, and depended on the types of political and social systems in the colonised territories as well as the timing of the intervention.[5] This has made understanding the impact of colonisation a very difficult and much-debated issue, with some scholars arguing that colonisation brought formal education and new technologies to the continent, thereby improving living standards, while others point to the subjugation and repression that many Africans had to endure under European rule and conclude that colonisation was clearly detrimental – and that it has never truly ended.

The reason there is so much debate is that there is no plausible research design. That is, almost all of Africa was colonised; we do not have sufficient observations of African territories that were not colonised. That makes our usual tools to measure the impact of a historical shock unsuitable and explains why there are so many different interpretations. As social scientists, though, it is our duty to think of innovative ways to answer this question in the most rigorous of ways. It means that we have to think hard about the counterfactual: what would have been the outcome if colonisation had not happened? That is what the economic historians Leander Heldring and James Robinson explore in 'Colonialism and economic development in Africa'.

Before we turn to their findings, it is perhaps useful to consider the type of question we will ask. In economic history we usually distinguish between positive and normative questions. Positive questions ask 'what happened'. They are interested in testable, refutable facts. Normative questions ask 'whether this was good or bad'. This implies a value judgement. These are much harder questions to answer because they are based on the norms and values of those asking the questions. And when there are different norms and values in a society, the same normative questions could have different answers, even if the facts are the same.

When the question about the impact of colonisation is considered, most people immediately jump to a normative interpretation: whether colonisation was 'good' or 'bad'. That is not what we want to answer here. We want instead to understand what colonisation was: how, where, when and by whom? What, when and why did Europeans intervene and how, when and why did Africans respond? If we know this, it will help us to ascertain how and why people (as individuals and groups) behaved the way they did. That is ultimately what we are interested in as social scientists: to construct better theories of human and social behaviour.

Although I have stressed that the experience of African colonisation varied substantially across the continent, it helps to categorise these diverse experiences. Heldring and Robinson identify three broad types of colonisation. The first concerns those regions with a centralised state at the time of colonisation. These include countries such as Botswana, Burundi, Ghana, Lesotho and Rwanda. The second concerns those regions characterised by European settlement. These are places like Kenya, Namibia, South Africa and Zimbabwe. The third concerns everywhere else: places with no centralised state, a mixture of centralised and decentralised states, and no European settlement. These are countries such as Nigeria, Uganda, Sierra Leone and Somalia.

Evaluating each of these three colonisation types, Heldring and Robinson argue that there is little evidence that colonisation brought more rapid development than would have happened in a counterfactual world where African states continued to govern their own territories. This is especially true for the first two colonisation types: those involving centralised African states and European settlement. The third case is more uncertain because it is unlikely that central states would have developed in these places. Colonial rule may have brought a more peaceful situation than the counterfactual in the short run, but perhaps that came at the cost of long-run peace, as the Michalopoulos and Papaioannou paper clearly demonstrates.

Despite the construction of railways and other forms of infrastructure geared towards European interests, and despite investment in formal education and medicine, Heldring and Robinson conclude that in each of the colonisation types they identify, the evidence suggests that colonisation had a detrimental effect on African living standards relative to the counterfactual case of no colonisation. In their own words: 'All in all, we find it difficult to bring the available evidence together with plausible counterfactuals to argue that there is any country today in sub-Saharan Africa which is more developed because it was colonised by Europeans. Quite the contrary.[6] Keep in mind that this does not deny that colonial powers did bring formal education, infrastructure or technology to some places – and that many Africans benefited from these investments. In Ghana, for example, African farmers profited greatly from the initial introduction of cash crops such as cocoa.[7] But given the favourable terms of trade for African commodities at the time, did this economic take-off happen because of or despite colonial rule? In other words, without British involvement, would it not have happened in any case? It seems very likely. Another aspect to keep in mind is that, as the economic historian Elise Huillery has demonstrated, often these colonial investments were funded not by the colonial powers but by taxes on Africans themselves.[8] And where taxes could not be raised, Africans were often coerced into forced labour.[9] Although we do not have accurate estimates for incomes before European arrival, the existing anthropometric evidence we have suggests that the heights of Africans declined during colonisation.[10] Taking all this evidence together, then, there is little doubt that European colonisation hurt rather than aided African development.

To understand just how debilitating colonisation could be, it helps to return to the Congo Free State, perhaps the most extreme version of colonisation in Africa. At the Berlin Conference France was 'given' the north bank of the Congo River (today, Congo-Brazzaville and the Central African Republic), while Portugal was given Angola. Leopold, in his personal capacity, was given the Congo (today the Democratic Republic of the Congo), an area larger than England, France, Germany, Italy and Spain combined.

When the demand for rubber increased suddenly because of John Dunlop's invention, Leopold saw an opportunity. He gave concessions to private companies and appointed a private army of Belgian and local soldiers – the Force Publique – to compel the more than 30 million inhabitants of the Congo to harvest wild rubber. Under colonial officials such as Léon Rom, a man who otherwise liked painting, writing and butterfly collecting, the Force Publique used any and every method to ensure a supply of wild rubber. Those who resisted the concession companies and armed forces were punished with torture, mutilation and murder. What began as a tool for extraction turned into genocide. While the numbers are imprecise, an estimated 10 million Congolese were killed, just as many as all the soldiers who died during the First World War and just below the total number of Africans shipped across the Atlantic as slaves. It was one of the worst human atrocities ever committed.

The economists Sara Lowes and Eduardo Montero wanted to know whether these historical concessions still affect living standards today, more than a century after they were shut down.[11] To find out, they surveyed residents living on either side of the border of the former rubber concessions. Congolese living inside these former concessions, they discovered, have lower levels of wealth, health and education. Village chiefs inside these borders also provide less infrastructure, are less democratic and are more likely to be hereditary. Leopold's ghost continues to haunt the Congo.

Leopold himself never paid for the atrocities committed in his name. When news of the genocide reached the West, Leopold was, after a delay of several years, finally forced to relinquish 'his' colony to the Belgian government. In *King Leopold's Ghost*, journalist Adam Hochschild discusses the terms of the handover agreement.[12] The Belgian government agreed to assume all 110 million francs of debt. It also agreed to pay 45.5 million francs towards completing Leopold's then unfinished pet building projects. And, on top of all this, the Belgian government agreed to pay their king another 50 million francs 'as a mark of gratitude for his great sacrifices made for the Congo'.

'Those funds were not expected to come from the Belgian taxpayer,' Hochschild notes. 'They were to be extracted from the Congo itself.'[13]

21 Who Wrote the Best Closing Line of Modern Literature?
The Great Depression and the New Deal

By November 1932 the United States economy was in a deep depression. The unemployment rate was above 20 per cent, the highest it had ever been, and the production of goods and services had fallen by 28 per cent since its peak in 1929. America needed fresh ideas.

It found them in a new president. During the first hundred days of his presidency Franklin D. Roosevelt, together with a largely Democratic Congress, instituted a broad range of spending and lending programmes and various new regulations that would collectively become known as the New Deal. The range of programmes included things such as state and local public works initiatives, temporary relief for the unemployed and the payment of farm subsidies. The programmes would, over the next eight years, be continually modified. Some initiatives were cancelled soon after their establishment, others continued until the end of the broader programme but were then discontinued, and still others, such as farm subsidies, were established as permanent programmes that remain in place today. In this chapter we discuss why some of these worked and others did not.

But first let's discuss why America was in such a deep depression in the first place. The Great Depression formally began in 1929 with the crash of the New York Stock Exchange on Wall Street. On 24 October – 'Black Thursday' – nervous investors began selling large volumes of shares, causing a huge fall in stock prices. Five days later, on 29 October – 'Black Tuesday' – another wave of panic swept the stock markets, this time with even bigger effects. By mid-November more than a third of the stock market's value was gone. Many shares ended up being entirely worthless. Millions of people lost all their savings, and thousands of banks that had granted unsecured loans to investors collapsed.

Why did this happen in the first place? What were the reasons for the crash? Why October 1929? How did so few see it coming? To answer these questions we need to go back a decade or two, to Henry Ford and the First World War.

The outbreak of war in 1914 ended the first era of globalisation. Before the war, goods and people could move easily across borders. That allowed capital-rich countries, such as Britain, to focus on producing manufactured goods while importing food from land-abundant countries such as America and Argentina. It also allowed thousands of Europeans to move to the New World, raising their own productivity, incomes and living standards and, perhaps surprisingly, also those of the people they left behind.

Then came the Great War. Borders closed. Capital that had funded new infrastructure now had to fund the war effort. New York, rather than London, became the new centre of the world's credit network. In 1918, after four years of war, the time was ripe for reintegrating the global economy. This was marked by a return to an era of low barriers, which were meant to buttress the shattered economies of Europe. Instead, the opposite happened. The Treaty of Versailles imposed heavy penalties on the perpetrators of the war. This in turn sank Germany into a prolonged period of stagflation. America turned inwards, raising trade tariffs and imposing barriers to immigration. The global economy of 1920 was in a far more fragile state than it had been just a decade earlier.

This was, however, not immediately obvious in the United States. After a short post-war and Spanish flu-induced recession, the American economy soared. Credit was cheap. Americans borrowed three times more than before the war, buying all kinds of expensive luxury items such as radios and refrigerators and, in particular, cars. No statistic can quite capture this age of exuberance as well as *The Great Gatsby*, F. Scott Fitzgerald's iconic book first published in 1925.[1]

It was not only demand that pushed the US economy forwards. Henry Ford's innovations in mass production pushed car prices to new lows. Americans of all ranks could now dream of owning something that had been reserved for the rich only two decades earlier. And because of cheap credit they could do so even if their salaries did not justify the extra debt. Chapter 19 noted that in 1920 one in every three American households owned a car. By the end of the decade the ratio was almost one to one. The surge in cars also boosted investments in new roads, the construction of suburban houses, and the opening of motels and diners to serve these new customers.

The Roaring Twenties would last until 1929. But even before then, the economy had shown signs that the surge in consumption was not sustainable. Americans were getting into too much debt, yet stock prices, largely because of insider trading and speculator manipulation – all legal at the time – continued to rise rapidly. Something had to give.

Black Thursday and Black Tuesday, and the further collapse of the stock market in the months that followed, devastated the American economy. A year earlier Herbert Hoover had been elected president. Hoover's response to the crisis was denial and, once it became abundantly clear that a depression was at hand, the best he could do was to request the private sector not to cut wages. For the laissez-faire Hoover, government spending was not even an option. The president also opposed any form of government relief. Even when bread-lines appeared across the country with long queues of hungry Americans, he maintained that such a programme risked plunging America 'into socialism and collectivism'.[2]

The same was true for those who ran the Federal Reserve, America's central bank. Today we know that in times of crisis monetary intervention is necessary to ensure enough liquidity in the financial market and prevent a run on banks. But the thinking at the time, of most policymakers and economists, was that an economy in crisis should be left alone, allowing the weaker banks and firms to perish. This, these experts argued, was to punish those who had made poor decisions during the good times: why should the mismanaged companies be bailed out? A depression was seen as a way to cleanse the economy of all the unproductive investments made during the boom years.

The problem was that the American economy just would not return to 'normal'. Those with some savings held onto them at all costs and the rest went hungry, scraping by to survive. A doctor working in a clinic remembered:

> The poor got some care, could go to free dispensaries. The rich got good care because they could afford it. There was this big middle class that was not getting any care. The middle class got very much in the position of the poor people ... People of that status would find it very difficult to accept charity ... Every day ... someone would faint on a streetcar. They'd bring him in, and they wouldn't ask any questions ... they knew what it was. Hunger. When he regained consciousness, they'd give him something to eat.[3]

The Great Depression had exposed a deep-rooted trend of the 1920s: America was becoming more unequal. Growth in manufacturing had increased the wages of skilled factory workers somewhat, but it especially benefited the owners, who earned large profits. Moreover, the worker in the city had to compete with increasing numbers of rural migrants. Increased mechanisation on farms and the low additional demand for food (a low income elasticity) reduced farmers' relative incomes. In short, the small farmers could not survive and were forced to move to the city, thus reducing the wages of the unskilled by flooding the labour market and therefore widening the gap between the rich and the poor.

The depression not only exposed but also exacerbated these fissures. Again, novelists can put into words what numbers often cannot. John Steinbeck, in *The Grapes of Wrath*, reflects on these inequalities:

> And the great owners, who must lose their land in an upheaval, the great owners with access to history, with eyes to read history and to know the great fact: when property accumulates in too few hands it is taken away. And that companion fact: when a majority of the people are hungry and cold they will take by force what they need. And the little screaming fact that sounds through all history: repression works only to strengthen and knit the repressed. The great owners ignored the three cries of history. The land fell into fewer hands, the number of the dispossessed increased,

and every effort of the great owners was directed at repression. The money was spent for arms, for gas to protect the great holdings, and spies were sent to catch the murmuring of revolt so that it might be stamped out. The changing economy was ignored, plans for the change ignored; and only means to destroy revolt were considered, while the causes of revolt went on.[4]

It is clear that in early 1933, when the depression was at its deepest, Americans were desperate for something different.

The first major relief programme that Roosevelt introduced after his election was the Federal Emergency Relief Administration, which provided immediate and direct government-funded income relief to households. Roosevelt also introduced massive public works programmes that funded things such as highway construction and flood control and hired workers for these projects at market wages. This funding was not evenly distributed. Political considerations were important to Roosevelt; more funds were allocated to districts that were more likely to swing towards voting for him. Other policies, such as the Agricultural Adjustment Act (AAA), which 'sought to raise farm prices by paying farmers to take land out of production for several types of goods, including cotton, tobacco, corn and wheat', did not benefit everyone equally.[5] While farmers gained from AAA payments, farm workers did not. In districts with more AAA spending, farm workers and the number of sharecroppers declined, and were replaced by machines. This then caused a decline in incomes and a rise in infant mortality rates.[6]

Despite these concerns, the New Deal largely stabilised a collapsing economy and turned it round. Between 1933 and 1937 the US economy grew at 7 per cent per year. As Eric Rauchway notes: 'This impressive rate of recovery reminds us how far the United Stated had to go to recover from the Hoover era.'[7] Economists who had believed that such policies were just one step away from socialism or, worse, communism suddenly needed to revise their models. It was John Maynard Keynes in 1935 who provided the intellectual rigour, in his book *The General Theory of Employment, Interest and Money*, that would justify government stimulus to revive a depressed economy.

Although the Great Depression was associated with severe poverty, a situation that Roosevelt's New Deal began to improve, it had exactly the opposite effect on levels of inequality. Wage inequality declined significantly between 1929 and 1933 as the middle classes joined the ranks of the poor, but by 1935 it had recovered to the same level as that before the Great Depression.[8] This mirrors the experience of many countries that see rapid poverty reduction. Not everyone grows out of poverty at an equal pace. While poverty declines, inequality may increase. It would be short-sighted to use only inequality as the barometer of policy success.

The New Deal did not end the American poverty created by the Great Depression: that would only happen when America joined the Second World War and ramped up military production. But a fundamental shift in the US economy had occurred. From a laissez-faire economy with limited government spending of less than 3 per cent of GDP, the New Deal transformed the role that government played to stabilise and grow the economy. By 1939, the year that the Second World War began, the US government spending was 8 per cent of its GDP. Although it briefly returned to lower levels during the war, it began a process of rising government transfers. By the 2010s just the operating expenses of the government were above 22 per cent of GDP.[9] In 2020, during the Covid-19 pandemic, the US government announced several fiscal programmes to support vulnerable households and businesses, pushing the ratio of operating expenses to GDP beyond 33 per cent and on course for its largest ever share in the US economy.

22 How Could a Movie Embarrass Stalin?
Russia and the Turn to Communism

Russia is the world's largest country by landmass, covering an area of 17 million square kilometres. Canada, the world's second-largest country, is less than 10 million square kilometres in size. At the beginning of 2022, before the invasion of Ukraine, Moscow, Russia's capital, was home to more billionaires than any other city on earth. Yet Russians are relatively poor compared with their western and eastern neighbours. The GDP per capita of Russians is only half that of Portugal, one of the poorest countries in Western Europe, and less than a quarter of that of Japan, its easternmost neighbour. Why is it that the average Russian has lagged behind, despite the nation's apparent opulence?

The answer lies in the country's economic institutions. By the beginning of the twentieth century Russia was already a poor country relative to its neighbours. It had only abolished serfdom in 1861. Serfdom, first introduced in the sixteenth century, was a system of labour coercion in which rural workers were forced to work for the landed elite, much like Western Europe's system of feudalism, which was already in decline by the time Russia imposed its version. And despite everything that befell Russia in the twentieth century, one should not lose sight of the fact that serfdom also had long-term consequences. The economic historians Johannes Buggle and Steven Nafziger have showed that households in districts where serfdom was widespread before 1861 are poorer today.[1] Why is this? The authors explain that the mechanism through which past serfdom affects present outcomes is industrialisation: in those places with high levels of former serfdom, firms are smaller, less productive, and more likely to be involved in agriculture than in manufacturing.

But serfdom was not the only economic institution to shape Russia's economic trajectory. When the serfs were emancipated in 1861 they used their freedom to move to the cities of Moscow and St Petersburg. But work in the cities was hard to come by, which meant that many lived in worsening squalor, hungry and destitute. With no jobs at hand and little hope of the situation improving, their anger reached a tipping point.

Their anger was directed at the monarchy. Ruled by the Romanov tsar Nicholas II, Russia was not only poor, but also deeply corrupt and oppressive. In 1904 it had entered an unpopular war against the Japanese that could only end in Russia's defeat. To appease his subjects, the tsar promised reforms. These did not materialise and, as a result, in January 1905 thousands of angry workers took to the streets in protest. Imperial forces opened fire in response, wounding and killing hundreds of demonstrators. The 'Bloody Sunday massacre' sparked national protests that finally ended when Nicholas promised to set up a representative assembly, or Duma.

When the First World War broke out, Russia was unprepared and ill-equipped to fight Germany's modern army. Russian casualties were greater than those of any country in any previous war. In 1915 Nicholas left the Russian capital, now renamed Petrograd (because St Petersburg sounded too German), to head the army, and left his unpopular wife Alexandra and her controversial (and somewhat mad) monk and adviser, Grigory Rasputin, in charge of running the country.

Nicholas had not learned from his earlier mistakes. Russia's losses in war, combined with an unpopular monarchy, were enough to fuel another wave of protests, this time with revolutionary consequences. The revolution began on 8 March 1917. Thousands of hungry Russians clashed with police in the streets, demanding food and a change in government. Despite many fatalities, the protests continued until Nicholas abdicated and a new government was formed.

Thirty-six-year-old Alexander Kerensky was one of the leaders of the revolution. An excellent orator, he became minister of war in the new socialist-liberal coalition government which

implemented various policies allowing free speech, trade-union formation and several other freedoms previously banned by the monarchy. As minister of war, Kerensky made the difficult decision to
continue Russia's participation in the war. It proved hugely unpopular with the soldiers and workers, who had believed that the new
government would end the war. By contrast, the more extreme
socialist party of Vladimir Lenin – the Bolsheviks – promised
'peace, land and bread'. On 6 and 7 November, when it was clear
that the policies introduced by the new government were not having
the desired effect, the Bolsheviks, now bolstered by many disgruntled
moderates, led an uprising against the Kerensky government in
the second revolution of 1917 – the October Revolution, or Red
October. (It is called the October Revolution because Russia was still
using the Julian calendar, which was about two weeks behind the
Gregorian calendar.)

Red October and the Bolshevik takeover plunged Russia
into a civil war that would last three years. On the one side was the
Red Army, backed by Lenin's Russian Communist Party, and on the
other side was the White Army, a coalition of monarchists, capitalists and supporters of social democracy. Lenin, who was by 1918 the
de facto leader of a one-party state, enacted economic policies that he
believed would signal the next and final phase of economic development. Lenin's communist policies included the nationalisation of all
manufacturing and industry and the requisitioning of surplus grain
from peasant farmers.

Before we discuss their consequences, it helps to understand
the intellectual origins of Lenin's communist policies. After he was
expelled from university, Lenin had been drawn to the writings of the
German philosopher Karl Marx. Marx believed that capitalism is
based on the exploitation of labour. The owners of the means of
production – capitalists – are able to extract the surplus value of this
labour for their own benefit, protected by the ruling regime and by
property rights. Marx believed that capitalism inevitably leads to
a class struggle, a struggle that can only end in revolution whereby
the means of production come to be owned by everyone equally. This
will allow 'a higher phase of communist society', Marx wrote:

> After the enslaving subordination of the individual to the
> division of labour ... has vanished; after labour has become

not only a means of life but life's prime want; after the productive forces have also increased with the all-round development of the individual, and all the springs of co-operative wealth flow more abundantly – only then can the narrow horizon of bourgeois right be crossed in its entirety and society inscribe on its banners: From each according to his ability, to each according to his needs![2]

Lenin believed that the Bolshevik Revolution in Russia had set an example of a workers' revolution that other countries would inevitably follow. But his optimism about collectivist policies was dashed when he witnessed the devastation they caused. Two years after the Communist Party came to power, farming and manufacturing output in Russia plummeted. While Americans were experiencing an era of unparalleled improvements in living standards – the Roaring Twenties – Russians were starving; in 1921 alone an estimated 5 million Russians died of famine. To prevent another revolution, Lenin announced a New Economic Policy that relaxed many of the War Communism policies, which included allowing peasants to sell their produce on the open market. While many Bolsheviks felt betrayed by these policies, scholars today suggest that the government would have been overthrown without them.

But Lenin was ill. In 1922 he appointed Joseph Stalin, a close ally, to the position of general secretary of the Communist Party. When Lenin had a stroke that partially paralysed him, Stalin became the de facto leader, making several important decisions, although still with Lenin's blessing. One was to incorporate fourteen countries, including Ukraine, Georgia, Latvia, Armenia and Kazakhstan, into a federation with Russia – the Union of Soviet Socialist Republics (the USSR) – which expanded Russia's influence greatly.

When Lenin died, there were multiple factions vying for power. On the left were Leon Trotsky and his supporters; on the right, holding the course with the New Economic Policy, was Stalin. Through clever alliances and appointments, by 1927 Stalin managed to gain control of the Central Committee of the Communist Party. Trotsky, his main rival, was deported in 1929.

As soon as he had gained control of the party, Stalin became more radical. He blamed the wealthier farmers (or kulaks), who had responded to the introduction of Lenin's New Economic Policy by increasing production, for hoarding grain and preventing its distribution to the cities where industrial workers needed it. He then sent the Red Army to confiscate all grain stores and arrest those farmers who opposed the measures. Violence broke out. By July 1930 more than 300,000 kulaks had been forced to flee or were shipped to penal camps in Siberia in what became known as the de-kulakisation policy. Many died on the way. With the kulaks out of the way, a policy of mass collectivisation of agriculture was introduced. Although it was officially voluntary, almost all peasants joined (for fear of punishment) or moved to the cities; between 1929 and 1931 1.4 million peasants abandoned their farms. The result was predictable: a major famine broke out in the winter of 1932–3, killing an estimated 5–7 million people.

The mass collectivisation of agriculture was one of two major initiatives in Stalin's Five-Year Plans. The other was the development of heavy industry and rapid industrialisation. Here Stalin achieved more success. In 1934, at the end of the first Five-Year Plan, industrial output was 50 per cent higher. Large new industrial centres were created overnight. These included Yekaterinburg with its heavy machine production facility, Magnitogorsk with its steel factory, and Chelyabinsk with its tractor plant.

Did this transformation of the Russian economy benefit the average Russian? Yes and no. Economic historian Robert Allen has calculated the changes in standards of living from 1928 to 1937 for both urban and rural Russians. He finds that those on the farms suffered: he quantifies 'the fall in living standards that occurred during collectivisation and shows that, by the late 1930s, the farm sector had only regained the consumption level of 1928'.[3] By contrast, the 'gains in average consumption in the 1930s were confined to urban residents and, to a lesser extent, accrued to peasants moving to the cities'.[4] He estimates that the gain for those in urban areas was about a 2 per cent annual increase in consumption.

But Stalin's apparent success in transforming the Soviet economy came at great cost. To entrench his position, Stalin executed more than 700,000 people between 1936 and 1938, including members of his own Communist Party, government officials, ethnic minorities and kulaks. The Great Purge, as it has become known, allowed Stalin to continue commanding more output with greater authority. His Five-Year Plans continued during the Second World

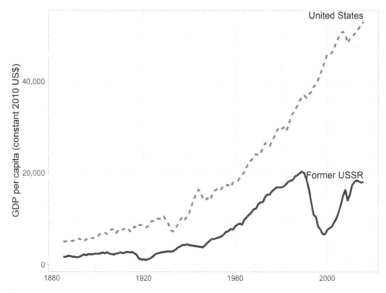

Figure 22.1 GDP per capita in the United States and the USSR, 1885–1995

War, when the focus was placed on the mechanisation of the military, and afterwards, when attention returned to heavy machinery and advanced industry.

If we consider only output, the industrialisation of the Soviet Union should be seen as a success story. From 1928 to 1970, as Figure 22.1 demonstrates, the USSR was arguably the second most successful economy in the world, after Japan.[5] But output should not be the only measure of success. Industrial output did not necessarily result in higher consumption. Consumer goods were limited to a small elite and were generally of poor quality. This was the consequence of firms not earning a profit – and thus having no incentive to compete for customers and invest in new products that would improve consumers' lives. While urban wages may have increased, the things these workers could buy were restricted to what the government believed was necessary for survival.

Output is only one indicator. Figure 22.2 plots the average life expectancy between 1960 and 2019 in former communist countries that were under the influence of the Soviet Union. The remarkable rise in life expectancy after the fall of the Berlin Wall is indicative of the poor quality of life under communism.

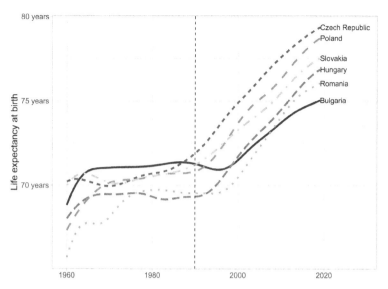

Figure 22.2 Average life expectancy in former Soviet-dominated communist countries, 1960–2019

This is best summarised by an anecdote. John Steinbeck's novel about the suffering during the Great Depression – *The Grapes of Wrath* – was released in 1939. The following year the book was turned into a film, with Henry Fonda as the lead character, Tom Joad. Although the film is considered one of the greatest American films of all time, its reception was not welcomed everywhere, especially not by the US government, which branded it 'socialist' and 'Marxist'.

In 1948, in an attempt to bolster sentiment against the capitalist system, Stalin thought it a good idea to show *The Grapes of Wrath* in the Soviet Union. Released there as *The Road to Wrath*, it produced a response that was very different from what Stalin had imagined. Audiences were in complete awe of the fact that even the poorest of the poor in the United States were able to afford an automobile. After showing for only a couple of weeks, it was quickly pulled from the circuit. Clearly, the definition of what constituted 'poor' was vastly different between the capitalism of America and the communism of the USSR.

23 Who Is the Perfect Soldier?
The Causes and Consequences of the Second World War

Walk into the Warsaw Uprising Museum in Poland's capital, and it won't be long before you'll begin to feel the eeriness that comes with being surrounded by death.[1] One exhibit allows visitors to cower inside a replica of the sewers where members of the Polish underground resistance used to hide while fighting the Nazis. Another exhibit shows original film footage of the destruction of Warsaw; by January 1945, after the Polish forces surrendered, 85 per cent of the city's buildings had been flattened. A third is dedicated to the child soldiers and nurses who died fighting for freedom. Around 16,000 members of the resistance were killed fighting in the streets. But the actual death toll was much larger. During and after the uprising, an estimated 150,000 civilian men, women and children died, mostly in mass executions.

The Warsaw Uprising was the largest military effort by a European resistance movement during the Second World War. It lasted sixty-three days. The Soviet Red Army, stationed on the outskirts of Warsaw, failed to provide support. And despite some low-level supply drops by British and South African aeroplanes, most of which fell in Nazi-occupied territories, the Polish underground resistance and their supporters received no military support from the Allied forces making their way to Berlin on the western front. It was an insurgency against a military industrial machine. Defeat was inevitable. After their surrender, almost all Polish forces were interrogated and imprisoned, sent to Gulags or executed. The entire civilian population of Warsaw was expelled and moved to a transit camp. A quarter of them were sent to labour camps in the Third Reich. A fifth were sent to concentration camps such as Auschwitz.

Four months later, on 2 May, Berlin fell to the invading Allied forces. Six days later, war ended in Europe. It would take another four months, and two atomic bombs, to bring the deadliest conflict in human history to an end. Between 1 September 1939, when Nazi Germany invaded Poland, and 2 September 1945, an estimated 80 million people died as a direct consequence of war. Many millions more perished due to starvation and disease.

Perhaps the most surprising thing about the Second World War is that it began only two decades after the Great War of 1914–18. Then, too, millions had died of conflict and disease. New technologies, such as machine guns, tanks and aircraft, produced warfare on a scale and with an intensity that was not possible with the cavalry lance, a weapon the British had been using against the Boers only a decade earlier.[2] Railways and the telegram made possible not only the assembly, organisation and supply of large armies, but also the rapid movement of people – and disease. In the final months of 'the war to end all wars', an influenza pandemic – the so-called Spanish flu of 1918 – spread globally as soldiers returned from the war front. To give one example of its scale: an estimated 20 million people in India, 6 per cent of its population, perished because of the flu.[3]

But why, one may ask, after so much death and destruction, would war erupt so soon? To answer this, it helps to understand the origins of Germany's Nazi Party and its far-right politics.

The Treaty of Versailles brought the First World War to an end. The treaty required Germany to accept responsibility for all losses and damages during the war, to disarm, and to pay reparations. These reparations amounted to about $442 billion (in 2021 prices). The former Boer War general and international statesman Jan Smuts, who would play an instrumental role in the creation of the League of Nations initially refused to sign the treaty, as he considered it too harsh. John Maynard Keynes, his friend and a prominent British economist, thought the treaty was counterproductive and predicted that it might lead to renewed conflict.

He was not far off the mark. To repay its debt the new Weimar Republic could either raise taxes or cut spending. Austerity, in a post-war Germany that required rebuilding, was not an option. The only alternative was to print money. The consequences were disastrous. In 1923 the value of the German mark collapsed. A loaf of bread, which cost only 260 marks in 1922, increased to 200,000,000,000 marks one year later. By the end of 1923 a 50-trillion-mark banknote was printed to ease exchange.

Yet the reparation payments and the hyperinflation did not immediately boost Nazi membership. In 1924 the National Socialist German Workers' (Nazi) Party was on the ballot for the federal elections. Its message was both anti-capitalist and anti-communist. It instead wanted a *Volksgemeinschaft*, a community of the people, the idea of a racially exclusive German nation that honoured its workers. But the party failed to receive widespread support; it won only 3 per cent of the vote. Four years later, now under the leadership of Adolf Hitler, it received 2.6 per cent. A commentator in 1928 would have found it difficult to predict its dramatic ascent to national politics. Yet that is exactly what happened. In the next federal elections, in 1932, Hitler's Nazi Party won 37 per cent of the vote, becoming Germany's largest party. What explains this remarkable growth?

One answer is fiscal austerity. The Great Depression finally forced the Weimar government to cut spending and raise taxes. As expected, the policy was hugely unpopular: one study finds that those German localities more affected by the austerity measures had a higher mortality rate between 1930 and 1933.[4] This had consequences: the same study shows that those localities that endured more suffering also had a higher vote share for the Nazi Party.

But austerity is not enough to explain the coming war. Technology played a role too. During the 1920s the Weimar government introduced a news programme on what was then a new form of technology: radio. These radio broadcasts contributed to a more informed – and less radical – populace. In fact, comparing localities inside reception areas with those just outside, one study shows that having access to this news broadcast weakened support for the Nazi Party.[5] But when Hitler was appointed chancellor, the public radio station began to broadcast only Nazi propaganda. This had the opposite effect: Germans inside reception areas were now more likely to vote for the Nazis than those outside.

It is worth pointing out that Germans weren't the only ones susceptible to the power of this new mode of communication. Economist Tianyi Wang studied the effects of Catholic priest Father Charles Coughlin's popular but pro-fascist radio programme which attracted a weekly audience of 30 million American listeners during the 1930s.[6] Wang shows that places more exposed to Father Coughlin's broadcasts were more likely to form a local branch of the pro-Nazi German-American Bund and sold fewer war bonds during the war. Six decades later, in Rwanda, radio propaganda would again be used to spread intolerance, violence and genocide, this time against the Tutsi minority.[7]

Another consequence of Nazi propaganda was to fuel the antisemitism that would ultimately culminate in the Holocaust, the genocide of an estimated 6 million Jews in German-occupied Europe. Economic history can help us understand why such anti-semitic views spread. One important feature of German antisemit-ism was that there was large variation across the country: some parts of Germany were deeply prejudiced while other regions were not. Remarkably, two economic historians, Nico Voigtländer and Hans-Joachim Voth, found the reason for the large differences between regions in events that happened almost six hundred years earlier, when the Black Death killed at least a third of Europe's population.[8] In the fourteenth century, Jewish communities were often blamed for local calamities such as epidemics. The authors show that the inhabitants of those places where Jews were mas-sacred during the Black Death of 1348–50 were also more likely to attack synagogues and to deport Jews to concentration camps in the 1930s. Prejudice and persecution, it seems, can persist over half a millennium.

Although Jews were frequently made the scapegoats for pandemics, the ultimate motive may have been economic. Economic historians Sascha Becker and Luigi Pascali explain that because of the Catholic ban on usury, Jews historically had an advantage in the money-lending sector.[9] Following the Protestant Reformation, however, Jews living in Protestant regions were sud-denly exposed to competition in the banking and finance sector with the Christian majority. The authors show that those cities that converted to Protestantism also saw an increase in antisemitic pog-roms (or organised massacres) and expulsions as well as an increase in the publication of anti-Jewish books. They then show that these effects persist: those cities that converted to Protestantism during the Reformation and faced competition from Jewish moneylenders were more likely to vote for the Nazis 400 years later.

When the Second World War ended, another war began. The Cold War was a period of geopolitical tension between the capitalist United States and the communist Soviet Union and their respective allies. It was 'cold' because there was no large-scale conflict, although there were several 'proxy wars' – from the 1953 Korean War, to the 1962 Cuban Missile Crisis, to civil conflict in countries as diverse as Angola, Cambodia, Afghanistan and Nicaragua. It ended with the fall of the Berlin Wall in 1989 and the dissolution of the Soviet Union in 1991.

Vietnam was one such 'proxy war'. Officially fought between North and South Vietnam, in reality it was a war between the Soviet Union, China and their communist allies backing the North and the United States, South Korea, Australia and various other anti-communist allies backing the South. It ended with the North Vietnam's Viet Cong capturing South Vietnam's capital, Saigon, on 30 April 1975.

The Viet Cong victory is all the more remarkable given the vast resources the United States invested to win the war. The Vietnam War included the most intense bombing campaign in military history, for example. The economists Edward Miguel and Gérard Roland wanted to know how the bombing affected economic development in Vietnam: did those regions under heavy bombardment, for example, decline in comparison to those regions not bombed? Surprisingly, they find no difference in consumption levels, infrastructure, literacy or population density three decades after the bombing.[10] What happened was that, after the war, the Vietnamese government reallocated substantial resources to rebuild those parts that were heavily affected; the massive destruction of physical capital is not a death sentence for a country.[11] The bombing did, however, have a different kind of long-lasting effect: one study finds that a 1 per cent increase in bombing intensity during 1965–75 increases the likelihood of severe mental illness in adults today.[12] Children are most likely to carry the scars of war.

Cold War 'proxy wars' were often fought in the poorest of countries. Mozambique is a tragic example. After a protracted war of independence against Portugal, Mozambique gained its independence in June 1975. Its first president, Samora Machel of the Mozambican Liberation Front (FRELIMO), had the unenviable task of turning around the fortunes of a country ravaged by war and conflict. He chose to establish a socialist, one-party state. An opposition insurgent force, RENAMO, supported by neighbouring and undemocratic South Africa and Rhodesia (later Zimbabwe), launched an insurgency. A fifteen-year civil war ensued, in which at least a million Mozambicans died and many more were displaced.

The weapon of choice during both the war of independence and the civil war that followed was the landmine, otherwise also known as the 'poor man's weapon'. It was for this reason that Pol Pot, leader of Cambodia's Khmer Rouge, the regime responsible for the death of at least 1.7 million Cambodians between 1975 and 1979, reportedly remarked that the 'landmine is a perfect soldier, it doesn't need food or water, it doesn't take any salary or rest, and it will lie in wait for its victim'.[13]

Landmines were strategically placed by both FRELIMO and RENAMO combatants to disrupt trade, protect vital infrastructure, and terrorise the civilian population. By the end of the Mozambican civil war in 1992 hundreds of thousands of landmines had been buried across the vast country. One study that investigated the effects of landmines in Angola, another former Portuguese colony that suffered a long Cold War-linked civil war, shows the devastating effects of landmines especially on children.[14]

But there is hope. Mozambique, despite being one of the poorest countries on earth, has done a remarkable job of clearing its landmines. With the help of international aid agencies and new landmine detection and removal technologies, Mozambique was officially declared 'landmine free' in September 2015. The economists Giorgio Chiovelli, Selios Michalopoulos and Elias Papaioannou calculate the economic value of this landmine clearance campaign.[15] In short, it is large, particularly in the most populated areas along trade routes. In fact, the authors conclude that the landmine clearance campaign in Mozambique was similar in size to some of the largest infrastructure projects in history, such as the construction of railways in the nineteenth-century United States that we discussed in Chapter 19.

War is costly, both for the generations who experience it and for those who are left behind. New technologies, from the radio to the landmine to the Internet, can intensify conflict. But technology can also help to heal, restore and build. Our economic freedom depends on cooperation. War and conflict destroy it. A prosperous future is one without war.

24 What Was the Great Leap Forward?
Mao Zedong, Famine and the Cultural Revolution

One of the most influential individuals of modern history is
Mao Zedong – or Chairman Mao. He lived an extraordinary life.
Influenced by the Marxist-Leninist ideology of communism while
a student at Peking University, Mao was a founding member of the
Communist Party of China (CPC) in 1927. He immediately led an
insurrection – the Autumn Harvest Uprising – that initiated a civil
war with the Kuomintang (KMT), the nationalist party that then
ruled China. It was a war that would last until 1949 (although
interrupted by the Second Sino-Japanese War from 1937 to 1945).
When Mao's CPC finally defeated the nationalists, the KMT and its
followers retreated to Taiwan. This is the reason that China still does
not recognise Taiwan as an independent country today.

With the defeat and exit of the KMT in 1949, Mao founded
the People's Republic of China, a one-party state controlled by the
CPC. He then began to implement his plans to transform the Chinese
economy. Although he had many plans, the most ambitious Five-
Year Plan was undoubtedly the Great Leap Forward, from 1958 to
1962.

Much like Stalin in the USSR, Mao thought that grain and
steel production was the key to transforming China from an agrarian
into an industrial power. He had seen the apparent success of the
Soviet Union's economic transformation and hoped to replicate it in
China. To do this, Mao established self-sufficient communes of
collective ownership and work. The plan was that these communes
would be tasked by the party's Politburo, another Soviet import, to
produce a certain quantity of grain and steel annually. Hard work

was key, Mao believed. There was no need for luxury items or consumables: the Maoist life was one of stoic work for the greater good of the party and country.

But hard work and stoicism were not enough. Mao wanted China to industrialise and, to do that, it needed to produce steel. Whereas Stalin had built large steel factories, Mao believed that steel output could be achieved within communes by using backyard steel furnaces. Millions of workers, most with no knowledge of metallurgy, were diverted from farming to operate these steel furnaces in the communes. Instead of reliable fuel such as coal, workers used wood from trees and, once that source was depleted, began using their home doors and furniture. To meet the wildly optimistic output projections, they often used their own pots, pans and other scrap metal as inputs.

Mao invested heavily in irrigation – these were large capital projects that lacked input from qualified engineers. Mao also imported pseudo-scientists from the Soviet Union who advocated unscientific beliefs aimed at increasing productivity and yields. One of these was close cropping, the false idea that by planting seeds closer together, seeds of the same type would not compete against each other. Another was deep ploughing, the belief that planting seeds up to 2 metres deep would yield plants with a stronger root system.

Despite these attempts at higher farm productivity (or perhaps because of them), grain output could never reach the high targets set by the Politburo. In fact, because so many workers were diverted to work on the steel furnaces, when it was time to harvest there were not enough agricultural workers available. A lot of grain was left on the fields. Nature responded: huge swarms of locusts descended on these crops, reducing the harvest even further.

The surprising thing was that few in the upper echelons of the CPC were aware of the looming disaster. This was because of the incentives that bureaucrats faced when they had to report grain output. Because no one wanted to report declining grain output – if they did, it would amount to an admission that the system was failing and the bearers of bad news would be replaced – they inflated the output figures. This happened at almost every level of state bureaucracy. The figures that were ultimately reported to the Politburo were very different from what was happening on the ground. The result was that a lot more grain was requisitioned for the cities than the countryside could afford to provide.

The consequences were devastating: between 1958 and 1962 at least 30 million Chinese died in one of the largest famines ever recorded in human history. Some estimate the number of dead as high as 45 million. This happened despite the fact that China was still exporting grain – Mao did not want to admit that there was a famine, and thought that continuing exports would help him to save face.

While the Great Leap Forward is considered one of the greatest human tragedies of recorded history, it is worth asking just which of Mao's many policies was responsible for the disaster. The economic historians Shuo Chen and Xiaohuan Lan show that one important precursor was the collectivisation movement, which ran from 1955 to 1957.[1] This movement involved the largest transfer of property in human history: 550 million peasants were organised into collectives and deprived of private ownership of land and draught animals. But while they could do little about their land, Chen and Lan show that peasants were reluctant to transfer their draught animals. As Figure 24.1 illustrates, they killed them instead.

Why would they do this? It was a matter of incentives. 'Faced with the prospect of losing the animals' future output, and unwilling to accept the low price paid in instalments that might never materialise, peasants chose to slaughter their animals to keep the meat and hide,' the authors explain.[2] Using an innovative econometric approach, they then calculate that almost 10 million draught animals were killed in the build-up to the Great Leap Forward. This provides another reason for the severity of the famine in 1959: peasants had far fewer draught animals that might have sustained them during a famine.

One would expect that a great human tragedy like the Great Leap Forward would initiate change. And, for a brief moment, this seemed possible. After the famine, many of the policies that had brought about the disaster were reversed. Mao, although still chairman of the party, was not in charge anymore. He was replaced by younger, more pragmatic men. But this situation did not last long. While out of power Mao had been contemplating the idea of 'continuous revolution'. In 1966, at a policy conference, Mao returned to power by calling many of the reformers enemies of the communist

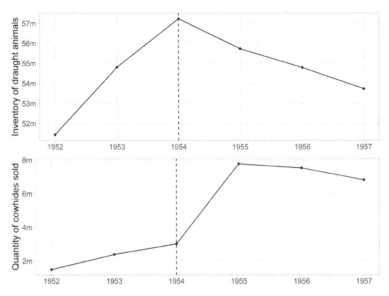

Figure 24.1 Changes in the number of draught animals and cowhides in China, 1952–1957

cause. He then launched the Cultural Revolution, which would last until 1976, the year of his death.

While the Great Leap Forward was an economic programme of land reform, the Cultural Revolution was an attempt at cultural reform with a focus on education. Here is one excerpt from the 'Sixteen Points' accepted by the party's Central Committee in 1966:

> Although the bourgeoisie has been overthrown, it is still trying to use the old ideas, culture, customs, and habits of the exploiting classes to corrupt the masses, capture their minds, and stage a comeback. The proletariat must do just the opposite: It must meet head-on every challenge of the bourgeoisie ... to change the outlook of society. Currently, our objective is to struggle against and crush those people in authority who are taking the capitalist road, to criticize and repudiate the reactionary bourgeois academic 'authorities' and the ideology of the bourgeoisie and all other exploiting classes and to transform education, literature and art, and

all other parts of the superstructure that do not correspond to the socialist economic base, so as to facilitate the consolidation and development of the socialist system.[3]

Academics and intellectuals were especially targeted. Three-quarters of all the senior members of the Chinese Academy of Sciences in Beijing were persecuted. Yao Tongbin, one of China's foremost missile engineers, was beaten to death by a mob in 1968. Many others were sent to labour camps where they were forced to do hard labour and 're-educate' themselves by studying Mao's socialist writings.

Schools and universities closed down at the start of the Cultural Revolution. Although some schools could reopen within a few months, most universities remained closed until 1972. An estimated 17 million 'educated youths' in the cities were forced to move to the countryside to be re-educated by the peasantry in agrarian matters. This cohort of Chinese students is often called the 'lost generation'.

The one thing the Great Leap Forward and Cultural Revolution did succeed in doing was to eradicate inequality in China. The redistribution of land and the elimination of education meant that physical and human capital were, by 1976, almost equally distributed. Five economists thought it worth asking whether this eradication of inequality has had any effect on inequality in China today. Four decades after the demise of Maoism, China has returned to a system of private ownership and has gradually opened its economy to the rest of the world.[4] The authors look at three generations – the grandparents (who were adults before the Great Leap Forward), the parents (the 'lost generation' of the Great Leap Forward and the Cultural Revolution) and the children (who are adults today). They then use digitised archival sources, household surveys and censuses today to link grandparents, parents and children to each other. This means that they can compare the grandchildren of rich and poor grandparents to see if any differences remain despite the wealth and income of the parents having being equalised.

Their results are startling. They show that the grandchildren of the pre-revolution elites earn 17 per cent more than the grandchildren of the pre-revolution non-elites. So, in short, if your grandparent was rich, you are more likely to be rich today. Remember, this wealth persisted despite the fact that your parents were not rich and did not receive an education, despite the most successful policy in human history to wipe out privilege and advantage.

The economists argue that this is because of the persistence of cultural values. 'The grandchildren of former landlords are more likely to express pro-market and individualistic values, such as approving of competition as an economic driving force, and willing to exert more effort at work and valuing education as an input into success.'[5] Despite Mao's best attempts at ridding Chinese society of any capitalist inclinations, positive attitudes towards the free market have survived. With the opening of the Chinese economy, these attitudes have been given the freedom to re-emerge and, it seems, have been pivotal in creating prosperity. China is home not only to the greatest human tragedy in recorded history, but also to the greatest human achievement: more than 850 million people have escaped poverty since the return to private ownership, education and the freedoms of a market economy.[6] The average Chinese citizen is today at least eight times more affluent than his or her parents were when Mao died in 1976.[7]

25 Why Should We Cry for Argentina?
A Country Reverses

Argentina was one of the richest countries in the world in 1900. Its GDP per capita, according to the Maddison Project database, was $4,583. At the same time, Germany's GDP per capita was $4,758, Sweden's was $3,320, and Japan's $2,123, the same as South Africa one year earlier, while Indonesia ($1,151) and India ($955) were comparatively poorer.[1]

More than a century later, in 2018, the situation was very different. While Argentina was four times as rich in 2018 as in 1900 ($18,556 vs. $4,583, adjusted for price increases), Germany was ten times richer in 2018 than in 1900 – a country, one must remember, that had suffered defeat in two world wars. Sweden was fourteen times richer. Indonesia was ten and India seven times richer. And Japan – a country that had seen two cities destroyed by atomic bombs in the middle of the century – was eighteen times richer. Even South Africa, with all its racial oppression and economic exclusion, was six times richer in 2018 than in 1900.

So what had happened to Argentina?

Let's begin by understanding why Argentina was so rich by the beginning of the twentieth century. The Industrial Revolution had made England the leading industrial power in the world. Several Western European countries, such as France and Germany, soon joined this process of industrialisation and experienced a rapid growth of their manufacturing sectors and a concomitant rise in the incomes of their populations. Higher incomes meant that Western Europeans could now afford to buy more consumables, which increased demand for not only manufactured goods (i.e. the things they were producing themselves), but also primary products, from food to fur.

It was this insatiable European demand for primary products that was the reason for Argentina's rising prosperity during the nineteenth century. Argentina was, of course, not the only country to export meat, wheat and other agricultural products to Europe, earning high incomes with relatively low levels of industrialisation. Other countries such as Uruguay, Canada, South Africa, Australia and New Zealand had also achieved prosperity based on three important things: exports of primary products; the integration of these export sectors with the rest of their economies; and the prevalence of broad-based economic and political rights.

Factor endowments – or what in Chapter 7 we simplistically called the land–labour ratio – help to explain this export-led growth model: countries that had a lot of natural resources, notably cheap and fertile land, were more likely to produce food. By contrast, European countries had abundant labour and capital, and therefore produced manufactured goods that used these things most intensively.[2] Argentina would thus export meat to England, and England would export equipment to Argentina.[3] As the economist David Ricardo had already predicted in the early nineteenth century, both benefited from the trade, which is why the reduction in trade barriers resulted in large increases in prosperity on both sides of the Atlantic.

It was not enough, however, for a country just to have raw materials. It was important for these sectors to be integrated into the rest of the country's economy. The extraction of mineral resources, for example, could be very lucrative, but often access to such mineral wealth was limited to a small subsection of the population. The same could be true of land. Many tropical countries had incredibly fertile land and produced commodities that were in high demand in Europe, but, as Engerman and Sokoloff explained (in Chapter 9), the lack of economic and political freedoms in the exporting countries meant that the returns were limited to the elites in these societies. Brazil's exports of lucrative commodities such as sugar and coffee relied heavily on slave labour; when slavery was abolished in Brazil in 1888, Argentina's GDP per capita was more than six times larger than Brazil's.

Given its relatively equal distribution of land and political rights, Argentina was as affluent as, if not more so than, the richest

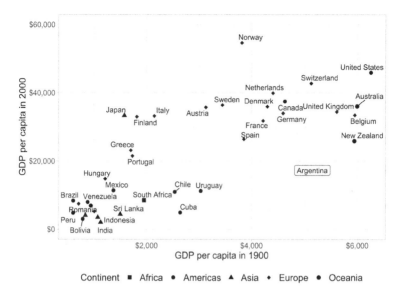

Figure 25.1 Correlations between GDP in 1900 and 2000 for various countries

European countries by the turn of the twentieth century. A visitor to Buenos Aires in 1900 'would have marvelled', writes the economic historian Alan Taylor, 'at the splendours of the city: the impressive opera house, the graceful architecture, the sophisticated railway system'.[4] But Figure 25.1 also shows that Argentina was unique in not maintaining its advantage over the course of the next century. Taylor continues:

> Today the city presents the same elegant facade, only frayed and decaying at the edges – and the visitor marvels that the city can function at all, given its dilapidated infrastructure. The satisfaction of living in one of the richest countries in the world is now a distant memory for the Argentines, who have struggled to come to terms with their sinking status. The downfall of this once developed country is ... an enigma for students of economic history ... More compelling and mysterious examples of failure than the ruination of Argentina are hard to imagine.[5]

So what explains the downfall?

As always, there are many theories. They all begin with measurement, as there is not even consensus on when the downfall began. Some argue that it started with the First World War, when international trade, a pillar of Argentina's economic growth, came to a halt and GDP fell precipitately. But all settler economies were badly hit by the Great War and the closing of international borders that accompanied it, so why did Australia and Canada, for example, recover but not Argentina?

Others look to the Great Depression and the Second World War as the causes of Argentina's woes. The import tariffs imposed by the Smoot–Hawley Tariff Act of 1930 in the United States, followed by similar trade restrictions from Europe, badly hurt the Argentinian economy, which needed the foreign exchange from its meat and wheat exports to pay for its manufactured imports. The Ottawa Treaty of 1932 allowed countries such as Australia, Canada and South Africa to export goods at lower tariff rates than other countries, undercutting products from Argentina, which had previously relied on the United Kingdom to buy a third of its exports. A trade agreement signed in 1933 to protect its share of the British market brought little relief.

Argentina turned to the United States as a possible outlet for its goods. But as a major wheat and meat producer itself, America was a competitor in many of the industries in which Argentina had an advantage. Attempts to sign a trade agreement with the United States in 1939 failed. It also did not help that Argentina refused to declare war on the Axis powers during the Second World War.

Finding no export markets, Argentina took a new direction: it turned inwards. It began with Juan Perón and the Perónist movement he founded. First elected president in 1946, a year after the end of the Second World War, at a time when Argentina's economy was struggling, the hugely popular Perón – aided, it must be said, by the popularity of his wife, Eva Perón, who was portrayed by Madonna in the movie *Evita* – introduced policies that gave a more active role for the state in the economy. To support the working class, his primary support base, he expanded social programmes and provided financial support for both labour unions and industrialists – measures which were aimed at redistributing income from the export (rural) sector to the industrial (urban) sector. Import-substitution industrialisation (or ISI), Perón believed, was the tool to make this happen, replacing imports of expensive manufactured goods with locally produced ones.

Perón would soon find intellectual support for this policy shift. In 1950 two economists, the Argentinian economist Paul Prebisch – who, ironically, had been forced to resign as head of the Argentinian central bank when the Perónists took over – and a German economist working at the United Nations, Hans Singer, separately developed a theory that would come to be known as the Prebisch–Singer hypothesis.[6] The theory proposes that the price of primary commodities, such as the meat and wheat that Argentina was exporting, will decline relative to the price of manufactured goods over the long run, causing the terms of trade of primary-goods-producing economies, such as Argentina, to deteriorate. The terms of trade is the ratio of export prices over import prices: basically, it measures how much imports an economy can buy for a unit of exports. If the price of exports rises more slowly than the price of imports, then the terms of trade will weaken. When Prebisch and Singer looked at trade data since the 1880s, they realised that this partly explained Argentina's weakening economic performance in the twentieth century, and they derived a general theory from it.

The Prebisch–Singer hypothesis did not offer a solution that would deal with the declining terms of trade. But Perón had a plan: his government would force structural reform through intervention in the markets.[7] Even before Prebisch and Singer had developed their theory, Perón implemented a Five-Year Plan to push Argentina away from primary-sector exports towards industrialisation. A new agency was established, for example, that would monopolise all agricultural exports by buying them in the local market and selling them abroad. Another new agency – the Secretariat of Industry and Commerce – imposed price controls for certain manufactured goods in the erroneous belief that this would ensure their availability. The Perónist government also supported industrialists by provided cheap loans (made possible after nationalising the central bank and bank deposits) and granting favourable exchange rates for raw materials and equipment imports.

Perón's interventions did have positive consequences for the poor. Workers received better protection than before and incomes increased, at least for a while. Perón saw himself as Argentina's Franklin Roosevelt; in his final speech as part of his presidential campaign in 1946, he quoted at length from Roosevelt's second inaugural address.

But his plans to industrialise the economy failed. By the end of the 1940s agricultural exports had collapsed. This caused a massive balance of payments crisis; put another way, Argentina's capacity to import halved between 1948 and 1952. Perón and his government tried to find a solution, and in the second Five-Year Plan agricultural exports were prioritised again. But it was too late. Three years later, in 1955, Perón's government was overthrown by the military and the Perónist party banned.

The ban did not end Perón's legacy of import-substituting industrialisation. The first open elections after the military coup of 1955 would only be held in 1973. Juan Perón was again elected, although he would die the next year, and was succeeded by his wife, who was deposed in a military coup two years later. In 2003 the Perónist Néstor Kirchner was elected president, followed by his wife, Cristina Fernández de Kirchner, from 2007 to 2015. The Kirchners' economic and trade policies mimicked their party's founder: nationalisation, large social-welfare programmes, opposition to free-trade agreements, and discouragement of importing goods that were also produced in Argentina.

But these populist policies, as before, had one predictable outcome: they burdened Argentina with huge debt obligations. Mauricio Macri, a former businessman turned politician, was elected president in 2015 to fix this. To do so, Macri implemented several reforms, including lifting exchange controls and opening the economy, but he could never keep the budget deficit down, and investors continued to distrust the ability of the Argentinian government to repay its debt. As a consequence, the peso collapsed and inflation soared, and Macri lost the 2019 election, again to a Perónist.

In 2019 Alberto Fernández was elected president, with Cristina Fernández de Kirchner, the former president, as vice president. They won the election on promises of reintroducing the spending that Macri had been forced to slash. Six months later, in May 2020, Argentina defaulted on its debt, for the ninth time in its history. One of the richest countries in the world at the start of the twentieth century was now insolvent, its current middle-income status evidence that the road to prosperity is not always linear – or even upwards.

26 Who Was the Last King of Scotland?
African Independence Struggles

When Milton Obote was inaugurated as Uganda's first prime minister in 1962, the future of the country that Winston Churchill had called 'the Pearl of Africa' looked brighter than ever. Independence from Britain had come with a carefully constructed federal constitution that gave some internal autonomy to the ancient kingdom of Buganda and its king, while Obote and his government could still maintain effective control of a country with diverse ethnic and interest groups.

Independence brought democratic institutions at a time when the economy was booming. The 'cash crop revolution' involving cotton and coffee that started with the construction of the railway from Uganda to the Kenyan port at Mombasa in 1901 had spread rapidly during the following half-century. In the first decade of independence, coffee exports more than doubled.[1]

But growth was not just a consequence of cotton and coffee. In the more fertile southern region of the country bananas were the staple crop, providing a decent standard of living to smallholder farmers. Uganda was also producing some of the world's highest-quality tea. Manufacturing was small but growing; it reached 6 per cent of GDP in 1965 and 7.3 per cent in 1971. The transportation system, including the railways, roads, airports and the steamer services that ran on Lake Victoria and the Nile River, was considered one of the best in sub-Saharan Africa. Copper had been discovered, and the abundant supply of water provided the means for water-powered electricity generation. GDP growth reflected the optimism that Ugandans experienced: real GDP growth averaged 4.8 per cent per year between 1965 and 1970.

The relative prosperity had also allowed for an expansive social-welfare programme. Uganda had an extensive health-care sector and had pioneered nutrition programmes for the poorest. Investment in primary education ensured that school class sizes were substantially below the African average.

Yet the optimism of the years that followed independence, as in many other regions of Africa, soon gave way to pessimism and, sadly, tragedy. Less than five years after he became prime minister, Milton Obote published a new constitution, arrested several ministers and suspended the National Assembly.[2] When leading members of the Buganda Kingdom tried to resist, he sent the army to attack the palace, forcing the king to flee to London. Hundreds of Baganda were detained without trial; in 1967 the kingdom of Buganda was abolished and divided into four administrative units.

Within five years Uganda had moved from a liberal democracy to a one-party state. Obote ruled by decree, with the support of the army and a new secret service, stocked with members of his own ethnic group. But Obote had underestimated his army commander, a man of enormous physical stature who was a former nine-time national heavyweight boxing champion and a rugby player, someone popular within army ranks. When Obote flew to Singapore in 1971 to attend a Commonwealth meeting, Idi Amin seized power.

Amin was initially welcomed as president. He freed political prisoners, stressed the temporary nature of military rule, promised new elections, and flew across the country to meet and listen to chiefs and elders. Yet Amin, who was largely illiterate and had no predilection for matters of government, was deeply insecure. He trusted no one and reacted to criticism in the only way he knew: by getting rid of those he thought were trying to oust him. Thousands of soldiers and police officers disappeared, killed by death squads that Amin had assembled, their bodies thrown into the Nile in the hope that crocodiles would destroy any evidence. Many simply washed up on the river's banks.

As the killings intensified, Amin's popularity waned. In reaction, Amin turned on the wealthy Indian community that controlled much of the country's trade and industry. In August 1972 he ordered them to leave Uganda within three months; an estimated

50,000 Indians out of a total of 80,000 left for the United Kingdom or Canada or returned to India. With their assets seized by Amin's army, industry collapsed; government revenues fell by 40 per cent within the year.

Amin's behaviour became increasingly erratic. He bestowed on himself the title 'His Excellency, President for Life, Field Marshal Al Hadji Doctor Idi Amin Dada, VC, DSO, MC, CBE, Lord of All the Beasts of the Earth and Fishes of the Seas and Conqueror of the British Empire in Africa in General and Uganda in Particular'. It is no wonder that *Time* magazine, in a 1977 piece, labelled him 'the Wild Man of Africa' and described him as a 'killer and clown, big-hearted buffoon and strutting martinet' – a description, to be fair, that would be equally true of Belgium's King Leopold II after his atrocious exploitation of the Congo almost a century earlier.[3] Amin also enjoyed being addressed as the 'Last King of Scotland', having apparently defeated the British. In a 2006 movie of the same name, Forest Whitaker portrays Amin, a performance which won him an Oscar.

Uganda was not the only African country to suffer at the hands of a tyrant. Across the continent the euphoria of independence soon gave way to military coups and, ultimately, the rise of dictators. Kwame Nkrumah of Ghana, the first African country to become independent, in 1957, was deposed by a military coup less than ten years later, in 1966. More coups would follow in Ghana in the ensuing decades. Nigeria, which became independent in 1960, experienced eight coups between 1966 and 1993. In 1966 the eccentric and ruthless Jean-Bédel Bokassa became the second president of the Central African Republic, formerly a colony of France, by overthrowing the incumbent, David Dacko. In 1976 he anointed himself Emperor of the Central African Empire, only to be ousted three years later. In the Democratic Republic of the Congo, which had gained independence from Belgium in 1960, Mobutu Sese Seko took power in 1966 after a second coup. He would rule until 1997. In Sudan, Omar Hassan Ahmad al-Bashir took power in 1989 and ruled until 2019. The long-time ruler of one of the last countries to gain independence, Robert Mugabe of Zimbabwe, was deposed in a coup in 2017, ending thirty-seven years of rule. Even in countries with no colonial presence, instability was common. Samuel Doe of Liberia overthrew William Tolbert in 1980 in a military coup, only to be deposed himself ten years later by Prince Johnson. Ethiopia had three coups in the 1970s alone.

It would be too easy, however, to blame the misfortunes of independent Africa on the rise of 'bad men' such as Amin, Bokassa, Sese Seko, al-Bashir and Mugabe. Weak political institutions certainly contributed to the malaise. Having maintained the former colonial boundaries, the newly independent African states had to deal not only with ethnic divisions – divisions that had often been amplified during the period of colonial rule – but also an ill-equipped and inexperienced state bureaucracy and an electorate illiterate in national politics. Besides, it took centuries of conflict for democratic institutions to emerge in Europe: why should we expect the process to be any less painful in Africa?

But economics played just as big a part in Africa's post-independence misfortunes as politics. In the years after the Second World War, the last phase of colonial rule, world prices for African commodities such as cocoa, cotton, coffee and copper soared to new levels. In Ghana, just as in Uganda, African smallholder farmers profited, using the colonial railways to ship their produce to international markets. Oil prices were low, at less than $2 per barrel, and debt was cheap. Even nature played along: good rains fell throughout the 1950s and early 1960s, boosting agricultural output. In 1961 Lake Chad and Lake Victoria reached their highest levels in the twentieth century.

Economic growth was also reflected in living standards. Economic historians Stephen Broadberry and Leigh Gardner calculate GDP per capita for eight Anglophone African countries since 1885.[4] They find that per capita incomes 'were above subsistence by the early twentieth century, on a par with the largest economies in Asia until the 1980s'. This is best reflected in wage data. As Figure 26.1 demonstrates, while the real wages of an East African unskilled labourer were on a par with those of labourers in major East Asian cities, West African urban labourers achieved welfare ratios – a ratio of household income to the poverty line – two to three times those of their Asian counterparts.[5] These high incomes inspired confidence in future growth. In 1967 the World Bank economist Andrew Kamarck wrote: 'I am confident that for most of Africa the economic future before the end of the century can be bright.'[6]

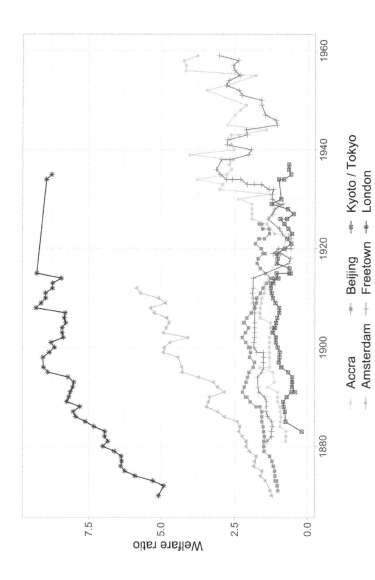

Figure 26.1 Welfare ratios calculated for various cities across the world, 1880–1960

When independence came the new leaders had to decide which economic strategies to adopt. Put yourself in the shoes of Kwame Nkrumah in 1957. Amidst the Cold War there were basically two options: the free-market capitalism of the West, which had less than three decades earlier suffered one of the largest depressions in history, or the communism of the Soviet Union, which had been rapidly transformed from an agricultural society into an industrial powerhouse (news of Stalin's atrocities were slow to emerge). For an ambitious leader, the socialist state-led approach seemed far more attractive.

The intellectual support for this came from a new subdiscipline of economics – development economics – and its disciples. Based on modernisation theory, development economists were critical of the laissez-faire approach of classical economists and in support of a larger role for government in the economy. One of its main proponents, the West Indian-born and later Nobel Prize-winning economist W. Arthur Lewis, was appointed as senior economic advisor in Nkrumah's new government. What was needed, Lewis and Nkrumah agreed, was a 'big push' strategy to industrialise, a Ghanaian Five-Year Plan. It was akin to the policies that, as we saw in the previous chapter, Argentina and other Latin American countries adopted.

But there was an important difference between Nkrumah and Lewis's views. In the West Indies, Egypt and India, Lewis argued, surplus labour could be redirected to the manufacturing sector. The constraint to development in those countries was inadequate investment in manufacturing.[7] Because Ghana was a labour-scarce country, there was no surplus labour. The solution, Lewis proposed, was to increase agricultural productivity first, so that surplus labour would be created to allow manufacturing to take off.

The point is that Nkrumah and Lewis had different types of 'big push' investment in mind. Both agreed to use the profits of agricultural marketing boards to cross-subsidise industrial investments. The marketing boards had been instituted to ensure a safety net for farmers – the boards would buy produce from cocoa farmers at fixed prices and would sell it on international markets at world prices. With the rise in world prices, however, marketing boards often did not increase the price they paid to farmers, generating huge revenues for the government. Lewis believed these revenues should be used to raise agricultural productivity. But his advice was unacceptable to the ambitious Nkrumah, who was determined that black Africa's first independent country would be a shining star for the rest of the continent.[8] Nkrumah, instead, wanted large projects that would support industrialisation. His flagship project was the Akosombo Dam on the Volta River, for example, creating the third-largest man-made lake in the world and supplying hydroelectric power to both Ghana and neighbouring Benin and Togo.

The Volta River Project, finished a month before Nkrumah was deposed in a coup, was the exception. Most of his projects had political rather than economic motives and included military spending and various vanity projects that were often rampantly corrupt. After fifteen months, in 1958, noting irreconcilable differences in approach, Lewis quit as adviser. Nkrumah attempted to explain his decisions in a letter: 'The advice you have given me, sound though it may be, is essentially from the economic point of view, and I have told you, on many occasions, that I cannot always follow this advice as I am a politician and must gamble on the future.'[9]

Using the profits of farmers to build factories failed to bring prosperity. Just as in Latin America, African markets were too small to realise the economies of scale necessary to make factories profitable. The trouble was compounded by African leaders borrowing prodigiously to fund their 'big push' strategies. All this borrowing could be repaid as long as their economies were growing, but by the 1970s growth began to falter. Global stagnation, the end of the Bretton Woods monetary system and an international oil crisis not only reduced commodity prices but also contributed to Africa's debt spiralling out of control. By the 1980s many African countries were close to insolvent, forced to approach the International Monetary Fund (IMF) and enter structural adjustment programmes. These reforms included severe budget cuts, improving monetary policy to reduce inflation, removing restrictions on international trade and lifting subsidies and state controls. The reforms came at a great cost, especially those that cut expenditure on education and health. This is why many Africans still not only consider these programmes unsuccessful – growth did not return immediately – but also see institutions such as the IMF and World Bank as evil. We return to the consequences of these reforms in Chapter 33.

The two decades between 1975 and 1995 are generally considered to be Africa's 'lost decades'. By 2000 the optimism about African prosperity had withered, replaced by a deep pessimism that Africa would never be able to grow – that it was a hopeless continent. That is a false belief. Half a century ago Africans were enjoying standards of living that were on a par with or often above those of their Asian counterparts. But three decades of dismal performance have meant that Africa now sits at the bottom of the global income-distribution tables.

This suggests that there is hope. If Africa's poverty is a consequence of the interaction of weak political institutions and poor economic policies following independence, combined with colonial policies that generally limited political and economic freedoms, then the happy message is that political institutions and economic policies can also be used to alleviate it. The point is that there is nothing inherent in Africa that predestines its people to perpetual poverty. The economic historian Morten Jerven summarised this idea best: 'The search for a root cause of African underdevelopment is futile, and ... such a search is based on asking the wrong question. There is a crucial difference between approaching the conundrum of African growth by asking why there has been a chronic growth failure and asking why African economies have sometimes grown and then regressed.'[10]

Asking the right question, as I pointed out in Chapter 1, is indeed a perspective that economic historians can offer. In Chapter 33 we turn to the surprising turnaround that has happened in Africa's fortunes, just when the rest of the world had given up.

27 How Did Einstein Help Create Eskom?
South Africa Industrialises

Just before the start of the First World War, Robert Millikan, professor of physics at the University of Chicago and a specialist in electron theory, travelled to Germany to present an academic paper. A few years earlier, in 1905, the scientist Albert Einstein had proposed a linear relationship between the wavelength of light and the maximum velocity of electrons emitted from irradiated metal. Einstein was developing quantum theory – and Millikan was adamant that he was wrong.

While visiting Dresden Millikan was introduced to a young researcher who had just completed his PhD. The young man was South African and could thus speak English – which is probably why he was asked to show Millikan around campus. They also shared a research interest, as the young researcher was also working on Einstein's theory. In fact, Hendrik van der Bijl had already found why it was so difficult to prove: the high velocities that Millikan had discovered did not prove that Einstein was wrong, but rather showed that the test had picked up a stray field.

Van der Bijl must have explained to Millikan that his attempt to prove Einstein wrong was futile. He reported that the news was 'a very great disappointment to [Millikan] but this disappointment was outweighed by the joy which naturally came to him as a true scientist when he found that my experiments confirmed the deductions from the Electron Theory. We remained great friends ever after.'[1] Millikan went on to change his opinion about Einstein's theory, and published a seminal paper confirming Einstein's results in 1916, although without any credit to van der Bijl. In 1923 he received the Nobel Prize in Physics.

Millikan did, however, repay the favour. Just before war broke out in Europe, he helped van der Bijl find a job at Western Electric in New York. Van der Bijl moved to the United States and soon began work on tube physics and electronics, technology that was used to build the first telephone line between New York and San Francisco. In 1914 he designed (without credit) the French TM and British R valve. Millions of these bulbs were produced. In 1920 he also published the seminal textbook on tube physics, which was used by a generation of students in American universities.

But van der Bijl had bigger things on his mind. Just as his textbook was published, he received an offer that would change the course of his career – and that of a country. It all started a year earlier. While South Africa's prime minister Jan Smuts was negotiating the Treaty of Versailles, he had read a paper by van der Bijl.[2] The paper was about how scientific research could be used to bolster industrial development. Smuts was so impressed that he invited van der Bijl to return to South Africa to become scientific and industrial adviser in the Department of Mines and Industries.

Much like the dreams that African independence leaders had for their own countries three decades later, van der Bijl's vision for South Africa was for it to become an industrial power. And for private industry to flourish, he believed, South Africa required substantial investments in transport and electric power. Here the government could play a role.

He began by creating an electricity company – the Electricity Supply Commission (Escom, today Eskom) – in 1923. Although it was the first South African parastatal, van der Bijl made it clear that he would run the company as if it were a private company. Its initial investment would come from private and state loans. It had multiple goals. The main one was to produce cheap electricity to support the mining industry, the largest contributor to state revenues, which fuelled the government's increasingly interventionist economic policies. Supporting the fledgling manufacturing industry was also a priority for him. At the same time, Escom was a way to provide employment for the thousands of 'poor whites' (a term largely used as a euphemism for Afrikaners at the time) who had moved to the cities in search of mining jobs but had lost out to lower-paid black labour. The sudden influx of large numbers of poor whites had political consequences; in 1924 the Pact government of the National Party and Labour Party, largely representing the interests of disgruntled white workers, came to power.

Fortunately, van der Bijl kept his job in government. And it did not take long before the new government adopted another of van der Bijl's ideas. This was to build a steel company, seen as a further cornerstone of industrialisation as well as a way to employ poor whites. The Iron and Steel Corporation, or Iscor, was founded in 1928, also under the leadership of Hendrik van der Bijl.

Managing the two opposing goals – of providing cheap inputs to the economy and providing jobs to poor whites – was a complicated balancing act. Van der Bijl succeeded largely in only one of them: to produce cheap electricity and steel. In 1939, only sixteen years after Escom was created, South Africa's total electricity output was six times greater than in 1922.[3] Half of this was used by the mines, but a growing share (14 per cent) was also used by industry. Iscor began production in 1934, producing 103,666 tons of steel in that year. Four years later production had risen to 1,031,495 tons. On the other hand, despite promises that Iscor would employ 'white labour entirely', by the end of the 1930s, more than half of all Iscor jobs were filled by black workers. At Escom, white workers formed 38 per cent of the labour force, which was the same share that white workers held in the rest of the economy.

But it was not only the state that contributed to South Africa's industrialisation. In 1941, during the darkest hours of the Second World War, a young Anton Rupert invested £10 in his new Johannesburg firm, Voorbrand Tabakmaatskappy, a tobacco company.[4] While some friends backed his decision by investing in it, others warned him against what they considered a terrible decision for someone with so much potential: why would anyone want to take on the behemoth United Tobacco Company, which controlled 90 per cent of the industry? But Rupert was emboldened by a new spirit in Afrikaner society. The 1938 centennial celebrations of the Great Trek had caused a cultural awakening. The first order of business discussed and debated in several 'congresses of the people' was the weak economic position of the Afrikaner. One estimate was that Afrikaner-owned businesses accounted for just 5 per cent of total output of trade, industry, finance and mining. Another estimate was that Afrikaner incomes were only 60 per cent of those of white English-speaking South Africans. This needed correction, Rupert believed, and the only way to do so was to get one's hands dirty.

Only four years after Rupert entered the tobacco industry he also invested in a struggling wine operation. He had little capital of his own, so he drove around the countryside persuading farmers to invest in his company. Almost all investment came from other Afrikaners, and in this way Distell was born.[5] Rupert's success came through partnerships. The company Voorbrand became Rembrandt through building a relationship with the UK-based Rothmans. Rembrandt would later turn into Richemont, acquiring luxury-goods brands such as Cartier, Alfred Dunhill, Vacheron Constantin and Montblanc. In 1945, the year the war ended, Rupert moved to Stellenbosch to be closer to his wine business – he had spent sixty-nine nights on the train between Johannesburg and Cape Town in the previous year. He purchased a house for 12,200 rand. Had the seller invested that money in Rupert's company, he would have owned 300 million rand's worth of shares by the turn of the century.

Although Rupert is the poster boy of the rise of Afrikaner entrepreneurs in the 1940s and 1950s, there were many others. In 1955 Renier van Rooyen purchased a single store – Bargain Shop – in Upington, a town in South Africa's Kalahari desert.[6] A decade later, after having established branches in several towns, he renamed the business Pep Stores, a company that would become a retail clothing giant. The question is whether the success of these Afrikaner entrepreneurs was due to state support – especially after the 1948 election victory of the National Party, which explicitly supported Afrikaner interests. There is no doubt that a black entrepreneur with the same talent, dedication and fortitude as Anton Rupert or Renier van Rooyen would not have been able to reach the heights they did. There were simply too many barriers in the way of black entrepreneurial success in South Africa at that time.

But it is also true that few of these Afrikaner business empires were built through government subsidies or tenders. Rupert's ideas about racial 'coexistence', a policy to replace apartheid, provoked the ire of the father of separate development, Hendrik Verwoerd, and subsequent apartheid leaders. In the 1970s Pep Stores built a thriving business in coloured neighbourhoods, selling shares to 871 coloured investors. When the scheme ended in the 1980s, eighteen years after it started, those investors received a return of 7,000 per cent on their initial investment.[7] Government and the profit motive of private business often did not see eye to eye. More interested in securing votes, the apartheid government was more enamoured of the white trade unions, which, in turn, were more interested in protecting white jobs than in growing the economy.

State support, instead, was directed at parastatals. In 1940 van der Bijl founded the Industrial Development Corporation (IDC), and two years after his death, in 1950, the IDC established Sasol. The plan was to produce oil from coal, an ambitious scheme with unproven technology that for much of the 1950s seemed a futile exercise. There was growing international pressure to isolate and sanction South Africa, especially after the Sharpeville massacre of 1960 in which police killed sixty-nine peaceful protesters, and the government's consequent desire for self-reliance ensured that Sasol continued to receive the financial and scientific support it needed to succeed. Success – the production of synthetic fuel – not only brought self-reliance but also esteem; it gave rise to what the historian Stephen Sparks has called a 'techno-nationalist "pioneering" discourse that celebrated the toil and ingenuity of South African engineers and scientists'.[8]

Self-reliance meant the production not only of oil, but also of weapons. In 1968 Armscor was established to manufacture armaments. In the 1970s and 1980s Armscor engineers produced six nuclear weapons, all of which were scrapped by F. W. de Klerk in 1991. South Africa remains the only country in the world to have voluntarily dismantled its own nuclear arsenal.

Many of these state companies would eventually become private enterprises. Sasol was the first to do so, partially in 1979, and fully in 2000. Iscor was sold for $3 billion in 1989. Denel was spun out of Armscor in 1992. Telkom, the telecommunications company that was created from the former Department of Post and Telecommunications, was partially privatised in 1996.

Sasol was 'a parastatal funded by taxpayers' money with an official regulatory regime heavily skewed to its advantage', Sparks concludes.[9] The same is true for many other parastatals established in an effort to industrialise South Africa. While they are often considered evidence of the success of state-led investments, the obvious question must be: at what cost? It is an almost impossible question to answer. What would have happened had the apartheid government not supported Sasol? Would entrepreneurs have filled the gap? It is unlikely that private capital, with its shorter time horizon, would have been willing to support the development of a technology that would only yield dividends a decade after its establishment. But then again, what other technologies could have been devised with the resources used to prop up Sasol for a decade? Imagine that funding going to universities or scientific institutions instead, or, through lower taxes, back into the pockets of visionary entrepreneurs like Rupert or van Rooyen, or to close the large funding gap between white and black education.

We will never know, of course. That is why counterfactual history is such a perilous scholarly exercise; as Einstein allegedly said, 'a man should look for what is, and not for what he thinks should be'. What we know is that South Africa industrialised because of state-led investments in infrastructure and science that allowed (white) entrepreneurs to flourish. These state-led investments were run on business principles and on belief in the benefits of science but were funded through high taxes on mining profits rather than by excessively taxing agriculture, as was the case in Latin America and elsewhere in Africa. As we will discover in the next chapter, those high mining profits depended on one critical element.

28 Why Would You Want to Eat Sushi in the Transkei?
The Economics of Apartheid

In December 1932, in the throes of a deep recession, South Africa left the gold standard. Britain had abandoned it the previous year – and a political battle within South Africa's government had ensured a delay that severely hurt the economy. The decision to leave had an immediate effect; instead of having the currency backed by gold, the South African pound depreciated, making South African exports more attractive to foreign buyers. It proved a huge boon to gold-mining companies. Gold prices rose rapidly and mining output expanded, increasing the demand for inputs and workers, and as a consequence government revenues increased significantly. In 1936, only three years later, the Johannesburg municipality could begin construction of the South-Western Townships, or Soweto, on the back of windfalls from the mining industry.

These mining windfalls – profits for shareholders and taxes for government – depended on one important factor: paying cheap wages. Wage disputes were the main reason that mine owners frequently clashed with white labour unions, which wanted their members to be paid a 'civilised' wage. In fact, white miner wages were some of the highest in the world, both because of high living costs in Johannesburg and also because of the miners' political importance as voters. One way white labour unions and their political supporters had managed to keep wages high was by introducing legislation known as the colour bar, reserving jobs classified as 'skilled' and 'semi-skilled' for white workers only.

To avoid paying these high wages, mine owners constantly looked for alternatives. One was simply to employ more black workers. But one concern of mine owners was that attracting more black workers to the cities would mean fewer workers on farms. This would lead to higher prices for staples such as maize and bread, which would result in demands for higher wages on the mines. Employing black South African workers could thus be counterproductive: the 'gold–maize alliance' between mine owners and farmers ensured that mines would not attract workers from the same labour catchment areas on which farmers depended.

The alternative that mine owners chose to solve this labour conundrum was to import workers. An early experiment to bring in 63,000 Chinese workers just after the Anglo-Boer War failed. They then set their sights on African labourers from neighbouring countries. The Chamber of Mines established the Witwatersrand Native Labour Association, a labour recruitment agency known as WNLA or simply Wenela, in 1900. Soon, young men from Lesotho, Eswatini, Malawi and, in particular, Mozambique began to arrive in Johannesburg. By the 1930s, when gold mining boomed, more than 300,000 labourers worked on the mines; at least half of them came from the Sul do Save district in Mozambique. These workers, as the historian Charles van Onselen explains, were delivered to the Highveld mines in train coaches that were often barred and locked, to live their working lives in enclosed, well-policed mine compounds.[1] Worst of all, because of a deferred pay system, with half of all wages paid out only once the migrant workers returned to Mozambique, and because of theft by those responsible for transporting the miners, it is estimated that miners received as little as 15 per cent of the wages they had earned on the mines when they finally arrived back in Mozambique.

Despite these conditions, African workers continued to make the journey to Johannesburg. There is some evidence that their wages, however meagre, did improve conditions for them and their families. In 1967 Malawi signed a new labour recruitment treaty that tripled the number of mine workers sent to South Africa's mines. Seven years later a plane carrying Malawian mine workers crashed, which led to Hastings Banda, Malawi's president, imposing a three-year ban on all labour recruitment in the country. The economists Taryn Dinkelman and Martine Mariotti have used the recruitment treaty and moratorium to estimate the effect of these income shocks on the children of those living close to mine-recruitment stations. They found that twenty years later, children whose fathers lived in recruitment areas (Wenela districts), and who were of school-going age in the seven-year period, were 5–7 per cent more likely to go to school. It makes sense: as more Malawian men migrated to Johannesburg to work on the mines, their wages increased, allowing their kids back home in Malawi to attend school.[2]

In a separate paper, Mariotti considered children born in South Africa's Transkei before and after 1974.[3] After the plane crash and Malawi's subsequent ban on labour recruitment, mine owners had to find alternative labour sources. The numbers of migrant workers from the Transkei rapidly increased. Mariotti found that children born in the Transkei in the years following their fathers' move to the mines are taller today than those born in the years immediately preceding that move – further anthropometric evidence in support of a rise in living standards from mine work. It is a sad indictment of the time that the terrible conditions on the mines were often a better alternative than the poverty of the home, whether in Malawi or the Transkei.

The constant competition between white and black labour became acute after the Second World War. White women and black men had filled the semi-skilled or even skilled jobs of the more than 200,000 white men who had given up work to fight in the war. In fact, factory owners soon realised that they could pay lower wages to white women and black men and achieve the same efficiency as with the higher-paid white men. Yet, when the white soldiers returned after the war they expected their jobs back, only to realise that they now had to compete with men and women they had never considered their equals. They responded in the only way they could: at the ballot box.

In 1948 the National Party – a small, populist party that had only come into existence a decade earlier and that catered mostly to lower-income Afrikaners – won the national elections with 37 per cent of the vote. Their opponents had no clear plan about how to deal with the race issues of the time. The National Party, in contrast, had a very clear vision of a country in which white and black people would live separately. The set of laws and policies they began to implement immediately after their victory – including the Group Areas Act (1950), which defined where South Africans could live and own property; the Population Registration Act (1950), which classified all South Africans into four race groups; and the Bantu Education Act (1953), which legislated differences in curriculum and funding between white and black schools – was known as apartheid. These discriminatory and repressive policies – many of them an extension or intensification of the segregationist policies introduced in the first half of the century – were condemned in 1973 by the United Nations as a crime against humanity.

One key tenet of apartheid was the creation of Bantustans or homelands. Although these had no international standing, all black South Africans were considered inhabitants of one or other of these 'countries' – and could therefore only move to the South African cities temporarily. For mine and factory owners in 'white South Africa', this created the problem of a labour shortage. This was particularly true for semi-skilled and skilled occupations. The first two decades after the National Party victory were a period of rapid growth in the economy: this was true not only in South Africa, but for much of the Western world. New technologies (often created for war purposes) improved productivity in many industries, leading to mechanisation and a demand for skilled jobs in the secondary and tertiary sectors.

But apartheid's masterminds had envisioned a very different society, one where better education for whites would allow them to fill the well-paid, skilled occupations while a large pool of cheap black labour would fill unskilled jobs. This was the model that had in effect been in place for the first half of the century. In fact, the Bantu Education Act was specifically designed to fulfil this objective: preparing black workers for unskilled work and white workers for skilled jobs. These actions show that the National Party policies were not only immoral, but also idiotic: the economy was transforming away from unskilled work just when the National Party hoped to produce more unskilled labourers. Something had to give.

Martine Mariotti shows that, despite legislation preventing black workers from taking up semi-skilled jobs, there were by the 1970s many black workers filling these types of occupations.[4] White trade unions were, of course, heavily opposed to any relaxation of the colour-bar legislation, and threatened to shift their support to the right-wing Conservative Party should the National Party consider doing so. An alternative plan was devised. If black workers could not move to the cities, the policymakers asked, why not take factories to the workers?

The plan was to build 'border industries' – in other words, factories on the edge of the Bantustans. The attraction to investors was the cheap labour available in the homelands. Here is Albert Luthuli, the 1961 Nobel Peace Prize recipient, in his book *Let My People Go*, on the poor economics of the plan:

> White industrialists are invited to place factories on the edges of the destitute Reserves. The bait is cheap labour. Nothing but cruelly underpaid labour could counteract the economic effect of putting factories out of reach of railheads and sources of power. We are told that these factories will enrich the Reserve population. We shall never have had it so good. We are even told what proportion of the populace will be employed in border industries, solely as unskilled workers. Quite arbitrarily, it is arranged that 40 per cent of the Reserve people will remain farmers, while 60 per cent will become industrial workers. The industrialists' response to the Government invitation so far is a few clothing factories and a few peanut factories ... Border industries cannot conceivably employ 60 per cent of the Reserve people. Economics will not obey racial blueprints.[5]

Luthuli was right, of course. For most firms, locating to the countryside was simply not an option; it was too expensive there to access production inputs and skilled workers, who wanted to live in cities within reach of the services and amenities that large agglomerations of people offered. There were exceptions, however. From the late 1970s large labour-intensive manufacturing from Asia began drifting towards these special economic zones in the rural homelands of South Africa.[6] With extensive 'bamboo networks', which connected them to supply chains in Taiwan, Hong Kong and South Korea, these firms provided rare success stories. At one stage the Transkei was the world's largest producer of chopsticks.

But despite some infrastructure investment (the IDC estimated that the costs of constructing this infrastructure equated to 1.5 per cent of GDP in each year from 1972 to 1979) and generous incentives, there was very little domestic interest in these rural home-land zones. When the tax and wage incentives ceased in 1996, so did the businesses.

Elsewhere in South Africa, instead of moving their location, factories mechanised by using (expensive) capital equipment to sub-stitute for labour. It was not only manufacturing that mechanised. Even agriculture – the sector that traditionally employed unskilled labour – began to transform. While the amount of farmland in cultivation declined between 1946 and 1976, the number of har-vester combines, a machine used for harvesting crops and a substitute for labour, increased more than tenfold from 1,722 to 23,767. This mechanisation across the economy had an important consequence, one that still haunts South Africa today: by reducing the need for unskilled labour, it gave rise to high levels of unemploy-ment. When black labour unions were unbanned and understandably began to push for higher wages, mechanisation and unemployment were further bolstered. If one includes both formal and informal employment, the unemployment rate increased from just above 10 per cent in 1976 to more than 50 per cent in 2000.

The economist Nicoli Nattrass has calculated the profitabil-ity rates of firms during the apartheid period.[7] She finds that low black wages during the 1940s and 1950s did indeed allow for growth in white wages and a rise in firm profits. But by the 1960s manufac-turing profits began to decline. Mining profits followed the down-ward trend by the 1970s. Instead of opening up the economy to encourage exports, the South African government chose the route of import-substitution because of international pressure and internal politics. This hurt not only workers, but also shareholders. Nattrass notes that during the 1970s and 1980s profitability 'continued to fall because of declining capital productivity. This, in turn, almost certainly stems from apartheid policies that encouraged greater capital intensity, notably racial restrictions on the labour market and subsidies to capital.'[8] Whereas average annual GDP growth had been 5 per cent between 1948 and 1974, it fell to just 1.5 per cent in the two decades that followed.[9]

Why, one has to ask, did it take so long for political change to come about when the economic situation was so dire? One, perhaps counterintuitive, answer is that it took so long *because* of the poor economy. This was a hot topic of discussion by the

1980s: would international sanctions that worsened the economic conditions – of both white and black South Africans – achieve their aim of a faster transition to democracy? In one sense it seems obvious that they should: if you hurt someone, they ought to change whatever they have been doing in order to reduce the pain. But economist Mats Lundahl explains why the sanctions might not have had the desired effect: 'Sanctions have different impacts on different groups, as does the apartheid system itself. Some groups gain while others lose. Thus, there is scope for conflicts of interests *within* the white community, and if those groups that stand to gain if sanctions are imposed are politically influential, the sanctions weapon may work in the completely wrong direction.'[10]

The international trade and investment boycotts, as the economist Merle Lipton found, strengthened the South African state vis-à-vis other sections of society.[11] It prolonged rather than put an end to apartheid. The same may have been true of Robert Mugabe's Zimbabwe. Sanctions gave him political legitimacy – he had an outside enemy to blame for the woes that Zimbabwe experienced after the land reform programme of 2000.

Ultimately, apartheid ended because, as Albert Luthuli had remarked, 'economics will not obey racial blueprints'. The costs of repressing black resistance, influx control and labour market policies that prevented black workers from filling semi-skilled and skilled jobs, education policies that created a mismatch between what firms demanded (skilled workers) and what was supplied (unskilled workers), and macroeconomic policies such as exchange control came to exceed the benefits to white South Africans, and left the last apartheid leaders with little alternative.[12] The system collapsed, ushering in a new, democratic era with the political freedom that so many black South Africans had been fighting for.

29 Why Do the Japanese Play Rugby?
The Rise of the East Asian Economies

On 9 August 1945 the United States dropped an atomic bomb on Nagasaki, a port city of Japan. Sumiteru Taniguchi was sixteen at the time, delivering post about a mile from ground zero. The force of the explosion threw him from his bicycle, melting his cotton shirt and searing the skin off his back and one arm. But Taniguchi survived, one of the fortunate few who did. Many thousands in Nagasaki and Hiroshima, the first city to be bombed, were not as fortunate. Japan surrendered six days later, thereby ending the Second World War.

Just like Taniguchi, who would become a lifelong advocate for the prohibition of nuclear weapons, Japan was left badly scarred after the war. But to understand the extent of the devastation, it helps to briefly discuss what came before the Second World War.

In 1872, the year that its first railway was built, Japan was still relatively poor; its citizens had roughly the same income as those of Peru, Poland and Portugal. The Japanese were poorer than Venezuelans or South Africans, and about half as rich as the French. The average American or Briton was about three times as rich as the average Japanese. But the transformation of the Japanese economy was already under way. It began in 1853 when US warships arrived in Japan to sign a treaty that would open the country to trade. Japan had been ruled by a military government, closed off to the outside world for more than two centuries. It had believed, much as the Chinese did a few centuries earlier, that outside influences, particularly Christian missionaries, would threaten the unique Japanese way of life. But when Commodore Matthew Perry sailed into Edo

Bay with his warships, the Japanese realised that their traditions and technologies were outdated. One Japanese elder reflected on their conundrum, saying: 'If we take the initiative, we can dominate; if we do not, we will be dominated.'[1]

Those pushing for reform won. The goal of the Meiji Restoration – meaning 'enlightened rule' – was to adopt modern systems and technologies from the West while preserving traditional values. On his second visit, in 1854, Perry brought a miniature steam locomotive to Japan. Eighteen years later the Meiji emperor opened the first railway between Tokyo and Yokohama. Japan did not only import new transport technologies: the merchants also introduced rugby to Japan, before the sport had even arrived in France, New Zealand or South Africa.

Japan's late nineteenth-century industrialisation was not just a consequence of imported institutions. Innovative new domestic institutions like the *zaibatsu* – large, family-owned conglomerates – were responsible for investing in capital-intensive technology. They could afford this capital-intensive approach because of their size (which gave them economies of scale), ownership structure (which allowed them to invest for the long run), diversified holdings (which spread the risk), high levels of education, and access to minerals such as coal.[2]

By 1939, then, on the eve of the Second World War, Japan's international ranking had changed. Japanese incomes were now above those of Peru, Poland and Portugal. It had surpassed Venezuela and South Africa. Britain was only twice as rich. Japan had become an industrial power.

But the war, and the two atomic bombs to end it, wiped out much of that progress. Industrial production declined to just 28 per cent of its pre-war level. Japanese incomes in 1945 were equal to what they had been on the eve of the First World War. Three decades' worth of economic growth had been obliterated.

Yet, in what has become known as the 'Japanese economic miracle', industrial production did not just bounce back, it accelerated. By 1980, one generation after the bombs had flattened the two cities, Japanese incomes were three times as large as incomes in Peru, and twice as large as incomes in Poland. Japanese GDP per capita was above the GDP per capita of Britain. And although Japan was the first, it was not the only East Asian country to experience an 'economic miracle'. South Korea and Taiwan soon followed, as well as the city-states of Hong Kong and Singapore – all countries collectively known as the Asian Tigers. By the twenty-first century Japan and the Asian Tigers had become high-income countries, their citizens attaining standards of living on a par with or even above those of Western Europe or the United States. At the same time, other countries that had been classed as developing in the middle of the twentieth century (as Japan had once been), including those in Latin America, Africa and South Asia, struggled to escape their middle-income-country status. In some cases they had even regressed. The Asian Tigers, joined by Thailand, Malaysia and, ultimately, China, came to form the fastest-growing – and poverty-eliminating – region worldwide.

What explains East Asia's remarkable transformation? The textbook explanation is straightforward: while other developing countries were looking inward – adopting the import-substitution policies we discussed in Chapters 24 and 25 – East Asian economies, despite some differences in timing and intensity, were generally looking outward. With no real natural resources to speak of, East Asia's economies had to turn to manufacturing. The formula was simple: import television sets, toasters and toys. Take them apart, copy and adjust the designs, and then produce them at a fraction of the import price for the export market.[3] Although initially applied predominantly to light manufacturing, the formula soon expanded to heavy industry, including the manufacture of motor vehicles.

The textbook explanation also acknowledges East Asia's politicians, often autocrats, for their contribution to the miracle. But textbook explanations are sometimes oversimplified. Not everyone agrees with this export-oriented interpretation of East Asia's success. Yes, argues economist Dani Rodrik, those countries did see a stellar increase in exports, but they started from such a small base that exports alone cannot explain the miracle.[4] Rodrik, instead, attributes success to a coherent investment strategy that was implemented by the state: 'In Korea the chief form of investment subsidy was the extension of credit to large business groups at negative real interest rates. In addition to providing subsidies, the Korean and Taiwanese governments also played a much more direct, hands-on role by organizing private entrepreneurs into investments that they may not have otherwise made.'[5]

Take the vehicle-manufacturing sector. In 1962 the South Korean government announced an automobile industry promotion policy. Foreign producers could only manufacture cars in Korea if they had a local partner. In the same year Japanese Mazda entered into a joint venture with Kia. The predecessor of SsangYong began operations in 1963. And Hyundai began as a partnership with Ford in 1968. But private-sector investment could only happen if cars could be produced profitably. This required cheap inputs. Here, too, government action helped. While car parts had to be imported initially, these imports were soon replaced with the products of local manufacturers, often also established with state support. Rodrik explains: 'Public enterprises played a very important role in enhancing the profitability of private investment in both [Korea and Taiwan] by ensuring that key inputs were available locally for private producers downstream. Not only did public enterprises account for a large share of manufacturing output and investment in each country, but their importance actually increased during the critical take-off years of the 1960s.'[6]

State intervention could range from industrial policies such as devaluing or unifying currencies, providing government loans and subsidising exports to creating consultative business councils, building an efficient bureaucracy and stamping out corruption. It is unclear – and still much debated – how important all these interventions were. In some cases, as Rodrik argues above, they were vital to nurturing a fledgling private sector. But many scholars argue that these same interventions also distorted markets, raised prices, lowered real wages and limited consumer choice; that workers ultimately 'paid' for the miracle by temporarily forgoing higher living standards, just as workers in England did during the Industrial Revolution. The only reason this was possible, the argument goes, is that there was consensus among the political and economic leaders to sacrifice the short-term well-being of their citizens for long-term development.

Others, again, point to Hong Kong, a Crown colony of Britain, as an example of the argument that state intervention was not necessary at all. In contrast to South Korea and Taiwan, the free market was allowed to operate relatively unchecked in Hong Kong. In 1960 the average per capita income of Hong Kong was 28 per cent of Britain's. By 1996, a year before Hong Kong officially reverted to

Chinese sovereignty, the average resident of Hong Kong, despite its population increasing tenfold from 600,000 to 6,000,000, was 37 per cent more affluent that the average Briton. The economist Milton Friedman frequently used Hong Kong as a case study for the success of free enterprise and free markets.

Whether or not you believe industrial policy was necessary, one form of state intervention that is generally agreed to have contributed substantially to the East Asian miracle is education. Two economists, Erik Hanushek and Ludger Woessmann, published a paper in *Science* in 2016, explaining that it was not the *quantity* of education that mattered (the number of years of schooling each student had), but the *quality* of education (how they actually performed on standardised tests).[7] Figure 29.1 shows two graphs: the first plots the average GDP growth rate between 1960 and 2000 against the average years of schooling. Although the correlation is positive, it is clear that there is large variation around the linear trendline; children in Chile, for example, spend more time in school than those in Singapore, yet Singapore's growth rate far exceeds the Chilean one. Compare that with the second correlation. It again plots average GDP growth, but now against test scores – a measure of education quality or outcomes. The correlation is stronger and the variance around the trend lower. Despite all the years children in Chile spend in school, their outcomes are dismal compared to those in Singapore.

The point that Hanushek and Woessmann make is that better-quality education – and not just more education – explains the Asian miracle. It was not just that wages were lower in East Asia than in Europe and North America – wages were cheap in many parts of the world, from Latin America to Africa to South Asia. Rather, workers were both affordable *and* skilled, with the result that labour productivity was high. This created a virtuous cycle: high labour productivity boosted profits, resulting in more investment, capital accumulation, innovation and higher labour productivity. Profits also meant higher tax revenues, which the Asian governments could then reinvest in education and industrial support.

One thing to keep in mind is that expanding the productivity of inputs is a great way to ignite an industrial transformation, but it cannot be done indefinitely. At some stage everyone will be educated and all land and capital will be used efficiently. What then? Does

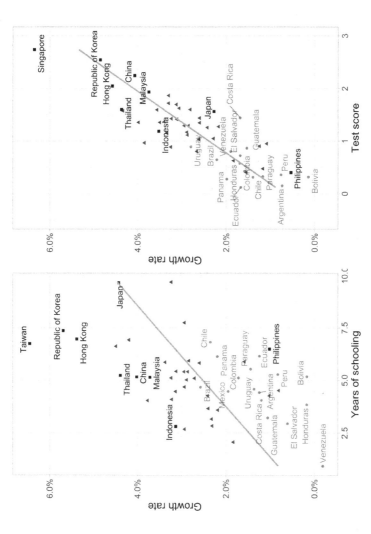

Figure 29.1 Correlations between schooling and economic growth, 1960–2000

growth reach a plateau? To some extent, this has happened in some of the East Asian economies. In the thirty years between 1961 and 1991 Japan grew at 6.1 per cent annually; in the twenty-seven years from 1992 to 2019 Japan grew at an average 0.9 per cent annually. In 2019, the year South Africa's Springboks beat England to win the Rugby World Cup in Japan, the Japanese economy grew at a dismal 0.7 per cent.

So how does one create sustained growth? The key is total factor productivity (TFP). This is the term economists give to the productivity increases not associated with more or better inputs in the production process. Such increases are entirely dependent on innovation in new technologies, new systems and new institutions. This is the heart of what makes a society prosperous.

As a result of increasing public and private investment in research and development, TFP growth has indeed been accelerating in several Asian Tigers, notably Hong Kong, South Korea, Singapore and Taiwan. The projections are that such TFP growth will continue to boost living standards, just as it has done in the last six decades. One astonishing statistic from anthropometrics summarises this transformation in living standards very well. The economic historian Sunyoung Pak shows that South and North Koreans born during the 1940s were of similar height.[8] The Korean War created two countries: one turning inward and the other, South Korea, turning outward. The height of men born today in North Korea is similar to what it was in the 1940s. By contrast, South Korean men today are, on average, 6 centimetres taller than their North Korean compatriots.

30 What Do Lego and the Greatest Invention of the Twentieth Century Have in Common?
The Second Era of Globalisation

The main reason for the long-lasting popularity of Lego bricks is their versatility. A back-of-the-envelope calculation will reveal that six bricks of 2 x 4 studs can be combined in almost 1 billion ways. And because Lego bricks made today still interlock with those first made in 1958, the year the toy was first patented, the possibilities for creative play are, quite literally, innumerable.

Two years before the patent that would turn Lego into the world's favourite toy company, a man called Malcom McLean made the same discovery as Ole Kirk Christiansen, the inventor of Lego. McLean was not in the business of making children's toys, however, but of shipping goods. On 26 April 1956 he was watching his idea come to fruition: in Newark, New Jersey, a crane was lifting fifty-eight aluminium metal boxes into an old tanker ship. Five days later McLean was in Houston to see the same ship, the *Ideal-X*, sail into the port with fifty-eight trucks waiting to take the boxes to their final destination. It was the first, tentative step towards what would arguably become the greatest invention of the twentieth century. It required no great design or engineering, nor any deep philosophical insights – at least, not anything beyond those of a Danish toymaker. What made the shipping container the greatest invention of the twentieth century was its impact. The box, as it would become known, would transform global trade patterns and, as a consequence, would be instrumental in alleviating global poverty and raising living standards to an unprecedented level. While McLean is now a footnote in history, he deserves to be celebrated.

Of course, McLean was not the first to have the idea that goods can be transported in boxes. In the 1930s, US freight companies experimented with using the same boxes on trains and ships. But it was McLean who realised that what was necessary was a total transformation of the freight industry. As the historian Marc Levinson explains in *The Box*, almost everyone in the shipping industry thought their business was shipping.[1] McLean realised that they were missing something important, that their business was not just carrying cargo across oceans, but that it was more about moving cargo from the point of production to the point of delivery. And this meant that every part of the transport system – ports, ships, cranes, storage facilities, trucks, trains, insurance and all the other aspects of moving goods – had to be containerised.

But for McLean, the first priority was to show that containerisation was worth the effort. He was happy to see the *Ideal-X* arrive in Houston, but anxious about whether it had been a financial success. Loading loose cargo on a medium-size cargo ship cost $5.83 per ton in 1956. After the boxes had reached their destination, McLean's experts tallied the costs of transport. They came in at 15.8 cents per ton, a saving of 97 per cent. It was an extraordinary triumph in cost saving – and a development that ushered in the second era of globalisation.

To understand the tremendous change of this second era, it helps to know something about the first. Although long-distance trade routes had existed for millennia – consider the Ishmaelite traders we met in Chapter 5, the Chinese trade voyages of Chapter 10 or the Atlantic slave traders of Chapter 11 – globalisation is generally considered to have begun during the second half of the nineteenth century.[2] This is because economic historians like to attach a very specific definition to globalisation: the economic integration of markets. One way to know whether markets are integrated is to test whether a shock in one market affects the price of the same commodity in another. Wheat prices in Cape Town, for example, began to co-move with London wheat prices around 1872.[3]

This is no coincidence. Technological improvements such as the steamship and railway were spreading rapidly around the globe, lowering transport costs.[4] An ideological shift towards free-trade policies lowered trade barriers such as import tariffs. It was suddenly much easier to ship everything from wheat to pianos halfway around the world, transporting the goods that rolled out of the factories of the Industrial Revolution into new, distant markets.

But the first era of globalisation was also characterised by another movement: that of people. Hundreds of thousands of Europeans migrated to the 'New World' of the Americas or the frontier colonies of Australia, New Zealand or South Africa, further boosting demand for industrial goods from the 'Old World'. The world had suddenly become a much smaller place.

The inter-war period slowed this integration. Not only was trade tricky when German U-boats lay in wait, but military production took precedence over civilian consumption. Instead of integration, autarky ruled. Towards the end of the Second World War, when Europe was beginning to imagine a post-war world, the need for deeper integration became once again glaringly obvious. The *raison d'être* for the first regional integration initiatives in Europe – the European Coal and Steel Community of 1950 and the Common Market of 1957 – was to encourage economic integration so as to make war unimaginable. Over the next four decades integration would deepen. In 1993, four years after the collapse of the Berlin Wall and the end of the Cold War, the European Union became a single market for the movement of goods, services, people and money. In 1999 the euro was adopted as a single currency for the region.

Such integration was not just happening within Europe. In 1944 delegates from forty-four Allied nations convened in Bretton Woods, New Hampshire, to decide about a new international monetary and financial order once the war was over. Three major decisions were made, although we generally celebrate only two of them. To regulate the foreign exchange market, the International Monetary Fund was created. To help with the reconstruction of Europe, the International Bank for Reconstruction and Development was founded (it was later renamed the World Bank). And to promote international trade, the International Trade Organisation was created. But the last body was stillborn, as it was never ratified by the US Senate. All that survived was an agreement – the GATT, or General Agreement on Tariffs and Trade – which stated that countries would voluntarily reduce the barriers to trade with participating nations.

But such a relaxation of tariffs required negotiation. The first meeting, in Geneva, involved 23 participating countries and yielded 45,000 tariff reductions, an impressive effort towards global trade liberalisation. Each successive 'trade round' further reduced tariffs, so that participating countries soon had very low levels of tariff protection. The goal of a tightly integrated world with goods moving freely between nations was becoming a reality.

Seeing the benefits of international trade, more countries joined the GATT. The Kennedy trade round of 1964 involved forty-five countries. The larger size did, however, complicate things: whereas the Geneva round took seven months to conclude, the Kennedy round took thirty-seven months. The next one, the Tokyo round, took seventy-four months, and the Uruguay round eighty-seven. The issues to discuss also widened in scope. Initially, tariff reductions were the only topic of discussion. But in the Kennedy round anti-dumping duties were added, and in Tokyo other non-tariff measures were added too. The Uruguay round, which began in 1986 and involved 123 countries, discussed all kinds of trade-related issues, including trade in services, intellectual property, and the creation in 1995 of the World Trade Organisation, which was to be a new international body to operate a system of trade rules.

The latest round, the Doha round, was opened with big fanfare in 2001. It has still not been concluded – and very likely never will be – because it has become almost impossible to get consensus among all members on contentious issues such as agricultural subsidies. These subsidies, paid to farmers in Western Europe and North America, distort agricultural prices, making it difficult for farmers in developing countries to sell their goods at competitive prices abroad. While agricultural subsidies are politically very popular – whenever there is talk of abolishing them, French farmers, in particular, have staged protests, often using their tractors to block major French highways – they have been shown to severely impoverish African farmers.[5]

To avoid the political stalemate of global trade negotiations, most countries have opted to sign regional agreements rather than attempting to negotiate one global agreement. The proliferation of regional trade agreements – an occurrence the economist Jagdish Bhagwati has termed the spaghetti bowl effect – has allowed countries to reach agreements more quickly.[6] But the downside is that smaller or poorer countries have been excluded; not only do they often not have the capacity to negotiate such agreements, but, given their size, they bring little to the table in negotiations with a large and rich country. A return to a multilateral system, which would benefit a greater number of countries, would be a fairer system.

But the ideological shift towards free trade and the consequent reduction in trade barriers alone cannot explain the surge in global trade during the second half of the twentieth century. Let us consider the evidence. Figure 30.1 shows that between 1950 and 2005 the volume of global exports increased more than twenty-fivefold. New technologies, like Malcom McLean's container or, as we'll explore in the next chapter, internet connectivity and the ICT revolution, explain much of this remarkable growth. It was not that these technologies simply reduced trade costs, but that they fundamentally reshaped the types of exchange possible. Before the second era of globalisation, almost all components were produced in the same country as the one where the final product was assembled. Today that rarely happens. Although local manufacturers do supply a wide range of parts to car-assembly plants in South

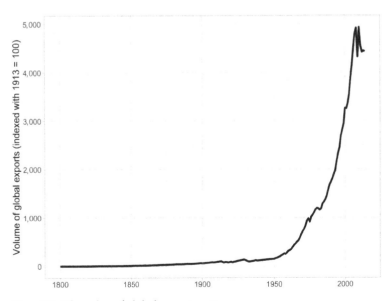

Figure 30.1 The value of global exports, 1800–2014

Africa, a fully assembled car that rolls off the production line nowadays has leather seats, gearboxes, tyres, electronics and various other components sourced from across the world. The same is true of assembly plants in all other countries. In short, value chains – the term used for all the firms involved in the assembly process of a product – have become far more integrated across national borders. Just as humans have become more specialised and, as a result, dependent on one another for survival, so too countries have become increasingly specialised in the production of certain components of the production process, and dependent on international cooperation and exchange. We thrive by relying more on others.

Another feature of the second era of globalisation is the shift towards trade in services. These services include all kinds of things, from the download of the latest *Grand Theft Auto* game by an Australian teenager, to Pakistani call-centre operators handling UK-based client queries, American tourists travelling to South Africa for plastic surgery, or Brazilian football players signing for a top Bundesliga team. This is all a consequence of technological innovation in the field of information and communications technology. It is very likely that trade in services will continue to thrive, especially after Covid-19. As we discuss in Chapter 33, this creates opportunities for African entrepreneurs.

But while goods and services (and capital) move freely today, people don't. This is in stark contrast to the first era of globalisation. In the inter-war period, governments started issuing passports to their citizens and began to impose limitations on cross-border movement. Today, even just travelling as a tourist from a developing country like South Africa to Europe or the United States requires a costly visit to an unfriendly and often privatised local visa issuer. Permanent emigration in the same direction is exorbitantly expensive. This is why, every year, more than a thousand African migrants lose their lives trying to cross the Mediterranean in search of a better life. Just as reducing the high barriers to trade brought huge benefits for the global economy, so too the reduction of the high barriers to the free movement of people would lead to global gains – and not just to those people in developing countries. In an exhaustive review of the migration literature, the economists Michael Clemens and Lant Pritchett conclude:

> Economics was born of studying the 18th-century efficiency losses from trade barriers. In the 21st century, the efficiency losses from remaining restrictions on trade are relatively small. Much larger, but much less studied, the recent literature suggests, are the efficiency losses from restrictions on migration. Wage gaps of hundreds of percent for similar workers between countries may imply large inefficiencies in the spatial allocation of labour, suggesting global costs of migration restrictions in the trillions of dollars per year.[7]

But while voters in the rich world have generally accepted the benefits of free trade, they have far bigger reservations about the free movement of people – of accepting immigrants. The rise of populism has exacerbated this belief; Donald Trump's 'Build a wall' campaign or the Brexit vote is anecdotal evidence of such resistance.

The rise of populism is itself, however, a consequence of the success of globalisation. The remarkable surge in international trade during the second half of the twentieth century has coincided with a period of dramatic declines in global poverty. As we have seen in Chapter 29, East Asian economies and, more recently, those of China and India have benefited immensely from a more open world and the technological innovations associated with it. But despite the many winners, this surge in trade has also created losers. Manufacturing and other blue-collar jobs have been outsourced to countries that pay lower wages for similar levels of productivity. In the United States, for example, the rich and the poor have become wealthier, while the middle class has been left behind. This has not only created populist sentiment, it has also prevented further liberalisation – notably the free movement of people – and has, in some cases, created a backlash against free trade itself.[8] On both sides of the political spectrum in much of the developed world, tariff restrictions are back in vogue.

Humanity has thrived because of the free movement of people and things across borders. But the overwhelming evidence from history is often not enough to convince politicians or voters. The case against free trade is gaining momentum. That will only hurt future generations.

31 | What Is Funny about Moore's Law?
ICT and the Fourth Industrial Revolution

You wouldn't call it a classic joke. It's more of a quip, to be honest; something you might hear at a computer-science convention. It is said that the number of people predicting the end of Moore's law doubles every two years. Lol.

For the uninitiated, Moore's law refers to Gordon Moore's prediction, in 1965, that the number of transistors on a computer microchip would double every two years while the cost of computers would be halved. It was a brave prediction to make when microprocessors and home computers were still just a distant dream. But despite the countless experts predicting the demise of Moore's law, as the quip insinuates, it has remained true for almost five decades, as Figure 31.1 demonstrates.

Today's microchips are millions of times stronger than those that guided *Apollo 11* to the moon in 1969. It gets even more bizarre: the smartphone in your pocket is now faster than the most famous supercomputer that has existed – IBM's 1997 Deep Blue, which beat Garry Kasparov in a historic chess showdown. That is the power of exponential growth.

This exponential growth of the computer chip has transformed our lives in ways that no one at the dawn of the ICT revolution could have imagined. We now open our smartphones – an invention of the 1990s – to read our daily news, order a lift or food delivery, make payments, watch videos and listen to music, have meetings, attend lectures and interact with friends via social media sites such as TikTok and Twitter. Sometimes we may even call someone to chat. But, surprising as it may be to us now, the benefits

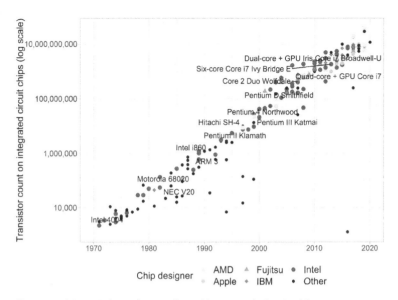

Figure 31.1 Moore's law: the number of integrated circuit chips, 1971–2018

of microchips and home computers were not immediately obvious to everyone. In fact, by the end of the 1980s economists were puzzled: why had productivity growth been so sluggish despite huge improvements in computing technology? The Nobel Prize-winning economist Robert Solow summarised the paradox at the time: 'You can see the computer age everywhere but in the productivity statistics.'[1]

In reflecting on this question, the economic historian Paul David did what any good economic historian would do: he turned to history.[2] Did the electric dynamo, David asked, the technological innovation at the heart of the electricity revolution that swept the world at the beginning of the twentieth century, have a similar delayed impact on productivity? And, if so, why? David's insight was that transformative technologies do not make an immediate impact. A visitor to the Paris Exhibition of 1900, where the dynamo and many of its applications were on display, could easily have imagined a bright future (literally and figuratively) for the device, but could also have thought to herself: many of these inventions, like the light bulb and the power station, were already more than two decades old. Why wasn't the dynamo immediately visible in the productivity statistics of the time? The simple answer is that, ironically, the larger the technological impact, the slower it is to take off. There are two reasons for this. As in the case of electricity, new technologies often require completely new infrastructure. A power plant only makes sense if enough users are connected to the grid. And building infrastructure takes time, especially during the initial phase when the technology is still improving. It often also requires government regulation, which can involve a slow process.

A second reason for the slow take-off of truly transformational technology is that most established firms play a wait-and-see game. Many managers argue that 'we should not fix something that is not broken'. They want to wait for the technology to reach maturity before they invest. That is partly why new technologies are so disruptive: new firms are nimbler and can adapt more quickly to the changing environment. Incumbents are often saddled with soon-to-be-obsolete systems and technologies, and prefer to hold on to those, frequently to their own detriment.

It was not long after the Paris Exhibition that the price of electricity began to decline precipitately. Between 1909 and 1929, as the technology standardised, electrification of US factories increased by 50 percentage points. And, as a consequence, so too did total-factor productivity and economic growth.

When David published his paper in 1990, it had been almost two decades since the dawn of the information age. Many were worried that it was a false hope; that the microchip and computer would be little more than playthings for the few. David notes that patience is a virtue:

> There is, on the one hand, the buoyant conviction that we are embarked on a pre-determined course of diffusion, leading swiftly and inexorably toward the successful transformation of the entire range of productive activities in a way that will render them palpably more efficient; and, on the other hand, there is the depressing suspicion that something has gone terrible awry, fostered by the disappointment of premature expectations about the information revolution's impact upon the conventional productivity indicators and our material standard of living. But, closer study of some economic history of technology should help us to avoid both the pitfall of undue sanguinity and the pitfall of unrealistic

impatience as we proceed on our journey into the information age.[3]

We now know that the computer and the World Wide Web (which was developed by the British computer scientist Tim Berners-Lee in the same year David wrote his paper) have indeed had profound political, social, cultural and, of course, economic consequences. Production and trade have changed in ways David could not have imagined. Microchips have accelerated automation to levels unimaginable only a few decades earlier. More recent developments in robotics – at the interface between computers and engineering – have further transformed the factory floor; Henry Ford's twentieth-century assembly line employing thousands of unskilled workers has now been displaced by machines operated by a few programmers. Computers and connectivity have created just-in-time (JIT) inventory systems. Based on a system originally developed by Toyota in the 1970s, JIT allows manufacturers to operate with low inventory levels, reducing the need for storage and cutting down on waste. And in the 1990s, as the internet spread across the globe, the outsourcing of production – or of parts of the production process – became a necessary cost-saving strategy for most firms in the developed world.

But the biggest impact of computers and the internet has been on the services sector. More than two-thirds of total value added globally is now in services, a sector that includes activities such as banking, retail, marketing, accounting, recreation, education, health and communication. Consider the industry that I work in: education. When I was a student in the early 2000s, my lecturers used to teach supply-and-demand graphs using transparencies and projectors. If they wanted to find information about the GDP of, say, Botswana, they had to visit the campus library and find the most recent World Bank report, in printed form. Many still wrote their papers by hand, submitting them to academic journals by postal mail. Just a decade or so earlier, many still had to draw graphs by hand or use punch cards to run statistical regressions.

Of course, things are different now. This book was written with extensive use of Google from the comfort of my home. When I needed access to books, I generally could find an electronic copy. I could easily download all the data from the Maddison or World

Bank databases, open a (freely downloadable) software package and plot my graphs. Covid-19 further accelerated the digital transformation. My classes began to be taught online, with students consulting slideshow summaries. And with everything moving online, my students – from as far away as Finland – could still participate. They all submitted essays on Turnitin, a website that automatically checks for plagiarism. It is easy to imagine that they will soon write tests graded by artificial intelligence software – more fairly and much faster (and with far less emotional drain) than I ever could.

The fear, just as with the eighteenth-century invention of the spinning jenny, is that these technologies will replace workers. And indeed, I would have had to spend much more time grading essays if technologies such as Turnitin did not exist. But in my profession, as in many others, technology is complementary rather than a substitute; it has boosted my productivity, allowing me to teach and research at a much higher quantity and quality than was possible before. Put simply, this book would not have been written had these technologies not been available.

One famous example of how technology can create jobs rather than shed them comes from banking. In the early 1990s, when ATMs were rolled out across the United States, the fear was that banking clerks would become obsolete, resulting in huge job losses. But exactly the opposite happened: instead of workers being displaced, the number of banking jobs increased.[4] The reason? The much cheaper ATMs allowed banks to set up many more local branches, build much bigger networks, and use their staff to provide other client services, such as selling insurance, rather than counting coins. Consumers profited not only from lower bank fees but also from a greater variety of financial services.

There *are* valid concerns regarding these technological developments. One of them is the concentration of market power among a few tech giants. Network industries are, by definition, monopolistic in nature. But it is useful to keep in mind that this monopolism is not new. Nineteenth-century railway lines or twentieth-century electricity grids were often under state control because it made sense to have only one provider. But the pervasive nature of today's network industries – from banking to broadcasting – has meant that many industries have concentrated around one or two firms. Google dominates the search-engine market, with more than 90 per cent market share. In several dozen countries Visa and Mastercard control more than 90 per cent of the market for debit and credit cards. Amazon sells more than 40 per cent of US ecommerce. Tencent takes half of all mobile game revenues in China. And these large market shares have allowed the companies to do incredibly well. Almost all of the world's largest companies – Apple, Amazon, Alphabet (Google), Microsoft, Meta (Facebook), Alibaba and Tencent – are tech companies, most of them created in the last three decades.

To maintain their market dominance, these giant companies buy up smaller companies. Between 2015 and 2019 Alphabet acquired a dozen firms, on average, every year. These range from Moodstocks, a French image-recognition company, to Halli Labs, an Indian artificial intelligence company, to Typhoon Studios, a Canadian video-game developer. In many cases, entrepreneurs today build businesses not to make profits, but for them to be sold to these tech conglomerates.

This would all be familiar to the business historian Alfred Chandler, who in the 1970s wrote about a similar phenomenon. In contrast to the perfectly competitive market that Adam Smith termed the 'invisible hand', Chandler wrote about the emergence of large, vertically integrated, managerially directed enterprises.[5] This phenomenon arose because large firms were more efficient: while small firms had to depend on the market to coordinate their purchases of inputs and sale of outputs, vertically integrated firms could integrate these functions internally through managerial hierarchies. But as the economic historians Naomi Lamoreaux, Daniel Raff and Peter Temin have pointed out, this turn towards 'big business' did not last.[6] In the 1980s and 1990s these large conglomerates were outperformed by smaller, nimbler firms that could adjust more easily in the rapidly changing ICT environment. It is not inevitable that the tech giants of today will remain giants forever. As new technologies evolve, and management of increasingly large entities becomes too cumbersome, new entrants emerge. And there is much to look forward to. With billions of people now connected via mobile devices, each more powerful than the most powerful computer only two decades ago, many argue that we have now entered another revolution – the Fourth Industrial Revolution. It remains to be seen to what extent the current giants will be able to maintain their advantage in the emerging fields of artificial intelligence, robotics, the metaverse, autonomous vehicles, 3D printing, nanotechnology, biotechnology, materials science, energy storage and quantum computing.

What is sure, though, is that these tech giants have not only created services from which we all benefit, but that they have also created immense wealth for their shareholders. Apple is a great example. It is now worth more than $2 trillion, yet this wealth is not concentrated in the hands of just a few founders. Its shares are owned by investment companies, such as the Vanguard Group, which, in turn, has more than 30 million investors. This means that millions of people around the world have a stake in Apple. Or take Tencent. In 2001 Koos Bekker, then a young CEO of Naspers, a largely unimpressive South African media company, purchased a 46.5 per cent stake in an unknown Chinese company. Tencent, founded just three years earlier, was the creator of an instant messaging platform called QQ at the time. Today Tencent is one of the largest companies in the world, and Naspers's 29 per cent share (held in Prosus, a company which was spun off in 2019), is now worth $170 billion.[7]

While Bekker himself has benefited handsomely from his foresight, so too have all South Africans who own Naspers and Prosus shares. And that is almost everyone with a pension fund, because Naspers and its spin-off makes up a large share of the Johannesburg Stock Exchange. In fact, a great example of digital transformation is the fact that South Africa, a country known for its wealth of gold and diamond resources, has created most of its wealth in the last decade from Chinese kids mining and scavenging for resources in online games such as *League of Legends* and *Fortnite*.

32 What Bubbles in Iceland?
The Global Financial Crisis of 2008

Iceland is a country of rugged beauty, volcanic mountains, countless waterfalls and, well, ice. Its inhabitants are even more exotic; 54 per cent of Icelanders, for example, believe in elves – or say it's possible that they exist. Travelling through the desolate landscape, one can easily imagine how such beliefs emerge: Iceland is a country with fewer than 400,000 residents. To put that in perspective, almost double the number of people live in the 33 square kilometres of Macau than in the 100,000 square kilometres of Iceland.

Iceland might seem like a strange place to start a story about the largest global financial crisis since the Great Depression. But Iceland exemplifies both the worst and best of the crisis. The story begins several years before 2008, when Iceland's bank managers saw an opportunity: they could attract the savings of Europeans, mostly residents of England and the Netherlands, by offering interest rates higher than those of the banks of those countries. The scheme seemed to work. Money poured in to such an extent that the three biggest banks grew to ten times the size of the economy, and twenty times the size of the government's budget. What did Iceland's banks do with all this money? They reinvested it abroad, buying all kinds of things, from foreign companies to foreign real estate – even foreign football teams. They also purchased what had become known as collateralised debt obligations, or CDOs. Think of a CDO this way: it pools the mortgage payments of many different home owners together. The attractive thing for an investor is that by pooling the mortgage payments of people across the United States, for example, the risk of non-payment is spread across many home owners and territories. If one home owner defaults, perhaps because of poor financial decisions or poor economic prospects in their area, the result is not so bad, because there are many others who will continue paying their mortgages. For that reason, a CDO can have a better risk rating than the underlying assets.

So, Iceland's banks invested their European clients' savings in the American housing market. These investments were fine while house prices were on the rise. And this was indeed the case for much of the first half of the 2000s. In fact, house prices were not only rising – they were skyrocketing. To cash in on the housing bubble many Americans had taken on second mortgages, at sub-prime interest rates, and used that money to speculate in the housing market. They often borrowed this money not from banks, but from financial institutions known as sub-prime lenders.

Sub-prime lenders were part of what was known as the shadow banking system in the United States. The liberalisation of financial regulations in the 1990s allowed new types of financial institutions to develop. These pseudo-banks were not subject to the same regulatory oversight as traditional banks and therefore could create complex financial instruments, such as CDOs, that separated the risks from the returns. In short, the high-risk sub-prime mortgages were creatively repackaged and disguised as CDOs and sold to bigger banks in the United States and Europe, including those cash-flush bankers in Iceland.

By early 2006, however, it was increasingly obvious that what had become a housing bubble was about to burst. House prices flattened and then declined. Home owners, such as those who had bought a second property hoping to sell at a higher price, could not find any buyers. Some began to default on their mortgage payments, leaving sub-prime lenders in the lurch. During the first few months of 2007 more than twenty-five US sub-prime lenders filed for bankruptcy. This had other knock-on effects. By August 2007 it was clear that the financial market could not solve the sub-prime crisis. Because of the interconnectedness of the banking system, the situation quickly spilled over into Europe. By the end of 2007, major European banks had announced substantial losses from sub-prime-related investments.

The worst was yet to come. When banks realised that the CDOs and other complex financial instruments they had purchased were actually not so safe, it caused what was equivalent to a run on the shadow banking system. Basically, everyone wanted to sell their CDOs as soon as possible, but no one wanted to buy them. The shadow banking sector collapsed. On 15 September 2008 Lehman Brothers, a global financial services firm founded in 1847 and the fourth-largest investment bank in the USA, with about 25,000 employees worldwide, filed for bankruptcy. Just a week earlier Fannie Mae and Freddie Mac were placed into conservatorship by the US Treasury. Fannie Mae (the Federal National Mortgage Association) had been founded in the aftermath of the Great Depression as a way to help Americans finance their home loans. It was privatised in the 1960s. In 1970 the Federal Home Loan Mortgage Corporation (or Freddie Mac) was founded to expand the secondary market for mortgages. When the housing bubble burst, Fannie Mae and Freddie Mac owned or guaranteed a large proportion of all home loans in the United States. Both were deemed too big to fail by government, and received government support to survive.

The collapse of a large part of the financial sector inevitably affected other parts of the economy too. Although the United States formally entered a recession in December 2007, during 2008 and 2009 the recession spread across the globe, becoming the Great Recession. International trade declined by 22 per cent in US dollar terms, commodity prices fell sharply, and unemployment increased. In 2009 global GDP declined for the first time since the Great Depression of the 1930s.

How did policymakers respond to the enveloping crisis? To sum it up: they told a story. In his presidential speech to the Economic History Association in 2012 the economist Barry Eichengreen explained that policymakers during the crisis had three options.[1] They could use deductive reasoning in deciding how to respond. This implied that they would use their macroeconomic models to determine their response. The problem with this approach is that there is much debate over which macroeconomic models best explain the economy, and, as a consequence, what to do when a crisis hits. Put very simplistically, the saltwater school (so named because all the major universities that support this approach are based next to the US's east and west coasts) would propose active monetary and fiscal policy intervention, while the freshwater school (notably the University of Chicago, which is based next to a lake) would propose limited government intervention.

A second approach was to use inductive reasoning. This would require one to collect as much evidence as possible about what was happening, and then respond in a pragmatic way. This is an approach attractive to many social scientists, yet it has one major limitation in a crisis: it takes time to collect accurate information about the state of the economy. It can easily take three months to devise an accurate estimate of GDP. By that time the policy response that would have been appropriate three months previously might no longer be relevant.

Eichengreen argued that during a crisis, such as the Great Recession of 2008, policymakers follow a third approach: they use analogical reasoning. And during the Great Recession, he said, they used the Great Depression of the 1930s as their analogy. They chose this approach to tell a story about what had gone wrong during the Great Depression and how we should 'learn from history'. This approach made sense for a couple of reasons. It was easy to get public support for something that most people could relate to. We all like to tell stories – and it is much easier to be convinced by a story than by a mathematical model or statistical evidence. Second, it is much easier to rely on a story when we disagree on theory, as was the case with the saltwater and freshwater economists. Third, it allows policymakers to move quickly.

As we discussed in Chapter 21, policymakers during the Great Depression were initially hesitant to intervene, hoping that the issue would solve itself. They believed that there was no need for fiscal or monetary policy, that in time the economy would revert to equilibrium. When this did not happen, Roosevelt introduced his New Deal. But it came four years after the initial Wall Street crash.

The crisis of 2008 was different. Ben Bernanke, who wrote his doctoral dissertation on the Great Depression while he was a student at MIT, was chair of the Federal Reserve, the central bank of the United States. He quickly realised that to avoid the same economic calamity as the Great Depression, he needed to act. In March 2009 the Federal Reserve quickly and resolutely adopted a policy of quantitative easing – the process of buying government bonds to inject money into the economy.

Monetary policy was not enough. A relatively unknown senator from Illinois, Barack Obama, had been elected president of the United States in the midst of the crisis. He, too, had learned from the past. He realised that if the banks and the companies that they serviced were allowed to fail, it would devastate the American economy. To counteract this he adopted a fiscal stimulus package to bail out insolvent banks and other companies. The combined effect of expansionary monetary and fiscal policy ensured that the crisis, although severe, was short-lived. The US economy shrank by 2.5 per cent in 2009. In stark contrast to the Great Depression, when negative economic growth persisted for several years, GDP growth bounced back the very next year, in 2010, recording a positive growth rate of 2.6 per cent.

Not all countries suffered equally from the fall-out. South Africa, for example, escaped much of the initial bank crisis. There was good reason for this. Only a few years earlier, in 2002, South Africa had experienced a 'small bank crisis', with several small banks, notably Saambou, filing for bankruptcy.[2] One consequence of this crisis was that the authorities imposed stricter banking regulations. South African banks were therefore far less exposed to the instruments issued by the sub-prime lenders in the United States. This does not mean that the country was unaffected. When America sneezes, the world catches a cold. During the crisis, the Johannesburg Stock Exchange contracted by 40 per cent. Lower commodity prices and a decline in global demand hurt South African exports substantially. GDP declined by 1.5 per cent in 2009, and unemployment and poverty increased, setting South Africa, as we will see in Chapter 34, on course for a decade of poor performance.

One question that has intrigued economists is how a future financial crisis can be averted. One clue is that these crises typically emerge because of some asset bubble: the Great Depression was preceded by massive speculation on the Dow Jones, and the Great Recession, as we have seen, was the result of a housing bubble.

Asset bubbles are, of course, not new events. One of the first and most famous bubbles was Tulipmania, which swept Holland in 1636. Tulipmania saw the price of rare tulips inflate in one year only to collapse by 90 per cent the following year, which devastated many tulip investors. Another was the South Sea Bubble of company stocks (including that of the South Sea Company) in the United Kingdom in 1720. And yet another was Bicycle Mania in 1895, which saw the rapid price appreciation of bicycle companies. Perhaps more familiar to us is the dot-com bubble of 2001, a stock-market bubble caused by excessive speculation in internet-related companies.

Financial historians William Quinn and John Turner explain that for a bubble to emerge, three things are necessary.[3] The first is marketability, or the ease with which an asset can be freely bought and sold. The second is low interest rates on traditional safe assets, which can force investors to 'reach for yield' in new asset classes. The third is speculation, the practice of buying an asset with the sole motivation of selling it later at a higher price. Although there is always speculation, Quinn and Turner note that during a bubble large numbers of novice investors join in as speculators.

The best recent example of how all three of these factors combine is the 2017–18 Bitcoin bubble. Bitcoin is a decentralised cryptocurrency that uses sophisticated blockchain technology to allow payments without the need for an intermediary. Bitcoin not only eases payments but is often also used as a store of value in countries that experience rapid currency depreciation. The bubble was brief but memorable. At the start of 2017 the price of one Bitcoin was below $1,000. By the end of that year it had reached almost $20,000. But the bubble burst, and it did so spectacularly in 2018. By the end of 2018 it had lost 72 per cent of its value.

This is not the end for Bitcoin and other cryptocurrencies, however. In March 2021 the price of one Bitcoin increased to above $60,000. A month earlier its market value had exceeded $1 trillion for the first time. Which brings us back to Iceland. Volcanoes and ice not only provide beautiful vistas, but are also a source of cheap energy and cold temperatures, a perfect combination for mining Bitcoin. As one journalist put it, 'effectively, a bunch of computers engage in a race to burn through the most electricity possible and, every 10 minutes, one wins a prize of 12.5 bitcoin for the effort'.[4] The cold Arctic air also reduces the need to invest in expensive air-conditioning for server rooms. As cryptocurrencies become more commonplace, displacing national currencies and allowing new types of transactions, Iceland may soon be at the forefront of global financial developments yet again.

33 What Did *The Economist* Get Spectacularly Wrong?
Africa after 2000

In May 2000 the world's leading financial weekly announced that there was little hope for the future of Africa. Under the headline 'The hopeless continent', *The Economist*'s cover showed a young man, presumably a rebel, carrying an anti-tank rocket launcher, over a cut-out of the region. The dark background spelled doom.

The Economist was not alone in its Afro-pessimism. In a seminal 1999 paper, development economists Paul Collier and Jan Willem Gunning attributed most of the malaise to Africa's poor integration in the global economy, a result of import-substitution and exchange controls. They concluded that African countries were left with challenges that 'are much more difficult to correct than exchange rate and trade policies, and so the policy reform effort needs to be intensified. However, even widespread policy reforms in this area might not be sufficient to induce a recovery in private investment, since recent economic reforms are never fully credible.'[1]

This bleak outlook was shared by other scholars. Academic journals frequently published papers using cross-country growth regressions – the fashion of the time – that included continental dummy variables which always yielded a negative coefficient for Africa, suggesting that, conditional on many other things, there was something uniquely wrong with Africa.[2]

And, indeed, there was much to be pessimistic about. As I noted in Chapter 26, many African countries had poor or negative economic growth; some were poorer in 2000 than they had been in 1960. The scourge of HIV/Aids had spread rapidly throughout

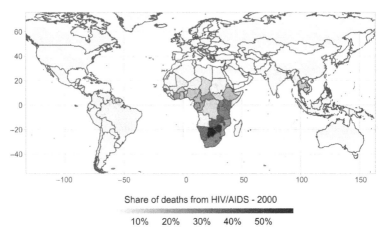

Share of deaths from HIV/AIDS - 2000

10%   20%   30%   40%   50%

Figure 33.1 Share of deaths from HIV/Aids across the globe, 2000

sub-Saharan Africa during the 1990s, with devastating consequences. As Figure 33.1 demonstrates, by 2000 the death of half of
all Zimbabweans was due to HIV/Aids. The figure was a third for
Namibia and a quarter for South Africa. The global average, on the
other hand, was 3 per cent.

The misery of HIV/Aids was compounded by the ineffect-
iveness of international aid. In the early 2000s Jeffrey Sachs, one of
the world's leading development economists and an eager contributor to understanding African poverty, proposed ending poverty
through massive spending: a 'big push' of international aid that
would drive investment, notably in infrastructure, boost productivity and raise living standards.[3] Although Sachs's efforts did help to
reduce the incidence of malaria, it had little effect on poverty allevi-
ation. In fact, some would argue that aid did more harm than good.
The development economist William Easterly has been especially
critical of Sachs's 'big push' strategy, arguing that there is little
evidence that the more than $500 billion spent on aid to Africa has
had any meaningful impact. This is because poverty, he argues, is not
solved through expert plans implemented from the top – but through
economic growth that empowers people from below.[4] The economist Dambisa Moyo, in her 2009 book *Dead Aid: Why Aid Is Not
Working and How There Is a Better Way for Africa*, concurred with
Easterly, arguing that foreign aid corrodes democratic institutions.[5]

The good intentions of foreign aid may in fact have resulted in perverse outcomes.

Things were not bad everywhere in Africa, of course. Between 1965 and 2000 Botswana had the highest rate of per capita economic growth of any country in the world. It is easy to simply attribute this exceptional performance – what many have now called an African growth miracle – to the discovery of diamonds. This assumption would ignore the strong market-friendly institutions – or, put differently, the lack of bad policies – that have been key to Botswana's success.[6] Other African countries, such as Sierra Leone, also have diamonds, yet they have not prospered; in 2018 the average citizen of Botswana was ten times richer than the average citizen of Sierra Leone.

But Botswana was the exception rather than the rule. In 2000, when *The Economist* wrote its unfortunate headline, most African countries were in bad shape. Fast-forward a decade to December 2011, when *The Economist* published another story on Africa, this time with a decidedly more optimistic outlook:

> Since *The Economist* regrettably labelled Africa 'the hopeless continent' a decade ago, a profound change has taken hold. Labour productivity has been rising. It is now growing by, on average, 2.7% a year. Trade between Africa and the rest of the world has increased by 200% since 2000. Inflation dropped from 22% in the 1990s to 8% in the past decade. Foreign debts declined by a quarter, budget deficits by two-thirds. In eight of the past ten years, according to the World Bank, sub-Saharan growth has been faster than East Asia's.
>
> Even after revising downward its 2012 forecast because of a slowdown in the northern hemisphere, the IMF still expects sub-Saharan Africa's economies to expand by 5.75% next year. Several big countries are likely to hit growth rates of 10%. The World Bank – not known for boosterism – said in a report this year that 'Africa could be on the brink of an economic take-off, much like China was 30 years ago and India 20 years ago,' though its officials think major poverty reduction will require higher growth than today's – a long-term average of 7% or more.[7]

What had caused this remarkable reversal? It helps to take a long-term view. The IMF's structural adjustment programmes of the 1980s and 1990s – policies intended to reduce bloated government budgets, reduce debt and stabilise things like inflation and exchange rates, reforms which later became known as the Washington Consensus – did not seem to yield immediate results. During the last two decades of the twentieth century growth in much of Africa remained dismal. And tragic outbreaks of famine – Ethiopia in 1984 – or genocide – Rwanda in 1994 – exacerbated the dire economic situation. This poor record of performance is why *The Economist* could justify its May 2000 headline and why both Africans and international experts doubted the efficacy of the Washington Consensus. In 2006 the economist Dani Rodrik wrote: 'Proponents and critics alike agree that the policies spawned by the Washington Consensus have not produced the desired results ... It is fair to say that nobody really believes in the Washington Consensus anymore. The debate now is not over whether the Washington Consensus is dead or alive, but over what will replace it.'[8]

But the apparent lack of success of the neoliberal reforms of the 1980s and 1990s should not be dismissed so quickly. In a 2019 working paper William Easterly quantifies the extent of 'bad policies' in Africa and elsewhere and measures their effect on later growth performance.[9] It turns out that when experts were making claims in the mid-2000s about the impact of the structural adjustment programmes, they were using a 2001 World Bank dataset that had not yet accounted for the rapid economic growth that many countries would experience from the 2000s onwards. Although Easterly himself was critical of the neoliberal reforms – in 2005, for example, he said that 'repeated (structural) adjustment lending ... fails to show any positive effect on policies or growth' – he was now happy to change his mind on the basis of new evidence.[10] The reforms, it seems, had a profound but delayed impact: fewer 'bad policies' did cause economic growth, particularly in those regions that were most likely to have had bad policies in the 1980s and earlier. Figure 33.2 shows the rapid decline in 'bad policies' in Latin America and Africa between 1990 and 2000. The lesson is obvious: the package of Washington Consensus policies was instrumental in getting rid of bad policies. Once they were removed, economies began to grow, although this growth was from a low base and was often deferred.[11]

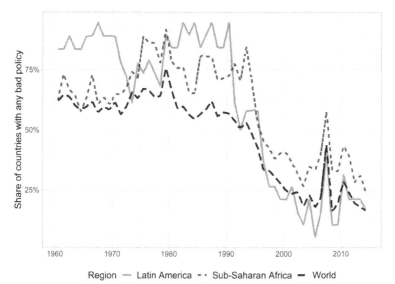

Figure 33.2 Share of countries with any 'bad policy', 1961–2015

It was not only a consequence of fewer bad policies that Africa's 'lost decades' from 1975 to 1995 were replaced by two decades of 'Africa rising'. The growth period was linked to the fact that commodity prices rose rapidly, a consequence of higher demand in fast-growing India, China and other Asian countries, thereby improving the terms of trade in many African economies and boosting commodity exports. To put the turnaround in perspective: between 2001 and 2010 six of the ten fastest-growing economies in the world were African – Angola, Nigeria, Ethiopia, Chad, Mozambique and Rwanda – and almost all were dependent on commodity exports. For some, this growth continued into the 2010s: Ethiopia was the fastest-growing economy between 2010 and 2019, growing at an incredible 9.5 per cent per annum. For others, growth slowed: Angola, an oil exporter, had negative growth rates between 2016 and 2019.

The fear is that African economies are just repeating the same boom-and-bust cycle they experienced in the 1950s and 1960s, which was also a period characterised by high commodity prices. Will African countries now finally be able to structurally transform their economies away from volatile commodity exports?

The economic historians Ewout Frankema and Marlous van Waijenburg caution against over-optimistic predictions of Africa's structural transformation.[12] They compare Africa today with Britain and Japan at the time of their transformation into manufacturing – and draw five lessons. First, the rapid industrialisation of Asian economies was based on a large labour cost gap between the West and the rest. No such gap exists today between the cost of labour in Africa and in Asia, where manufacturing is still increasing. Second, even if African countries were to push towards industrialisation, it is unlikely that this will immediately translate into higher living standards. It took almost half a century in Britain and Japan for living standards to improve after the shift to manufacturing. Third, population growth is higher in Africa and, in contrast to Britain and Japan, there is no 'escape valve', such as colonies or new territories to which surplus labour could move. This suggests that Africa will have a larger pool of labourers, which would widen the gap between industrialisation take-off and increases in living standards. Fourth, because of the focus on export commodities, Africa has lost many of its traditional artisanal skills. How quickly modern education can replace such skills remains to be seen. Fifth, and most importantly, industrialisation in Britain and Japan was backed by governments willing to forgo the human rights of its citizens, as well as to suppress wages for decades to ensure international competitiveness. Strong labour movements in Africa make such policies unlikely. This gloomy outlook is best summarised by the economic historian Morten Jerven: 'The dependency of African economies on export volumes and prices makes their development path one of recurring growth and recession.'[13]

But there is also cause for optimism. Information and communications technology, as we discussed in Chapter 31, has transformed the traditional path of economic development. Africa has embraced the digital revolution at a bewildering speed. In 2000 only 1 in every 200 Rwandans had a mobile phone. In 2017 3 in every 4 Rwandans had one. This rapid and deep penetration of mobile technology has opened two opportunities: first, the closer integration of domestic markets; and second, the opening of new export sectors.

Frankema and van Waijenburg discuss the first of these: a larger, more integrated market. Lower information, communication and transaction costs have brought producers, traders and consumers closer together, expanding domestic markets to those who were often excluded by distance or low density. Smallholder farmers in Kenya can now easily access market prices and weather updates on their mobile phones, making them more productive.[14] Mobile payment systems such as M-Pesa open up banking and insurance services that would have been too costly for any bricks-and-mortar equivalent.[15] And the changes are not only because of mobile technology. Drones have reduced transport costs for vaccines and other medical supplies.[16] Solar power enables countries to avoid building large power generators with their expensive power-transmission infrastructure. The point is that technological innovation is rapidly leading to more integrated and empowered local, national and regional networks, allowing producers to scale up production, reducing prices and expanding consumer choice.

The second reason for optimism is that technology allows for new export industries, notably in the services sector. Tourism is the most obvious industry in which many African countries already have a comparative advantage and into which new technology platforms, such as Uber or Airbnb, can easily expand. Thanks to the continent's rich natural and cultural heritage, many places are high on the list of must-see destinations. Indeed, for countries such as Madagascar (15%), the Gambia (20%), Mauritius (25%), Cape Verde (46%) and Seychelles (67%), tourism is the driving force of the economy.

But new technologies also allow for the export of other service types. Consider the Zambian accountant who is accredited in Britain. Based in Lusaka, she has a team that flies to London, does the audits, and then returns to Zambia to complete the paperwork. She charges a quarter of what a British auditor would ask – and provides the same high-quality service. These types of service exports can range from highly skilled (business and financial, engineering, education) to less skilled (from business process outsourcing – or call centres – to entertainment). There are several reasons why Africa, rather than Asia or Latin America, can fill this gap: the continent lies in the same time zone as Europe, and Africans speak two of the largest European languages, French and English.

It remains to be seen to what extent countries can skip industrialisation and shift directly from agriculture to services. The only countries that have managed to do so are city-states such as

Hong Kong and Singapore. But the type of technological change brought about by the Fourth Industrial Revolution now allows another route to prosperity. If Africa is to avoid the path of recurring growth and recession dependent on the commodity cycle, it needs to prevent the recurrence of the policy disasters of the past and embrace the opportunities that technological innovation offers.

34 Will Madiba's Long Walk to Freedom Ever End?

The First Twenty-Five Years of Democracy and the Future of South Africa

On 27 April 1994 Nelson Mandela's long walk to political freedom came to an end. On that fresh autumn morning 22 million South Africans headed to their nearest voting booths to cast their votes, many for the first time, in the country's first democratic elections. The mood was festive. After almost a century of political exclusion, black South Africans now had an equal political voice – and they made it count: the African National Congress won 63 per cent of the total vote. Mandela was sworn in a few days later as the country's first democratically elected president.

But not all freedoms were fulfilled on Freedom Day (as that first democratic election is known). Many South Africans at the time were living in abject poverty, unable to achieve the life they wanted. Almost all of them were black. The new rainbow nation was characterised by stark levels of inequality. In 1998 then-deputy president Thabo Mbeki described South Africa as a 'two-nation' society: 'One of these nations is white, relatively prosperous, regardless of gender or geographic dispersal ... The second and larger nation ... is black and poor, with the worst-affected being women in the rural areas.'[1] Mbeki was both right and wrong. White South Africans were indeed far more affluent than black South Africans. In 1996, the year of the first democratic census and the year South Africa adopted its new constitution, of the richest 22% in South Africa, 10% were black while 65% were white. Poverty, of course, was almost an entirely black experience: of the poorest 10% in South Africa, 90% were black.[2]

But by the time Mbeki described South Africa as a 'two-nation' society, inequality was changing, and had been doing so for at least the three preceding decades. In 1975 only 2% of the richest 10% of South Africans were black. Within two decades the share of black South Africans who formed part of the elite would increase tenfold. Inequality was increasing more within race groups than between them: 62% of inequality in South Africa in 1975 could be explained by the gap between black and white incomes; by 1996 this had fallen to 33% – still large, but far less important.[3]

That these changes were happening during the last two decades of apartheid should not be surprising. The National Party, in an attempt to placate black unrest, had begun to expand social transfers to black South Africans too. By 1993 white and black state pensions had equalised. Many of the restrictions that had limited black economic freedom, such as influx control, the colour bar and the ban on trade unions, had been relaxed during the 1980s or early 1990s.

There is no denying, however, that the ANC faced an immense challenge to build a better life for all. In 1993 it adopted its first policy document, called the Reconstruction and Development Programme, which promised 'a decent living standard and economic security'. This would be achieved largely through fiscal redistribution, using tax revenues to build housing and provide other social services. Many of the public housing projects on the outskirts of South African towns and cities are still known as RDP houses. But in 1996 the ANC switched gears, adopting the Growth, Employment and Redistribution (GEAR) plan, which shifted the government's priorities to macroeconomic stability and economic growth. This made sense at the time. Not only had the new government inherited high levels of debt and price volatility, making it difficult to pay for the social services it wished to provide, but it also had no track record to convince potential investors of its capacity to govern. It urgently needed investment in an economy that had stagnated for almost a decade – investment that could only come from the international community, which was sceptical of the ANC's socialist roots. GEAR was its plan.

It worked. For one thing, the timing was fortunate. The end of the Cold War, rapid globalisation and high rates of growth in the developed world created an appetite for investments in developing countries. And there is no doubt that South Africa's 'political miracle', with Mandela as its figurehead, helped convince the sceptics that the country was on the way up. Yet it was not Mandela who was largely responsible for GEAR's success. That honour would fall to the three TMs: Thabo Mbeki, as second president of the Republic, Trevor Manuel, as minister of finance, and Tito Mboweni, as governor of the Reserve Bank. Although GEAR was not an immediate success – and the 1998 Asian financial crisis, the 2001 depreciation of the rand and the 2002–3 'small bank crisis' did not help – the overall economic outlook improved markedly between 1994 and 2006. Between 2004 and 2007 economic growth averaged above 5% per annum. Inflation, a measure of price increases, was down. In the decade leading up to 1994 average inflation was 14%; over the next decade inflation averaged 6.4%. Debt as a percentage of GDP was down too, from 49.5% in 1996 to 26.5% in 2008. Government revenue increased faster than expenditure; after many years of budget deficits, in February 2007, Minister Manuel could announce a budget surplus.

Part of this period of success can, of course, be ascribed to higher global commodity prices. As the world's largest producer of platinum – six times bigger than Russia, the second largest – commodity prices still shape the fortunes of South Africa, just as gold shaped its fortunes in the twentieth century. But the economic growth achieved during this period was not exclusively due to commodities; innovation was key too. Just consider the following news article from *Wired* magazine, published in October 2008: 'On the 15th anniversary of Nelson Mandela receiving the Nobel Peace Prize, South Africa is gaining attention for another world-friendly achievement. This time, it's an electric car from Cape Town-based Optimal Energy that's grabbing headlines. The Joule has been the darling of the Paris Auto Show, and it's easy to see why.'[4] In the same year that Tesla, headed by Elon Musk, a South African immigrant to the United States, built its first car, an impractical and expensive all-electric roadster, it was the Joule's long-range, six-passenger capacity and quirky design that attracted all the attention.[5]

The economic growth achieved in the 2000s raised living standards too. Higher revenue meant that government spending on social grants could increase from 1.9 per cent of GDP in 2000 to

3.3 per cent in 2007. South Africa had – and still has – some of the best-targeted grant systems in the world. This simply means that the grants actually reach the poorest who need them. And the expanding economy and more stable macro-environment gave more people a safety net, what the development economist and Nobel Prize-winning economist Amartya Sen calls the freedom of 'economic protection'. The result was that poverty declined. Using a standard money metric, development economists Arden Finn, Murray Leibbrandt and Ingrid Woolard calculate that between 1993 and 2010 the poverty rate in South Africa fell from 37% to 28%.[6] If a multidimensional index is used that also accounts for things such as housing, electricity, water and sanitation, the numbers are even more impressive: from 37% to 8%. A better life for all, indeed.

All was not perfect, however. Although the decline in poverty was impressive, there were still not enough jobs for everyone. This was because South Africa's integration into the global economy necessitated changes in many firms. Gone was the 'protection' that apartheid isolation offered; South African firms suddenly had to compete against far more efficient foreign competitors. To improve their efficiency, the South African firms cut jobs. Economists at the time called the early 2000s a period of 'jobless growth'. More efficient firms meant higher labour productivity for those employees who remained behind – and higher wages – but it also meant a growing gap between those with and those without jobs. This led to increasing inequality.

Inequality was further exacerbated by a school system unable to produce good-quality graduates. Although the large funding gap between black and white schools had been eliminated soon after 1994, school outcomes were still very different. In 2007 education economist Servaas van der Berg summarised this trend: 'Despite massive resource shifts to black schools, overall matriculation results did not improve in the post-apartheid period. Thus, the school system contributes little to supporting the upward mobility of poor children in the labour market.'[7]

The first thirteen years of democracy, from 1994 to 2007, stand in stark contrast to the next thirteen. The global financial crisis of 2008, although it did not have the same disastrous impact on South Africa's financial sector as it did in other parts of the world, still hurt the economy badly. It led to a short recession and higher debt levels in the country. But rather than a global recession, it was local politics that would transform the South African economy from one that was imperfect but optimistic to one that was decidedly bleak; from one where South Africans could dream about improvement to one where they had to cope with immiseration.

In September 2008, with about nine months left of his second term as president, Thabo Mbeki was recalled by the National Executive Committee of the ANC. He resigned and was replaced by Kgalema Motlanthe as interim president, who in turn was succeeded by Jacob Zuma after the 2009 elections. The country soon found itself heading in a new direction. The first and most obvious change was the rapid increase in the size of government. Not only did the number of government employees increase in the first five years of Zuma's presidency, from around 2.2 million to 2.7 million, but their wages increased much more than inflation – in fact, some estimates show that they achieved a premium of 22 per cent over private-sector workers at the wage-negotiation table. The consequence was that the budget surpluses of the Manuel years quickly turned into large (and unsustainable) deficits. It also became increasingly clear that the action plans drawn up by government – notably the ambitious and admirable National Development Plan (NDP), which aimed to eliminate poverty and reduce inequality by 2030 – were paid little more than lip service.

One key component of the NDP was the strengthening of state-owned enterprises such as Eskom and Transnet. Exactly the opposite happened under Zuma's leadership. In what has become known as a process of state capture, political cronies affiliated with the ANC leadership were appointed to positions of power. A 2017 report – entitled 'Betrayal of the Promise' – explains the strategy:

> From about 2012 onwards the Zuma-centred power elite has sought to centralise the control of rents to eliminate lower-order, rent-seeking competitors. The ultimate prize was control of the National Treasury to gain control of the Financial Intelligence Centre (which monitors illicit flows of finance), the Chief Procurement Office (which regulates procurement and activates legal action against corrupt practices), the Public Investment Corporation (the second largest

shareholder on the Johannesburg Securities Exchange), the boards of key development finance institutions, and the guarantee system.[8]

The consequence was that many state-owned enterprises collapsed. The most significant of these was Eskom. Although the first power cuts occurred for a short time in late 2007 and early 2008, as a consequence of underinvestment they returned in 2014 and again, more frequently, in 2019. A country that does not have a reliable source of energy, the most important input in almost any production process, cannot grow. And that is exactly what happened. In Zuma's first term of office, per capita GDP growth averaged less than 1 per cent; in his second term, which lasted from 2014 to 2018 (when he, too, was recalled by the ANC), per capita GDP growth was negative. The implication was that the average South African became poorer. This was borne out by poverty statistics. In contrast to the sharp declines in poverty during the Mbeki era – an era, it should be stressed, that witnessed the rapid spread of HIV/ Aids, largely due to Mbeki's unwillingness to tackle the issue – the share of people below the poverty line increased substantially during Zuma's presidency. Figure 34.1 demonstrates this reversal quite clearly.

In 2018 Cyril Ramaphosa was elected as the fifth president of South Africa. His task was immense: to turn around the fortunes of a country scarred by a bitter past and a burgled decade. To see how far South Africa has fallen, compare the country's performance with its more famous BRICS partners – Brazil, Russia, India and China. Between 1994 and 2018 only Brazil, at 2.1% per annum, grew at a slower pace than South Africa, at 2.9%. Russia (4.4%), India (4.7%) and China (5.4%) experienced rapid catch-up growth. China's GDP per capita, as recently as 1990, was half of South Africa's; by 2016 China was richer on a per-capita basis. South Africa's poor economic performance, especially in the 2010s, raises questions about its inclusion in BRICS. Nigeria, as the largest economy and most populous country on the African continent, achieved 4.5% growth between 1994 and 2018. Perhaps BRINC is a more appropriate acronym.

What can be done to elevate South Africa's growth path to those of our peers? There is no doubt that, just as in 1996, South

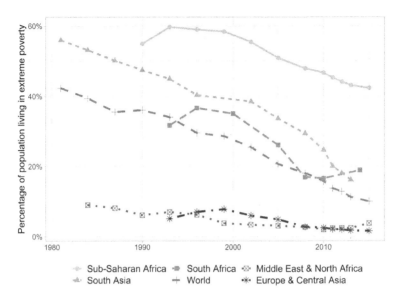

Figure 34.1 Share of population living in extreme poverty by region, 1980–2015

Africa needs to get the macroeconomic fundamentals right – a task made extra difficult by the impact of Covid-19. Investment in renewable energies would not only ease the burden on the fledgling electricity network, but also shift South Africa, a heavy polluter, towards carbon neutrality. But we also need creative solutions that improve economic freedom.[9] These can range from affordable family planning that empowers young mothers to make their own decisions, to early childhood-development programmes, to a voucher programme for schools that will encourage innovation in education, to making it easy for skilled migrants to establish businesses. Covid-19 has also accelerated the digital transformation of our lives. It should be top of the government's list of priorities to reduce the digital divide.

The first twenty-five years of the 'new South Africa' were what sports enthusiasts might call a game of two halves. During the first half economic freedoms were extended to those who had for centuries been denied access to them. To do this, the ANC government implemented sound economic policies that created economic growth. The benefits were growing prosperity and a better life for all. The second half, unfortunately, was less rosy. Extracting rents became the government's priority. The poorest, who depend most on a capable government, lost out, and their lives became a daily struggle for food, jobs and service delivery. Nelson Mandela's long walk to economic freedom went down a wrong path. Let's hope we can find our way back.

35 What Should No Scholar Ever Do?
Predicting the Future

Predicting the future is a perilous exercise. But that has not stopped us trying. Hunter-gatherers carefully studied their natural environment to predict food availability. The earliest farmers developed sophisticated ways to predict rain. In the eighth century BCE the oracle of Delphi attracted to her temple those who wanted to know the future. Others have searched for clues to future events in bones, marbles, cards and crystal balls. For a quick fix, just page to the horoscope section in your daily newspaper.

It makes sense to want to know the future. Knowledge is power. And power is money. Entrepreneurs must predict the future demands of their customers, the behaviour of their competitors, and the cost of their inputs. In more volatile environments, prediction is more difficult, which increases risk and requires higher reward. That is why it is so difficult to attract investment in unstable times. It is also why there's a lot of money in prediction – and why the tools we use have become increasingly sophisticated. Financial analysts and traders use elaborate econometric and Big Data techniques to forecast stock prices. A better forecast yields higher returns. Epidemiologists, as Covid-19 has shown, build mathematically complex models to predict the spread of diseases. Climatologists do the same to study weather patterns and climate change. Even governments need accurate predictions of the future: a sudden economic downturn could result in a surge in unemployment insurance applications and a collapse of tax revenue.

Despite all this effort to understand the future, we remain pretty bad at predicting it. That is because we are human. The future depends on millions of daily decisions made by billions of humans. But even if these things were predictable, our predictions are biased in ways we are unaware of. Between 1956 and 1962 the psychologist Kurt Danziger asked 436 South African students to imagine how the twentieth century might unfold. Two-thirds of black South African students imagined that apartheid would end; only 4 per cent of white Afrikaners did.[1] His point was clear: we are likelier to predict what we want to see happen. Our biases are programmed into our DNA.

The rigorous forecasting methods we use to circumvent these biases only take us so far. We may be able to predict fairly accurately the weather or the price of oil next week, but the complexity of the world we live in reduces our ability to forecast far into the future. Our models struggle to comprehend the compounding effect of innovation, for example. Globalisation amplifies this. The telephone took more than seventy years to reach 100 million users worldwide and the mobile phone fifteen. Instagram reached 100 million users within two-and-a-half years. Who knows how quickly the next app developed in Bangladesh, Bolivia or Botswana could spread next week?

Does this mean we should just give up trying to predict the future? Not if we use history as our guide. We study history, as we have done in this book, to help us understand the world we live in. To make sense of all the noise, we construct theories of human and social behaviour. Our theories, then, have predictive power. But it is useful to keep in mind that these are not precise forecasts like those of the weatherman or the financial analyst. Any theory or model is, at best, a simplified representation of the world, a map. We use these maps to navigate our way through the complexity. On the basis of these theories, we can delineate a map of the future. The map will be imprecise and frequently wrong, but when we are wrong we update our map – our theories – and we become more confident in our next prediction.

Let us, then, return to a theory we introduced early in this book. In Chapter 5 I explained that there are three ways to solve the economic problems of production and distribution: custom, command and the market. We can now apply these to our reality. The three solutions become the three domains of social life: command becomes the government, which typically relies on hierarchy and coercive forms of authority; the market becomes the private sector, which organises cooperation and the allocation of goods and services through competition; and custom becomes civil society, which can be defined as formal and informal institutions, organisations or cultures that affect our beliefs and behaviour. These may include anything from family units to global religious denominations, from book clubs to environmental-activist organisations, from amateur sports teams to academic societies.

All three of these domains are important for successful societies. In *The Narrow Corridor*, Daron Acemoglu and James Robinson argue that only a very few societies in history have managed to grow and become prosperous.[2] This is because most could not find a balance between the power of government and the power of citizens. In many societies throughout history, citizens had too much power, and thus a government that provides the public goods that a prosperous society requires could never be formed. In those places where governments could form, it often gained too much power, and would just extract rents from its citizens to benefit the powerful elite. What is necessary, then, is for societies to find the narrow corridor, a delicate power balance between government and citizens.

How we find the balance between government and citizens will be affected by technological change. When we think of economic systems we tend to think of a continuum, with socialism (where everything is owned by the state) at the one extreme and free-market capitalism (where everything is owned privately) at the other. But the triangle helps us to understand that ownership is not only a choice between free markets and government. When we want to think of the future, therefore, it might be more useful to consider the many ways that technology could change the way we think about ownership.

Ownership refers to the right to possess something. The concept of ownership has changed considerably throughout human history. For much of our history, as we discussed in Chapters 7, 11 and 14, people owned other people. It is only in the recent past that we have considered this an abhorrent practice, a crime against humanity. And although the practice still exists in many guises today, from sex trafficking and forced marriages to child labour, it is a hidden crime, very different from its public practice only two centuries ago.

Yet we may see ownership of people re-emerge in future, although we will hardly recognise it. Consider the world's top football players. An investor can now perfectly legally own 'all or part of the financial rights to a player'. Hedge funds now acquire the rights to young players, and cash in when the best ones are sold to top clubs. If it works in football, why not elsewhere? Could a brilliant young mathematician without the resources to study at university sell a part of her future income to an investor? Crowd-funding platforms already allow this possibility. It is not impossible to imagine that stock markets will develop where shares in people are sold. New technologies could take such human ownership to the extreme: what if governments were to abolish personal income taxes and simply 'own' a tenth of all newborn babies in their territories? Would politicians then not have an incentive to invest in the health and education of young people so that future government revenue would be higher? And what about parents? If parents could use the shares they own in their children as their pensions, would they not be more willing to invest in their children's development? There is little doubt that these possibilities will raise knotty ethical issues, issues that civil society would have to solve.

Such debates are not new. Philosophers have debated the ethics of land ownership from the time of the earliest agricultural societies. Beliefs about land rights varied – and continue to vary. In some parts of the world all land is privately owned. In others most land is communally owned, or owned by the state. In Chapter 6, for example, we discussed how most land in feudal Europe was the property of princes, vassals and the Church, with serfs, the actual farmers, having no ownership rights. I argued that this is not too different from the land rights of those living in South Africa's former homelands today.

What we do learn from history is that, although private property rights are not sufficient for economic development (and some would argue they are not even necessary), where private property rights have expanded, so too has productivity. When the return on our effort goes into our own pocket, our output is likely to increase. The opposite is, of course, equally true. In Chapter 22 we showed how collectivisation in the USSR caused catastrophic famines. And in Chapter 24 we discussed how the Great Leap Forward in

China abolished property rights in cattle, only for people to start culling theirs, thereby killing productivity.

That property rights can affect behaviour may also help us to respond to one of humanity's greatest challenges: climate change. We now know that the release of carbon dioxide causes the earth's climate to heat up, leading to both more frequent and larger natural disasters, ecosystem destruction and poorer health for people. In fact, we can even put a number on it: one additional ton of carbon dioxide today will lead to an increase of $36.6 in future global mortality risk, a figure much higher than we had previously thought.[3] But there is hope. When we tax the ownership of pollution, firms will produce less of it. A global carbon tax is essential if we are to preserve both our natural environment and our high levels of prosperity.

Taxes are one way to jolt productivity. Higher asset taxes may force us to use the assets we own more productively (or, if taxes are too high, get rid of them entirely). Our houses are empty while we are at the office. Our cars sit idly in parking garages. Governments own many things – land, buildings, patents – that are not used optimally. Technology can change that. Uber allows car owners to be matched to car users. Airbnb is the world's largest hotel chain without owning any hotels; it has created so much wealth for ordinary people, not because it owns properties, but because it uses technology to make existing assets more productive and profitable. Expect more of such asset utilisation apps that lift the returns on capital.

Technology will allow us not only to borrow the weed eater from our neighbour's house, but also to reach for the stars. We will soon settle on other planets. We will do so faster if we can make money from it. Elon Musk is already building a planetary transport system. Jeff Bezos envisages our moving all heavy industry to the moon and Mars. But there are many questions unanswered: Who would lay claim to these lands? Who will pay for the (mis)adventures of the pioneer settlers? Will governments, much as we discussed in Chapter 10, grant charters to private firms? Will it give rise to a new class of interplanetary haves and earthly have-nots? As Mark Twain said, history may not repeat itself, but it often rhymes.

Until we have discovered the riches of these foreign lands, the most valuable commodity at home is not land but data. Some

98 per cent of all Facebook revenue comes from targeted advertisements – targeted because of the data its users generate. Who owns this data? On its own, tracking my online behaviour is not of much value to anyone. But combine it across millions of users and, with quantum computing and artificial intelligence, it becomes extraordinarily valuable, not only to market but also to manipulate. Algorithms developed by Californian teenagers now determine our daily moods. And as the Bell Pottinger saga in South Africa or Facebook's Cambridge Analytica scandal have so vividly demonstrated, our data can be weaponised against us for devious ends.

The irony of data aggregated across millions of users is that ownership is often in the hands of a few. Market concentration within the tech industry, as we suggested in Chapter 31, is worrying. It means that large firms can collude with governments to create what Shoshana Zuboff has called 'surveillance capitalism'.[4] What is needed, indeed, is broader participation of civil society in counteracting these monopolising forces.

One obvious tool to spread ownership and broaden participation in the economy is to give citizens a monthly cash stipend, with no questions asked. The economic security a Basic Income Grant provides is certainly worth considering – and many developed countries have launched pilots to test its efficacy. But the evidence remains inconclusive. To make a difference the monthly stipend must be large, and developing countries often do not have the fiscal capacity to afford it. And it's not just about money: there is dignity in work. What will people do with their lives when robots are simply better at everything? Just giving cash stipends is a start, but we need smarter and more innovative solutions to expand economic freedoms.

One obvious thing to do is to expand ownership rights. A central theme of this book is that living standards have suffered when economic participation in the economy, including the ownership of assets, has been suspended or suppressed. Consider colonisation in Latin America or Africa (which expropriated land and labour from locals), or Idi Amin's post-independence Uganda (which expropriated the assets of European and Asian residents), or apartheid South Africa (which denied ownership rights to black South Africans). Imagine what would happen if instead of paying corporate taxes to government, companies 'paid' their taxes by giving shares to every citizen, just as many companies now give share options to their employees. For this reason, it is more important than ever that more of the tech giants list publicly. The profits of an unlisted firm only benefit the founders and a few shareholders, but anyone, from small-scale investors to pension funds, can own Apple or Alphabet, Tencent or Tesla. This changes corporate behaviour. Responsible investing integrates environmental, social and corporate governance (ESG) factors, such as climate change, diversity, human rights and animal welfare, into investment strategies. It is civil society that keeps the abuses of both government and the private sector in check.

Even if everyone can be empowered, some may still benefit more than others. While the last half-century's globalisation has undoubtedly made all of us more prosperous, it has done so more for the very rich and the very poor than for those in the middle. This creates resentment among the 'losers', a feeling that is often followed by the emergence of politicians who exploit the frustrations of ordinary people. Such populism usually leads to exaggerated nationalism, isolationism, inward-looking policies – policies that exclude rather than include. The sad truth is that those policies are back in vogue. If history is any guide, they are likely to impede our long walk to economic freedom.

Such economic frustrations have political repercussions. One is the idea of the nation-state. As the size and power of central governments increase, many citizens may feel unrepresented by a political elite in a distant capital city. Social media allow them to connect to like-minded people. Independence movements in many parts of the world indicate that national boundaries – often those forged through conquest or colonial rule – are being increasingly questioned. Residents want to see their taxes used in their own communities. They want control over decisions that affect them directly. Local government elections may soon become more important than national elections.

When people cannot make their voices heard at the ballot box, they will vote with their feet. Despite the high walls many countries are building – literally and figuratively – pressures to migrate from the developing to the developed countries will only grow. And it will be necessary: the rich world is growing older. Predictions suggest that the Japanese population will decline by 30 million people in the next half-century.

The cultural clashes associated with migration will, however, further feed the frustrations of those feeling disempowered. The demand for higher walls will rise. This populist trap, much like climate change and pandemic responses, cannot be addressed at the local level. Because these problems affect all of humanity, they require global solutions. This is where civil society will have to intervene. Governments currently have little incentive to introduce expensive remedial measures when the benefits will only materialise after the next election cycle.

One way to do that is through the media, a sector which has changed substantially over the last two decades. We now consume most of our news online, often on social media where fake news is peddled alongside credible reporting. Distinguishing between 'deep fake' videos and reality will become increasingly difficult. Algorithms will amplify echo chambers. Malicious attacks to divide us will become more frequent. Media watchdogs will have to find a delicate balance between freedom of speech and protection against predators. The only cure against bullying – bullying that can come from both corporates and governments – is broad-based economic participation.

Economic participation will also aid the pursuit of scientific knowledge. Science spans the entire triad of business, government and civil society. Firms invest in research and development; governments fund research at public universities and research institutes; and civil society, most crucially, not only provides the infrastructure that nurtures scientists and disseminates their findings, but fosters the values and beliefs that underpin science. These values and beliefs are important, because too much government involvement or too much private-sector power can lead to perverse outcomes.

As history shows again and again, the countries most successful in escaping the bonds of poverty and entropy are the ones where government, the private sector and civil society collectively endorse the pursuit of useful science. These societies cultivated – as the Enlightenment philosophers discovered and as Joel Mokyr has so eloquently phrased it – the belief that our understanding of nature can and should be used to advance the material conditions of humanity. We are rich because we have learned how to use nature to provide for our needs.

But it is not just about efficiency. We have discovered that governments are there to serve not just the rich and powerful, but society at large. Yes, scientific knowledge has made us prosperous beyond the wildest imaginings of our ancestors, but it was not only science: many of us live longer, better and more meaningful lives because economic freedoms have been expanded beyond just a tiny elite.

The beliefs that knowledge should be used to make us more prosperous and that governments should serve the needs of the poorest have made the world a better place. True, not everyone shares in the benefits of our scientific accomplishments equally. There is still much work to do, especially for those of us who live on the continent I call home. But the lesson from history is clear. As long as we continue to empower ordinary people to contribute to and benefit from the remarkable advances in scientific knowledge, the future, for Africa and beyond, will be bright.

Epilogue
How Do You Win a World Cup?

One of my favourite memories is taking a road trip with friends to watch four games of the FIFA World Cup in 2010. We started in Cape Town, drove to Johannesburg to watch David Villas score two goals for Spain against Honduras, and on the way back stopped in Bloemfontein to watch South Africa's Bafana Bafana beat a hapless France. The World Cup was a moment that brought South Africans together as only sport can do. Indeed, as Nelson Mandela said, sport 'has the power to unite people in a way that little else does'. I experienced it very vividly that day in the City of Roses.

Throughout the road trip, though, I was thinking of a question that a visiting geography professor – whose name I, sadly, forget – had asked at a University of Cape Town seminar only a few months earlier: How do you win a World Cup? Do you, he suggested, appoint a very expensive coach? This is, of course, exactly what South Africa had done in preparation for the big event. The Brazilian Carlos Alberto Parreira was appointed in 2006 at R3 million per month – or almost $500,000 at the time. South Africa, although only losing one game at the tournament, could not reach the round of sixteen. While the event was a massive success, the performance of Bafana Bafana was somewhat disappointing.

Or do you, the visiting scholar continued, give every child in South Africa a soccer ball? That will not make much of a difference a year or two before a global tournament. It will also do little for South Africa's chances at the 2014 or 2018 event, he explained. But by 2022 an entire new generation would have grown up playing football. Some of them would have excelled. They would have been recruited to play for South Africa's premier soccer clubs, a few even for prestigious European clubs such as Arsenal, Barcelona or Chelsea. The Bafana Bafana team at the FIFA World Cup in Qatar would have been filled with young stars. By 2026 South Africa would have had a World Cup-winning team.

The same can be applied to building a prosperous society. If history has taught us anything, it is that wealth is created by empowering ordinary people with the freedoms to help them build better lives. Technology can assist. Instead of building a big-budget coal-fired power station, we should give everyone a solar panel. Instead of funding a state broadcaster, we should provide free and fast internet access. Instead of designing another top-down economic strategy, we should get children into good schools so they can design their own. Want to win the economic World Cup? Empower every child with an economic soccer ball.

Where does one start? Quality health care and education – the building blocks of human capital – are an obvious first step on the journey towards economic freedom. Give women the freedom to make the family-planning decisions that are best for them. Give parents the freedom to choose which nurseries and schools to send their children to. Involve the private sector, but do not leave the task exclusively to it. The jobs of tomorrow cannot depend on children educated with yesterday's tools.

Science and technology will play a pivotal role. We have become remarkably rich by standing on the shoulders of giants. We learn by trying things, testing our hypotheses against the evidence, and discarding what is wrong. In science and in life, pursue active incrementalism. Create safety nets and incentives that encourage even the poorest to invest, learn from failure and try again. Building a prosperous society is hard, but it is entirely achievable.

The Fourth Industrial Revolution will make us even more productive than we can possibly imagine, allowing us to live longer, happier and more meaningful lives. But it will also exclude. Freedoms will become easier to give but also easier to take away. Nurture democracy. Make sure everyone counts. Be sceptical of those who promise too much or success that comes too easily. Big business can be just as evil as big government; both will want to control what we see and hear – and shape our behaviour accordingly.

Never forget that we do not have to play a game of *Monopoly*. Wealth begets wealth. The world is not a zero-sum game. We grow more prosperous, counterintuitively, the more we rely on others. Nelson Mandela recognised this: 'For to be free is not merely to cast off one's chains, but to live in a way that respects and enhances the freedom of others.' Again, this is not easy. It requires trust, cooperation, even faith. The good news is that the more we interact and exchange – the more we break down barriers – the easier it gets.

And that is why the future belongs to the optimists. At the end of his *magnum opus, The Wealth and Poverty of Nations*, the economic historian David Landes concludes: 'In this world, the optimists have it, not because they are always right, but because they are positive. Even when wrong, they are positive, and that is the way of achievement, correction, improvement, and success. Educated, eyes-open optimism pays; pessimism can only offer the empty consolation of being right.'[1]

Madiba would have agreed: 'Part of being optimistic is keeping one's head pointed toward the sun, one's feet moving forward.' The future belongs to those who believe in a better tomorrow.

Notes

How Do We Thrive? An Introduction

1 C. J. Norris, The negativity bias, revisited: Evidence from neuroscience measures and an individual differences approach, *Social Neuroscience*, 16 (1), 2021, 68–82.
2 D. N. McCloskey, The great enrichment: A humanistic and social scientific account, *Social Science History*, 40 (4), 2016, 583–98.
3 As we do not have a definitive GDP per capita estimate for the entire world, I assume a comparatively high level in 1800 of $800 per capita (2011 US dollars).
4 I say 'generally' for a reason. In the 1970s Richard Easterlin pointed out that while happiness tends to be positively correlated with income within and among countries at a specific point in time, this is not true across time. This has become known as the Easterlin paradox.

1 Who Are the Architects of Wakanda? African Economic Historians and the Stories We Tell

1 The next two paragraphs are loosely based on Anton Howes's introductory lecture at King's College London. See https://medium.com/@antonhowes/why-study-economic-history-ef747767be25. Howes writes a fascinating economic history newsletter, which you can subscribe to on his website: antonhowes.com.
2 A. G. Hopkins, Fifty years of African economic history, *Economic History of Developing Regions*, 34 (1), 2019, 1–15.
3 W. Rodney, *How Europe Underdeveloped Africa* (Dar es Salaam: Tanzania Publishing House, 1972).
4 Hopkins, Fifty years, 6.
5 Ibid., 8.
6 Ibid.

7 J. Fourie, The data revolution in African economic history, *Journal of Interdisciplinary History*, 47 (2), 2016, 193–212.

8 J. Fourie and N. Obikili, Decolonizing with data: The cliometric turn in African economic history, in *Handbook of Cliometrics*, edited by C. Diebolt and M. Haupert (Heidelberg: Springer Reference, 2019), 1–25.

9 J. Fourie, Who writes African economic history? *Economic History of Developing Regions*, 34 (2), 2019, 111–31.

10 This does not mean, of course, that poverty is history; $1.90 is still a very low level of income. To get a fuller extent of the income distribution, consider that half of all humans (in 2017) lived on less than $6.70 per day; 85% of the global population earn less than $30 per day. I would venture to guess that most readers of this book are in the top 4% of global income earners, earning more than $70 per day.

11 I am, of course, not the first to do so. See also Johan Norberg's *Progress* (London: Oneworld, 2016); Steven Pinker's *Enlightenment Now* (New York: Viking, 2018); and Hans Rosling's *Factfulness* (New York: Flatiron Books, 2018).

12 M. Wilson, Meet the designer who created *Black Panther*'s Wakanda (2018), www.fastcompany.com/90161418/meet-the-designer-who-created-black-panthers-wakanda.

2 What Happened at Blombos in 70,000 BCE? The Out-of-Africa Hypothesis and the Peopling of the World

1 R. M. Wragg Sykes, *Kindred: Neanderthal Life, Love, Death and Art* (London: Bloomsbury, 2020).

2 Q. Ashraf and O. Galor, The 'Out of Africa' hypothesis, human genetic diversity, and comparative economic development, *American Economic Review*, 103 (1), 2013, 1–46.

3 J. D. A. Guedes, T. C. Bestor, D. Carrasco, R. Flad, E. Fosse, M. Herzfeld, C. C. Lamberg-Karlovsky, C. M. Lewis, M. Liebmann, R. Meadow and N. Patterson, Is poverty in our genes? A critique of Ashraf and Galor, 'The "Out of Africa" hypothesis, human genetic diversity, and comparative economic development', American Economic Review (forthcoming), *Current Anthropology*, 54 (1), 2013, 71–9.

4 Ibid., 71.

5 C. S. Henshilwood, F. d'Errico, K. L. van Niekerk, L. Dayet, A. Queffelec and L. Pollarolo, An abstract drawing from the 73,000-year-old levels at Blombos Cave, South Africa, *Nature*, 562 (7725), 2018, 115–18, at 115.

3 Why Are the Danes So Individualistic? The Neolithic Revolution and the Rise of Civilisations

1 Y. N. Harari, *Sapiens: A Brief History of Humankind* (London: Random House, 2014), 91.

2 J. C. Scott, *Against the Grain: A Deep History of the Earliest States* (New Haven: Yale University Press, 2017).

3 O. Olsson and C. Paik, Long-run cultural divergence: Evidence from the Neolithic Revolution, *Journal of Development Economics*, 122, 2016, 197–213.

4 O. Olsson and C. Paik, A western reversal since the Neolithic? The long-run impact of early agriculture, *Journal of Economic History*, 80 (1), 2020, 100–35.

4 Why Does isiXhosa Have Clicks? The Bantu Migration

1 This description is largely based on J. Diamond, *Guns, Germs and Steel* (New York: Vintage, 1997), ch. 19: How Africa became black, 367–401.

2 A 2021 paper by economist Arthur Blouin finds empirical support for Diamond's hypothesis. Blouin reports that those Africans 'whose ancestors could consistently keep livestock and produce traditional dry-crops throughout their multigenerational migration journey are more likely to engage in these activities today'. See A. Blouin, Axis-orientation and knowledge transmission: Evidence from the Bantu expansion, *Journal of Economic Growth*, 26, 2021, 359–84, at 359.

3 For those wondering, ostriches can only be tamed (or partially domesticated), and this was done on a large scale about 150 years ago in South Africa. Ostriches that are farmed are still very close to their wild ancestors, as any ostrich farmer would attest to.

4 Diamond, *Guns, Germs and Steel*, 401.

5 How Did Joseph and His Eleven Brothers Solve the Three Economic Problems? Custom and Command in the Ancient World

1 This example is borrowed from Robert Heilbroner's bestselling classic (still highly recommended) *The Worldly Philosophers: The Lives, Times, and Ideas of the Great Economic Thinkers* (New York: Simon & Schuster/Touchstone, 1999 [1953]).

2   S. G. Marks, *The Information Nexus: Global Capitalism from the Renaissance to the Present* (Cambridge: Cambridge University Press, 2016).

6 What Do Charlemagne and King Zwelithini Have in Common? Feudalism

1   The Carolingian empire, as it would later become known, would only last until 888, when it split owing to internal rivalries and external threats.
2   W. H. McNeill, *Plagues and Peoples* (Garden City, NJ: Anchor Press, 1976).
3   The first 600 years, up to 1000 CE, are sometimes called the Dark Ages.
4   M. Bloch, *Feudal Society*, trans. L. A. Manyon, 2 vols. (Chicago: University of Chicago Press, 1961).
5   Even in 1840, 70 per cent of all employees in the USA worked in agriculture.
6   A haberdasher is a seller of small articles for sewing, dressmaking and knitting, such as buttons or ribbons.
7   S. Ogilvie, The economics of guilds, *Journal of Economic Perspectives*, 28 (4), 2014, 169–92.

7 Why Do Indians Have Dowry and Africans Lobola? Pre-Colonial African Economic Systems

1   Numbers calculated from United Nations Population Division.
2   G. Austin, Resources, techniques, and strategies south of the Sahara: Revising the factor endowments perspective on African economic development, 1500–2000, *Economic History Review*, 61 (3), 2008, 587–624.
3   The next section relies heavily on Erik Green's *Production Systems in Pre-Colonial Africa*, ch. 3: The history of African development (online textbook), www.aehnetwork.org/textbook/production-systems-in-pre-colonial-africa/.
4   M. Alsan, The effect of the tsetse fly on African development, *American Economic Review*, 105 (1), 2015, 382–410.
5   J. Cherniwchan and J. Moreno-Cruz, Maize and precolonial Africa, *Journal of Development Economics*, 136, 2019, 137–50.
6   Green, *Production Systems in Pre-Colonial Africa*, 12.

8 Who Was the Richest Man Ever to Live? The Spread of Islam in Africa and the Crusades

1   M. Hamidullah, Muslim discovery of America before Columbus, *Journal of the Muslim Students' Association of the United States and Canada*, 4 (2), 1968, 7–9.

2 M. Saleh, On the road to heaven: Taxation, conversions, and the Coptic–Muslim socioeconomic gap in medieval Egypt, *Journal of Economic History*, 78 (2), 2018, 394–434.

3 Paul Lovejoy makes a similar point for nineteenth-century long-distance kola trade between the Asante and the Sokoto caliphate. See P. E. Lovejoy, Long-distance trade and Islam: The case of the nineteenth-century Hausa kola trade, *Journal of the Historical Society of Nigeria*, 5 (4), 1971, 537–47.

4 L. Blaydes and C. Paik, The impact of Holy Land Crusades on state formation: War mobilization, trade integration, and political development in medieval Europe, *International Organization*, 70 (3), 2016, 551–86.

5 Ibid., 552.

9 How Did 168 Spanish Conquistadores Capture an Empire? Europeans in the New World

1 These figures are calculated using the Maddison Project GDP estimates. The World Bank's World Development Indicators also suggest a sizeable gap – the average American earns twenty-two times as much as the average Haitian – although it is not quite as large as the Maddison Project calculation suggests.

2 We will learn more about the Atlantic slave trade in Chapter 11.

3 S. L. Engerman and K. L. Sokoloff, *Economic Development in the Americas since 1500: Endowments and Institutions* (Cambridge: Cambridge University Press, 2012).

4 K. L. Sokoloff and S. L. Engerman, Institutions, factor endowments, and paths of development in the New World, *Journal of Economic perspectives*, 14 (3), 2000, 217–32, at 230.

10 Why Was a Giraffe the Perfect Gift for the Chinese Emperor? The Indian Ocean Trade and European Imperialism

1 E. Pollard and O. C. Kinyera, The Swahili coast and the Indian Ocean trade patterns in the 7th–10th centuries CE, *Journal of Southern African Studies*, 43 (5), 2017, 927–47.

2 J. de Vries, The limits of globalization in the early modern world, *Economic History Review*, 63 (3), 2010, 710–33, at 726.

3 S. Hejeebu, The colonial transition and the decline of the East India Company, c.1746–1784, in *A New Economic History of Colonial India*,

edited by L. Chaudhary, B. Gupta, T. Roy and A. V. Swamy (London: Routledge, 2015), 33–51.

4 De Vries, The limits of globalization in the early modern world, 731.

11 Who Visited Gorée Island on 27 June 2013? The Atlantic Slave Trade and Africa's Long-Run Development

1 Available at obamawhitehouse.archives.gov.

2 P. Manning, *Slavery and African Life: Occidental, Oriental, and African Slave Trades* (Cambridge: Cambridge University Press, 1990).

3 It helped that Africans were also more resistant than Europeans to many of the tropical diseases, notably malaria.

4 W. C. Whatley, The gun–slave hypothesis and the 18th century British slave trade, *Explorations in Economic History*, 67, 2018, 80–104.

5 M. H. Wanamaker, 150 years of economic progress for African American men: Measuring outcomes and sizing up roadblocks, *Economic History of Developing Regions*, 32 (3), 2017, 211–20.

6 S. Beckett, *Empire of Cotton: A Global History* (London: Vintage, 2015).

7 A. L. Olmstead and P. W. Rhode, Cotton, slavery, and the new history of capitalism, *Explorations in Economic History*, 67, 2018, 1–17.

8 Ibid., 5.

9 A. L. Olmstead and P. W. Rhode, Biological innovation and productivity growth in the antebellum cotton economy, *Journal of Economic History*, 68 (4), 2008, 1123–71.

10 G. Wright, Slavery and Anglo-American capitalism revisited, *Economic History Review*, 73 (2), 2020, 353–83.

11 E. E. Baptist, *The Half Has Never Been Told: Slavery and the Making of American Capitalism* (London: Hachette, 2016).

12 A. Smith, *An Inquiry into the Nature and Causes of the Wealth of Nations*, edited by E. Cannan (London: Methuen & Co., 1904), IV.7, 46.

13 N. Palma, A. Papadia, T. Pereira and L. Weller, Slavery and development in nineteenth century Brazil, *Capitalism: A Journal of History and Economics*, 2 (2), 2021, 372–426.

14 P. Manning, African population: Projections, 1850–1960, in *The Demographics of Empire: The Colonial Order and the Creation of Knowledge*, edited by K. Ittmann, D. D. Cordell and G. H. Maddox (Athens: Ohio University Press, 2010), 245–75. See also E. Frankema and M. Jerven, Writing history backwards or sideways: Towards

a consensus on African population, 1850–2010, *Economic History Review*, 67 (4), 2014, 907–31, for a discussion of historical population estimates.

15 N. Nunn, The long-term effects of Africa's slave trades, *Quarterly Journal of Economics*, 123 (1), 2008, 139–76.

16 How did he do this? He made use of an instrumental variable approach in his statistical regression analysis. In short, he used the distance from Africa to the Americas as a proxy for the number of slaves exported. He first showed that there is a high correlation between the distance and the number of slaves shipped. That makes sense: the European traders would have wanted to reduce transport costs (it was, after all, a profit-making enterprise) and so would have chosen the shortest route to the Americas. That establishes the first condition of a good instrument. Second, there is no reason why the distance between Africa and the Americas should have any effect on living standards in Africa today. Yet this is exactly what Nunn found in his regression analysis. The result suggests that slavery from the fifteenth to the nineteenth centuries causally explains lower levels of development today.

17 N. Nunn and D. Puga, Ruggedness: The blessing of bad geography in Africa, *Review of Economics and Statistics*, 94 (1), 2012, 20–36.

18 N. Nunn and L. Wantchekon, The slave trade and the origins of mistrust in Africa, *American Economic Review*, 101 (7), 2011, 3221–52.

19 N. Obikili, The trans-Atlantic slave trade and local political fragmentation in Africa, *Economic History Review*, 69 (4), 2016, 1157–77; L. Pierce and J. A. Snyder, The historical slave trade and firm access to finance in Africa, *Review of Financial Studies*, 31 (1), 2018, 142–74; R. Levine, C. Lin and W. Xie, The African slave trade and modern household finance, *Economic Journal*, 130 (630), 2020, 1817–41.

20 G. Austin, The 'reversal of fortune' thesis and the compression of history: Perspectives from African and comparative economic history, *Journal of International Development*, 20 (8), 2008, 996–1027.

21 This test is performed in a working paper by Marlous van Waijenburg and Ewout Frankema. The test is not included in the published version of the paper. See M. van Waijenburg and E. Frankema, Structural impediments to African growth? New evidence from real wages in British Africa, 1880–1965 (CGEH Working Paper no. 24, 2011).

22 Available at obamawhitehouse.archives.gov.

12 What Is an Incunabulum? Book Printing and the Reformation

1 Available at www.luther.de/en/95thesen.html.

2 Here I rely on S. O. Becker, S. Pfaff and J. Rubin, Causes and consequences of the Protestant Reformation, *Explorations in Economic History*, 62, 2016, 1–25.

3 J. Baten and J. L. van Zanden, Book production and the onset of modern economic growth, *Journal of Economic Growth*, 13 (3), 2008, 217–35.

4 J. Rubin, *Rulers, Religion, and Riches: Why the West Got Rich and the Middle East Did Not* (Cambridge: Cambridge University Press, 2017), 129.

5 J. Rubin, Printing and Protestants: An empirical test of the role of printing in the Reformation, *Review of Economics and Statistics*, 96 (2), 2014, 270–86.

6 F. Valencia Caicedo, The mission: Human capital transmission, economic persistence, and culture in South America, *Quarterly Journal of Economics*, 134 (1), 2019, 507–56.

7 F. A. Gallego and R. Woodberry, Christian missionaries and education in former African colonies: How competition mattered, *Journal of African Economies*, 19 (3), 2010, 294–329.

8 J. Cagé and V. Rueda, Sex and the mission: The conflicting effects of early Christian missions on HIV in sub-Saharan Africa, *Journal of Demographic Economics*, 86 (3), 2020, 213–57; D. Okoye, Things fall apart? Missions, institutions, and interpersonal trust, *Journal of Development Economics*, 148, 2021, 102568.

9 R. Jedwab, F. Meier zu Selhausen and A. Moradi, Christianization without economic development: Evidence from missions in Ghana, *Journal of Economic Behavior and Organization*, 190, 2021, 573–96.

10 R. Jedwab, F. Meier zu Selhausen and A. Moradi, The economics of missionary expansion: Evidence from Africa and implications for development, *Journal of Economic Growth* (forthcoming, 2022).

13 Who Was Autshumao's Niece? The Arrival of Europeans in South Africa and the Demise of the Khoesan

1 I am a descendant of Louis Fourie's twentieth child, ten generations ago.

2 M. H. de Kock, *Selected Subjects in the Economic History of South Africa* (Cape Town: Juta & Co., 1924), 24, 40.

3 P. van Duin and R. Ross, *The Economy of the Cape Colony in the 18th Century* (Leiden: Centre for the Study of European Expansion, 1987), 1.

4 J. Fourie, An inquiry into the nature, causes and distribution of wealth in the Cape Colony, 1652–1795 (PhD thesis, Utrecht University, 2012).

5 J. Fourie, The remarkable wealth of the Dutch Cape Colony: Measurements from eighteenth-century probate inventories, *Economic History Review*, 66 (2), 2013, 419–48.

6 J. Fourie and F. Garmon, The settlers' fortunes: Comparing tax censuses in the Cape Colony and early American Republic (mimeo, 2022).

7 After the death of Maddison in 2010, the Maddison Project hosted by the University of Groningen continues to be updated and improved. Visit www.rug.nl/ggdc/historicaldevelopment/maddison/.

8 S. Broadberry, H. Guan and D. Li, China, Europe, and the Great Divergence: A restatement, *Journal of Economic History*, 81 (3), 2021, 958–74.

9 J. Fourie and J. L. van Zanden, GDP in the Dutch Cape Colony: The national accounts of a slave-based society, *South African Journal of Economics*, 81 (4), 2013, 467–90.

10 W. H. Boshoff and J. Fourie, The significance of the Cape trade route to economic activity in the Cape Colony: A medium-term business cycle analysis, *European Review of Economic History*, 14 (3), 2010, 469–503.

11 J. Fourie and D. von Fintel, Settler skills and colonial development: The Huguenot wine-makers in eighteenth-century Dutch South Africa, *Economic History Review*, 67 (4), 2014, 932–63.

12 J. Fourie, The quantitative Cape: A review of the new historiography of the Dutch Cape Colony, *South African Historical Journal*, 66 (1), 2014, 142–68.

13 J. Fourie and E. Green, The missing people: Accounting for the productivity of indigenous populations in Cape colonial history, *Journal of African History*, 56 (2), 2015, 195–215.

14 And given that my great-grandfather married a Zaaiman, I, too, am a descendant of Krotoa.

14 What Did Thomson, Watson & Co. Purchase? The Emancipation of the Enslaved

1 This section relies on research by Delia Robertson's First Fifty Years project, www.e-family.co.za/ffy/g8/p8919.htm.

2 A century later Constantia sweet wine would be sought after across the world, most famously by Napoleon after he was exiled on the Atlantic island of St Helena.

3 R. C. H. Shell, *Children of Bondage: A Social History of the Slave Society at the Cape of Good Hope, 1652–1838* (Hanover, NH, and London: Wesleyan University Press, 1994), 40.

4 E. Green, *Creating the Cape Colony: The Political Economy of Settler Colonisation* (London: Bloomsbury, 2022).

5 E. Green, The economics of slavery in the eighteenth-century Cape Colony: Revising the Nieboer–Domar hypothesis, *International Review of Social History*, 59 (1), 2014, 39–70.

6 The careful reader would observe another reason for their opposition to greater numbers of European immigrants at the Cape: in Chapter 9 we discussed the implications of the Engerman–Sokoloff hypothesis. In a highly unequal society the elite would want to protect their privileges, and one way of doing so is to limit immigration.

7 K. Ekama, Bondsmen: Slave collateral in the 19th-century Cape Colony, *Journal of Southern African Studies*, 47 (3), 2021, 437–53.

8 R. Hornbeck and T. Logan, The great American productivity gain: Emancipation and aggregate productivity growth (working paper, 2022).

9 Compensation of the slave owners rather than the enslaved was the general rule during all emancipations. There are few exceptions. In Jaffna, Sri Lanka, mothers received a small amount for each child manumitted. See N. Wickramasinghe, *Slave in a Palanquin: Colonial Servitude and Resistance in Sri Lanka* (New York: Columbia University Press, 2020).

10 R. Ross and L.-C. Martin, Accommodation and resistance: The housing of Cape Town's enslaved and freed population before and after emancipation, *Journal of Southern African Studies*, 47 (3), 2021, 417–35.

15 What Do an Indonesian Volcano, Frankenstein and Shaka Zulu Have in Common? The Mfecane and the Great Trek

1 G. D. A. Wood, *Tambora: The Eruption that Changed the World* (Princeton: Princeton University Press, 2014).

2 M. Garstang, A. D. Coleman and M. Therrell, Climate and the Mfecane, *South African Journal of Science*, 110 (5–6), 2014, 1–6.

3 D. von Fintel and J. Fourie, The great divergence in South Africa: Population and wealth dynamics over two centuries, *Journal of Comparative Economics*, 47 (4), 2019, 759–73.

16 Why Was the Spinning Jenny Not Invented in India? Science, Technology and the Industrial Revolution

1 J. Mokyr, *A Culture of Growth: The Origins of the Modern Economy* (Princeton: Princeton University Press, 2016), 19.

2 T. R. Malthus, *An Essay on the Principle of Population As It Affects the Future Improvement of Society, with Remarks on the Speculations of Mr. Goodwin, M. Condorcet and Other Writers* (London: J. Johnson in St Paul's Church-yard, 1798).

3 Ibid., 13.

4 R. C. Allen, The Industrial Revolution in miniature: The spinning jenny in Britain, France, and India, *Journal of Economic History*, 69 (4), 2009, 901–27.

5 Mokyr, *A Culture of Growth*.

6 N. Nunn, Culture and the historical process, *Economic History of Developing Regions*, 27 (sup-1), 2012, 108–26.

7 D. N. McCloskey, *Bourgeois Dignity: Why Economics Can't Explain the Modern World* (Chicago: University of Chicago Press, 2010).

8 Mokyr, *A Culture of Growth*, 339.

17 Why Did Railways Hurt Basotho Farmers? South Africa's Mineral Revolution

1 R. Germond, *Chronicles of Basutoland: A Running Commentary on the Events of the Years 1830–1902* (Morija: Morija Sesuto Book Depot, 1967), 46.

2 A. Herranz-Loncán and J. Fourie, 'For the public benefit'? Railways in the British Cape Colony, *European Review of Economic History*, 22 (1), 2018, 73–100, at 96.

3 D. Donaldson, Railroads of the Raj: Estimating the impact of transportation infrastructure, *American Economic Review*, 108 (4–5), 2018, 899–934.

4 A. Herranz-Loncán, The role of railways in export-led growth: The case of Uruguay, 1870–1913, *Economic History of Developing Regions*, 26 (2), 2011, 1–32; J. P. Tang, Railroad expansion and

industrialization: Evidence from Meiji Japan, *Journal of Economic History*, 74 (3), 2014, 863–86; R. Jedwab and A. Moradi, The permanent effects of transportation revolutions in poor countries: Evidence from Africa, *Review of Economics and Statistics*, 98 (2), 2016, 268–84; L. Maravall, The impact of a 'colonizing river': Colonial railways and the indigenous population in French Algeria at the turn of the century, *Economic History of Developing Regions*, 34 (1), 2019, 16–47; T. Berger, Railroads and rural industrialization: Evidence from a historical policy experiment, *Explorations in Economic History*, 74, 2019, 101277; C. Paik and J. Vechbanyongratana, Reform, rails and rice: Thailand's political railroads and economic development in the 20th century (working paper, 2021).

5   A. Gwaindepi and J. Fourie, Public sector growth in the British Cape Colony: Evidence from new data on expenditure and foreign debt, 1830–1910, *South African Journal of Economics*, 88 (3), 2020, 341–67.

6   Cape Hansard, Budget debate, 1902, in Cape of Good Hope, *Debates in the House of Assembly* (Cape Town: May Murray & Leger Printers, 1902), 158.

18 What Did Sol Plaatje Find on His Journey through South Africa? Property Rights and Labour Coercion

1   S. Plaatje, *Native Life in South Africa* (Johannesburg: Picador Africa, 2007), 21.

2   W. Beinart and P. Delius, The historical context and legacy of the Natives Land Act of 1913, *Journal of Southern African Studies*, 40 (4), 2014, 667–88.

3   F. Nyika and J. Fourie, Black disenfranchisement in the Cape Colony, c.1887–1909: Challenging the numbers, *Journal of Southern African Studies*, 46 (3), 2020, 455–69.

4   Plaatje, *Native Life in South Africa*, 24.

5   M. Dell, The persistent effects of Peru's mining mita, *Econometrica*, 78 (6), 2010, 1863–1903.

6   Plaatje, *Native Life in South Africa*, 70.

7   B. Mpeta, J. Fourie and K. Inwood, Black living standards in South Africa before democracy: New evidence from height, *South African Journal of Science*, 114 (1–2), 2018, 1–8.

19 Why Can You Have Any Car as Long as It Is Black? The Rise of American Industry

1 N. Rosenberg and M. Trajtenberg, A general-purpose technology at work: The Corliss steam engine in the late-nineteenth-century United States, *Journal of Economic History*, 64 (1), 2004, 61–99.

2 D. Donaldson and R. Hornbeck, Railroads and American economic growth: A 'market access' approach, *Quarterly Journal of Economics*, 131 (2), 2016, 799–858.

3 Ibid., 854.

4 M. A. Carlson, S. Correia and S. Luck, The effects of banking competition on growth and financial stability: Evidence from the national banking era (working paper SSRN 3202489, 2019).

5 M. Alsan and C. Goldin, Watersheds in child mortality: The role of effective water and sewerage infrastructure, 1880–1920, *Journal of Political Economy*, 127 (2), 2019, 586–638.

6 This per capita income is roughly the same as Bosnia and Herzegovina, Ecuador or Uzbekistan today.

20 What Does a Butterfly Collector Do in the Congo? The Berlin Conference and the Colonisation of Africa

1 E. Frankema, J. Williamson and P. Woltjer, An economic rationale for the West African scramble? The commercial transition and the commodity price boom of 1835–1885, *Journal of Economic History*, 78 (1), 2018, 231–67.

2 S. Michalopoulos and E. Papaioannou, The long-run effects of the Scramble for Africa, *American Economic Review*, 106 (7), 2016, 1802–48.

3 Ibid., 1804.

4 Ibid., 1844.

5 L. Heldring and J. Robinson, Colonialism and economic development in Africa, in *The Oxford Handbook of the Politics of Development*, edited by C. Lancaster and N. van de Walle (Oxford: Oxford University Press, 2018), 295–327.

6 Heldring and Robinson, Colonialism and economic development in Africa, 300.

7 P. Y. Aboagye and J. Bolt, Long-term trends in income inequality: Winners and losers of economic change in Ghana, 1891–1960, *Explorations in Economic History*, 2021, 101405.

8 E. Huillery, The black man's burden: The cost of colonization of French West Africa, *Journal of Economic History*, 74 (1), 2014, 1–38.

9 M. van Waijenburg, Financing the African colonial state: The revenue imperative and forced labor, *Journal of Economic History*, 78 (1), 2018, 40–80.

10 J. Baten and L. Maravall, The influence of colonialism on Africa's welfare: An anthropometric study, *Journal of Comparative Economics*, 2021 (in press).

11 S. Lowes and E. Montero, Concessions, violence, and indirect rule: Evidence from the Congo Free State, *Quarterly Journal of Economics*, 136 (4), 2021, 2047–91.

12 A. Hochschild, *King Leopold's Ghost: A Story of Greed, Terror, and Heroism in Colonial Africa* (London: Folio Society, 2017 [1998]).

13 Ibid., 272.

21 Who Wrote the Best Closing Line of Modern Literature? The Great Depression and the New Deal

1 Fitzgerald ends *The Great Gatsby* with one of the most popular (and poignant) lines of modern literature: 'So we beat on, boats against the current, borne back ceaselessly into the past' (F. S. Fitzgerald, *The Great Gatsby* (London: Penguin, 1974 [1926]), 188). Even our best attempts fail to divorce us from (our) history.

2 J. H. Wilson, *Herbert Hoover: Forgotten Progressive* (Long Grove: Waveland Press, 1992), 151.

3 S. Terkel, *Hard Times: An Oral History of the Great Depression* (New York: The New Press, 2000), 145.

4 J. Steinbeck, *The Grapes of Wrath* (New York: Viking, 1939), 238.

5 P. Fishback, The newest on the New Deal, *Essays in Economic and Business History*, 36, 2018, 1–22, at 5.

6 B. Depew, P. V. Fishback and P. W. Rhode, New Deal or no deal in the Cotton South: The effect of the AAA on the agricultural labor structure, *Explorations in Economic History*, 50 (4), 2013, 466–86.

7 E. Rauchway, *The Great Depression and the New Deal: A Very Short Introduction* (Oxford: Oxford University Press, 2008), 5–6.

8 F. Benguria, C. Vickers and N. L. Ziebarth, Labor earnings inequality in manufacturing during the Great Depression, *Journal of Economic History*, 80 (2), 2020, 531–63.

9 Here I use the World Development Indicator series of 'Expense (% of GDP)'. It captures all cash payments for operating activities of the

US government in providing goods and services. It includes compensation of employees (such as wages and salaries), interest and subsidies, grants, social benefits, and other expenses such as rent and dividends.

22 How Could a Movie Embarrass Stalin? Russia and the Turn to Communism

1 J. C. Buggle and S. Nafziger, The slow road from serfdom: Labor coercion and long-run development in the former Russian Empire, *Review of Economics and Statistics*, 103 (1), 2021, 1–7.
2 K. Marx, *Critique of the Gotha Programme*, edited by C. P. Dutt (New York: International Publishers, 1938 [1875]), 5.
3 R. C. Allen, The standard of living in the Soviet Union, 1928–1940, *Journal of Economic History*, 58 (4), 1998, 1063–89, at 1065.
4 Ibid.
5 R. C. Allen, The rise and decline of the Soviet economy, *Canadian Journal of Economics*, 34 (4), 2001, 859–81.

23 Who Is the Perfect Soldier? The Causes and Consequences of the Second World War

1 The direct translation from Polish is the Warsaw Rising Museum, which is also how it is used on the museum's website.
2 J. Fourie, K. Inwood and M. Mariotti, Military technology and sample selection bias, *Social Science History*, 44 (3), 2020, 485–500.
3 C. Tumbe, *The Age of Pandemics, 1817–1920: How They Shaped India and the World* (New Delhi: HarperCollins India, 2020).
4 G. Galofré-Vilà, C. M. Meissner, M. McKee and D. Stuckler, Austerity and the rise of the Nazi Party, *Journal of Economic History*, 81 (1), 2021, 81–113.
5 M. Adena, R. Enikolopov, M. Petrova, V. Santarosa and E. Zhuravskaya, Radio and the rise of the Nazis in prewar Germany, *Quarterly Journal of Economics*, 130 (4), 2015, 1885–1939.
6 T. Wang, Media, pulpit, and populist persuasion: Evidence from Father Coughlin, *American Economic Review*, 111 (9), 2021, 3064–92.

7   D. Yanagizawa-Drott, Propaganda and conflict: Evidence from the Rwandan genocide, *Quarterly Journal of Economics*, 129 (4), 2014, 1947–94.

8   N. Voigtländer and H. J. Voth, Persecution perpetuated: The medieval origins of anti-Semitic violence in Nazi Germany, *Quarterly Journal of Economics*, 127 (3), 2012, 1339–92.

9   S. O. Becker and L. Pascali, Religion, division of labor, and conflict: Anti-Semitism in Germany over 600 years, *American Economic Review*, 109 (5), 2019, 1764–1804.

10 E. Miguel and G. Roland, The long-run impact of bombing Vietnam, *Journal of Development Economics*, 96 (1), 2011, 1–15.

11 As Chapter 29 explains, despite fighting on the side of the Axis powers and despite the atomic bombs that flattened two major cities, Japan also experienced a remarkable recovery.

12 S. Singhal, Early life shocks and mental health: The long-term effect of war in Vietnam, *Journal of Development Economics*, 141, 2019, 102244.

13 G. Chiovelli, S. Michalopoulos and E. Papaioannou, Landmines and spatial development (National Bureau of Economic Research working paper no. w24758, 2018), 3.

14 J. L. Arcand, A.S. Rodella-Boitreaud and M. Rieger, The impact of land mines on child health: Evidence from Angola, *Economic Development and Cultural Change*, 63 (2), 2015, 249–79.

15 Chiovelli et al., Landmines and spatial development.

24 What Was the Great Leap Forward? Mao Zedong, Famine and the Cultural Revolution

1   S. Chen and X. Lan, There will be killing: Collectivization and death of draft animals, *American Economic Journal: Applied Economics*, 9 (4), 2017, 58–77.

2   Ibid., 59.

3   Quoted from www.marxists.org/subject/china/peking-review/1966/PR1966-33g.htm.

4   A. F. Alesina, M. Seror, D. Y. Yang, Y. You and W. Zeng, Persistence through revolutions (National Bureau of Economic Research working paper no. 27053, 2020).

5   Ibid., 39.

6   The poverty rate fell from 88% in 1985 to 0.7% in 2015.

7   From $1,519 in 1976 to $13,102 in 2018. This is a conservative estimate. The World Development Indicators reported by the World

Bank shows an increase from $264 to $8,405, or an increase of thirty-two times!

25 Why Should We Cry for Argentina? A Country Reverses

1 Because of the Anglo-Boer War, I use the GDP per capita estimate of South Africa in 1899 (so as not to overstate South Africa's twentieth-century economic performance).

2 In international trade this is known as the Heckscher–Ohlin trade theory.

3 The economic historians Vicente Pinilla and Agustina Rayes show convincingly that Argentina had a successful agro-export sector because it offered a diverse basket of products to the different European and American countries that consumed them. In other words, grains and meat, which became stronger after the final decade of the nineteenth century, joined the livestock products that Argentina traditionally exported: V. Pinilla and A. Rayes, How Argentina became a super-exporter of agricultural and food products during the First Globalisation (1880–1929), *Cliometrica*, 13 (3), 2019, 443–69.

4 A. M. Taylor, External dependence, demographic burdens, and Argentine economic decline after the Belle Epoque, *Journal of Economic History*, 52 (4), 1992, 907–36, at 908.

5 Ibid.

6 J. F. Toye and R. Toye, The origins and interpretation of the Prebisch–Singer thesis, *History of Political Economy*, 35 (3), 2003, 437–67.

7 C. Belini, Industrial exports and Peronist economic policies in post-war Argentina, *Journal of Latin American Studies*, 44 (2), 2012, 285–317.

26 Who Was the Last King of Scotland? African Independence Struggles

1 M. de Haas, Measuring rural welfare in colonial Africa: Did Uganda's smallholders thrive? *Economic History Review*, 70 (2), 2017, 605–31.

2 M. Meredith, *The State of Africa: A History of the Continent since Independence* (New York: Simon & Schuster, 2011).

3 *Time* Magazine, 7 March 1977, http://content.time.com/time/sub scriber/article/0,33009,918762,00.html.

4 S. Broadberry and L. Gardner, Economic growth in Sub-Saharan Africa, 1885–2008: Evidence from eight countries, *Explorations in Economic History*, 83, 2022, 101424.

5　E. Frankema and M. van Waijenburg, Structural impediments to African growth? New evidence from real wages in British Africa, 1880–1965, *Journal of Economic History*, 72 (4), 2012, 895–926.

6　Andrew Kamarck, *The Economics of African Development* (New York: Praeger, 1967), 248.

7　W. A. Lewis, Economic development with unlimited supplies of labour, *Manchester School*, 22 (2), 1954, 139–91.

8　E. Akyeampong, African socialism; or the search for an indigenous model, *Economic History of Developing Regions*, 33 (1), 2018, 69–87.

9　R. L. Tignor, *W. Arthur Lewis and the Birth of Development Economics* (Princeton: Princeton University Press, 2006), 173.

10　M. Jerven, African growth recurring: An economic history perspective on African growth episodes, 1690–2010, *Economic History of Developing Regions*, 25 (2), 2010, 127–54, at 147.

27 How Did Einstein Help Create Eskom? South Africa Industrialises

1　Dirk Vermeulen, The remarkable Dr Hendrik van der Bijl, *Proceedings of the IEEE*, 86 (12), 1998, 2445–54, at 2448.

2　The Nobel laureate for Chemistry Lord Todd, Master of Christ's College at the University of Cambridge, said in 1970 that 'in 500 years of the College's history, of all its members, past and present, three had been truly outstanding: John Milton, Charles Darwin and Jan Smuts.'

3　N. L. Clark, *Manufacturing Apartheid: State Corporations in South Africa* (New Haven: Yale University Press, 1994), 103.

4　E. Dommisse and W. P. Esterhuyse, *Anton Rupert: A Biography* (Cape Town: Tafelberg, 2005).

5　At the time of writing, the Dutch brewing company Heineken had announced plans to acquire Distell.

6　A. Ehlers, Renier van Rooyen and Pep Stores Limited: The genesis of a South African entrepreneur and retail empire, *South African Historical Journal*, 60 (3), 2008, 422–51.

7　A. Ehlers, Business, state and society – doing business apartheid style: The case of Pep Stores Peninsula Limited, *New Contree*, 63, 2012, 35–66.

8　S. J. Sparks, Apartheid modern: South Africa's oil from coal project and the history of a company town (PhD thesis, University of Michigan, 2012), 7.

9   Stephen Sparks, Between 'artificial economics' and the 'discipline of the market': Sasol from parastatal to privatization, *Journal of Southern African Studies*, 42 (4), 2016, 711–24, at 724.

28 Why Would You Want to Eat Sushi in the Transkei? The Economics of Apartheid

1   C. van Onselen, *The Night Trains: Moving Mozambican Miners to and from the Witwatersrand Mines, circa 1902–1955* (Cape Town: Jonathan Ball, 2019).
2   Taryn Dinkelman and Martine Mariotti, The long-run effects of labor migration on human capital formation in communities of origin, *American Economic Journal: Applied Economics*, 8 (4), 2016, 1–35.
3   Martine Mariotti, Fathers' employment and sons' stature: The long-run effects of a positive regional employment shock in South Africa's mining industry, *Economic Development and Cultural Change*, 63 (3), 2015, 485–514.
4   Martine Mariotti, Labour markets during apartheid in South Africa 1, *Economic History Review*, 65 (3), 2012, 1100–22.
5   A. Luthuli, *Let My People Go* (London: Fontana, 1982), 180.
6   E. Kerby, Bamboo shoots: Asian migration, trade and business networks in South Africa, *Studies in Economics and Econometrics*, 42 (2), 2018, 103–37.
7   N. Nattrass, Deconstructing profitability under apartheid: 1960–1989, *Economic History of Developing Regions*, 29 (2), 2014, 245–67.
8   Ibid., 264.
9   W. H. Boshoff and J. Fourie, The South African economy in the twentieth century, in *Business Cycles and Structural Change in South Africa*, edited by Willem Boshoff (Cham: Springer, 2020), 49–70.
10 M. O. Lundahl, *Apartheid in Theory and Practice: An Economic Analysis* (London: Routledge, 2019), 218.
11 M. Lipton, *Capitalism and Apartheid: South Africa, 1910–1986* (Cape Town: David Philip, 1986).
12 A. D. Lowenberg, Why South Africa's apartheid economy failed, *Contemporary Economic Policy*, 15 (3), 1997, 62–72.

29 Why Do the Japanese Play Rugby? The Rise of the East Asian Economies

1   R. H. Wade, East Asia, in *Asian Transformations*, edited by D. Nayyar (Oxford: Oxford University Press, 2019), 477–503, at 482.

2 J. P. Tang, Technological leadership and late development: Evidence from Meiji Japan, 1868–1912, *Economic History Review*, 64 (1), 2011, 99–116.

3 The Japanese did it so well that they sometimes changed the language of importing countries. To this day, the Dutch call a calculator a *zakjapanner* – a pocket Japanese.

4 D. Rodrik, East Asian mysteries: Past and present, National Bureau of Economic Research, The Reporter, no. 2, www.nber.org/reporter/spring-1999/east-asian-mysteries-past-and-present.

5 Ibid.

6 Ibid.

7 E. A. Hanushek and L. Woessmann, Knowledge capital, growth, and the East Asian miracle, *Science*, 351 (6271), 2016, 344–5.

8 S. Pak, The biological standard of living in the two Koreas, *Economics and Human Biology*, 2 (3), 2004, 511–21.

30 What Do Lego and the Greatest Invention of the Twentieth Century Have in Common? The Second Era of Globalisation

1 M. Levinson, *The Box: How the Shipping Container Made the World Smaller and the World Economy Bigger* (Princeton: Princeton University Press, 2016).

2 K. H. O'Rourke and J. Williamson, When did globalisation begin? *European Review of Economic History*, 6 (1), 2002, 23–50.

3 W. H. Boshoff and J. Fourie, When did South African markets integrate into the global economy? *Studies in Economics and Econometrics*, 41 (1), 2017, 19–32.

4 L. Pascali, The wind of change: Maritime technology, trade, and economic development, *American Economic Review*, 107 (9), 2017, 2821–54.

5 E. W. F. Peterson, *A Billion Dollars a Day: The Economics and Politics of Agricultural Subsidies* (Oxford: John Wiley & Sons, 2009).

6 J. Bhagwati, *Termites in the Trading System: How Preferential Agreements Undermine Free Trade* (Oxford: Oxford University Press, 2008).

7 M. A. Clemens and L. Pritchett, The new economic case for migration restrictions: An assessment, *Journal of Development Economics*, 138, 2019, 153–64, at 153.

8 D. Rodrik, Populism and the economics of globalization, *Journal of International Business Policy*, 1 (1), 2018, 12–33.

31 What Is Funny about Moore's Law? ICT and the Fourth Industrial Revolution

1 His comment appears in a 1987 *New York Times Book Review* article.
2 P. A. David, The dynamo and the computer: An historical perspective on the modern productivity paradox, *American Economic Review*, 80 (2), 1990, 355–61.
3 This lengthy quotation is from a presentation of his working paper at the Warwick Economics Summer Workshop in July 1989. The quote sadly did not make it into the published version: P. A. David, Computer and dynamo: The modern productivity paradox in a not-too distant mirror (working paper, 1989), 31.
4 B. Bátiz-Lazo, *Cash and Dash: How ATMs and Computers Changed Banking* (Oxford: Oxford University Press, 2018).
5 A. D. Chandler, *The Visible Hand: The Managerial Revolution in American Business* (Cambridge, MA: Belknap Press of Harvard University Press, 1977).
6 N. R. Lamoreaux, D. M. Raff and P. Temin, Beyond markets and hierarchies: Toward a new synthesis of American business history, *American Historical Review*, 108 (2), 2003, 404–33.
7 These figures were accurate at the time of writing in November 2021.

32 What Bubbles in Iceland? The Global Financial Crisis of 2008

1 B. Eichengreen, Economic history and economic policy, *Journal of Economic History*, 72 (2), 2012, 289–307.
2 R. Havemann, The South African small banks' crisis of 2002/3, *Economic History of Developing Regions*, 36 (2), 2021, 313–38.
3 W. Quinn and J. D. Turner, *Boom and Bust: A Global History of Financial Bubbles* (Cambridge: Cambridge University Press, 2020).
4 A. Hern, How Iceland became the Bitcoin miners' paradise, *The Guardian*, 13 February 2018, www.theguardian.com/world/2018/feb/13/how-iceland-became-the-bitcoin-miners-paradise.

33 What Did *The Economist* Get Spectacularly Wrong? Africa after 2000

1 P. Collier and J. W. Gunning, Why has Africa grown slowly? *Journal of Economic Perspectives*, 13 (3), 1999, 3–22.

2   P. Englebert, Solving the mystery of the AFRICA dummy, *World Development*, 28 (10), 2000, 1821–35.

3   J. D. Sachs, *The End of Poverty: Economic Possibilities for Our Time* (London: Penguin, 2006).

4   W. Easterly, *The White Man's Burden: Why the West's Efforts to Aid the Rest Have Done So Much Ill and So Little Good* (London: Penguin, 2006).

5   D. Moyo, *Dead Aid: Why Aid Is Not Working and How There Is a Better Way for Africa* (New York: Farrar, Straus & Giroux, 2009).

6   E. Hillbom, Diamonds or development? A structural assessment of Botswana's forty years of success, *Journal of Modern African Studies*, 46 (2), 2008, 191–214.

7   The sun shines bright, *The Economist*, 3 December 2011, www .economist.com/briefing/2011/12/03/the-sun-shines-bright.

8   D. Rodrik, Goodbye Washington Consensus, hello Washington confusion? A review of the World Bank's economic growth in the 1990s: learning from a decade of reform, *Journal of Economic Literature*, 44 (4), 2006, 973–87.

9   W. Easterly, In search of reforms for growth: New stylized facts on policy and growth outcomes (National Bureau of Economic Research, working paper no. w26318, 2019).

10   W. Easterly, What did structural adjustment adjust? The association of policies and growth with repeated IMF and World Bank adjustment loans, *Journal of Development Economics*, 76 (1), 2005, 1–22, at 1.

11   See also K. B. Grier and R. M. Grier, The Washington Consensus works: Causal effects of reform, 1970–2015, *Journal of Comparative Economics*, 49 (1), 2021, 59–72; and B. Archibong, B. Coulibaly and N. Okonjo-Iweala, Washington Consensus reforms and lessons for economic performance in sub-Saharan Africa (working paper, 2021).

12   E. Frankema and M. van Waijenburg, Africa rising? A historical perspective, *African Affairs*, 117 (469), 2018, 543–68.

13   M. Jerven, African growth recurring: An economic history perspective on African growth episodes, 1690–2010, *Economic History of Developing Regions*, 25 (2), 2010, 127–54, at 147.

14   N. T. Krell, S. A. Giroux, Z. Guido, C. Hannah, S. E. Lopus, K. K. Caylor and T. P. Evans, Smallholder farmers' use of mobile phone services in central Kenya, *Climate and Development*, 2020, 1–13.

15   I. Mbiti and D. N. Weil, The home economics of e-money: Velocity, cash management, and discount rates of M-Pesa users, *American Economic Review*, 103 (3), 2013, 369–74.

16   L. A. Haidari, S. T. Brown, M. Ferguson, E. Bancroft, M. Spiker, A. Wilcox, R. Ambikapathi, V. Sampath, D. L. Connor and B. Y. Lee,

The economic and operational value of using drones to transport vaccines, *Vaccine*, 34 (34), 2016, 4062–7.

34 Will Madiba's Long Walk to Freedom Ever End? The First Twenty-Five Years of Democracy and the Future of South Africa

1 Available at www.dirco.gov.za/docs/speeches/1998/mbek0529.htm.
2 N. Nattrass and J. Seekings, 'Two nations'? Race and economic inequality in South Africa today, *Daedalus*, 130 (1), 2001, 45–70.
3 A. Whiteford and D. van Seventer, Understanding contemporary household inequality in South Africa, *Studies in Economics and Econometrics*, 24 (3), 2000, 7–30.
4 K. Barry, South African electric car the Crown Joule of Paris Auto Show, *Wired*, 10 October 2008, www.wired.com/2008/10/south-african-e/.
5 The Joule, just like other electric cars, depended on government subsidies. Sadly, that support ended during the financial crisis. By contrast, Tesla would become one of the largest companies in the world. Few in South Africa today remember that we once built an electric car.
6 A. Finn, M. Leibbrandt and I. Woolard, What happened to multidimensional poverty in South Africa between 1993 and 2010? (SALDRU working paper no. 99, University of Cape Town, 2013).
7 S. van der Berg, Apartheid's enduring legacy: Inequalities in education, *Journal of African Economies*, 16 (5), 2007, 849–80, at 849.
8 M. Swilling, Betrayal of the promise: How South Africa is being stolen (State Capacity Research Project, 2017).
9 J. Fourie, The long walk to economic freedom after apartheid, and the road ahead, *Southern Journal for Contemporary History*, 42 (1), 2017, 59–80.

35 What Should No Scholar Ever Do? Predicting the Future

1 K. Danziger, The psychological future of an oppressed group, *Social Forces*, 42 (1), 1963, 31–40.
2 D. Acemoglu and J. A. Robinson, *The Narrow Corridor: States, Societies, and the Fate of Liberty* (London: Penguin, 2020).
3 T. A. Carleton, A. Jina, M. T. Delgado, M. Greenstone, T. Houser, S. M. Hsiang, A. Hultgren, R. E. Kopp, K. E. McCusker, I. B. Nath and J. Rising, Valuing the global mortality consequences of climate

change accounting for adaptation costs and benefits (National Bureau of Economic Research working paper no. 27599, 2020).

4   S. Zuboff, Big other: Surveillance capitalism and the prospects of an information civilization, *Journal of Information Technology*, 30 (1), 2015, 75–89.

Epilogue: How Do You Win a World Cup?

1   D. S. Landes, *The Wealth and Poverty of Nations: Why Some Are so Rich and Some so Poor* (New York: W. W. Norton, 1998), 524.

Bibliography

Aboagye, P. Y. and J. Bolt. Long-term trends in income inequality: Winners and losers of economic change in Ghana, 1891–1960. *Explorations in Economic History*, 2021, 101405.

Acemoglu, D. and J. A. Robinson. *The Narrow Corridor: States, Societies, and the Fate of Liberty*. London: Penguin, 2020.

Adena, M., R. Enikolopov, M. Petrova, V. Santarosa and E. Zhuravskaya. Radio and the rise of the Nazis in prewar Germany. *Quarterly Journal of Economics*, 130 (4), 2015, 1885–1939.

Akyeampong, E. African socialism; or the search for an indigenous model. *Economic History of Developing Regions*, 33 (1), 2018, 69–87.

Alesina, A. F., M. Seror, D. Y. Yang, Y. You and W. Zeng. Persistence through revolutions. National Bureau of Economic Research working paper no. 27053, 2020.

Allen, R. C. The Industrial Revolution in miniature: The spinning jenny in Britain, France, and India. *Journal of Economic History*, 69 (4), 2009, 901–27.

Allen, R. C. The rise and decline of the Soviet economy. *Canadian Journal of Economics*, 34 (4), 2001, 859–81.

Allen, R. C. The standard of living in the Soviet Union, 1928–1940. *Journal of Economic History*, 58 (4), 1998, 1063–89.

Alsan, M. The effect of the tsetse fly on African development. *American Economic Review*, 105 (1), 2015, 382–410.

Alsan, M. and C. Goldin. Watersheds in child mortality: The role of effective water and sewerage infrastructure, 1880–1920. *Journal of Political Economy*, 127 (2), 2019, 586–638.

Arcand, J. L., A. S. Rodella-Boitreaud and M. Rieger. The impact of land mines on child health: Evidence from Angola. *Economic Development and Cultural Change*, 63 (2), 2015, 249–79.

Archibong, B., B. Coulibaly and N. Okonjo-Iweala. Washington Consensus reforms and lessons for economic performance in sub-Saharan Africa. Working paper, 2021.

Ashraf, Q. and O. Galor, The 'Out of Africa' hypothesis, human genetic diversity, and comparative economic development. *American Economic Review*, 103 (1), 2013, 1–46.

Austin, G. Resources, techniques, and strategies south of the Sahara: Revising the factor endowments perspective on African economic development, 1500–2000. *Economic History Review*, 61 (3), 2008, 587–624.

Austin, G. The 'reversal of fortune' thesis and the compression of history: Perspectives from African and comparative economic history. *Journal of International Development*, 20 (8), 2008, 996–1027.

Baptist, E. E. *The Half Has Never Been Told: Slavery and the Making of American Capitalism*. London: Hachette, 2016.

Baten, J. and J. L. van Zanden. Book production and the onset of modern economic growth. *Journal of Economic Growth*, 13 (3), 2008, 217–35.

Baten, J. and L. Maravall. The influence of colonialism on Africa's welfare: An anthropometric study. *Journal of Comparative Economics*, 2021 (in press).

Bátiz-Lazo, B. *Cash and Dash: How ATMs and Computers Changed Banking*. Oxford: Oxford University Press, 2018.

Becker, S. O. and L. Pascali. Religion, division of labor, and conflict: Anti-Semitism in Germany over 600 years. *American Economic Review*, 109 (5), 2019, 1764–1804.

Becker, S. O., S. Pfaff and J. Rubin. Causes and consequences of the Protestant Reformation. *Explorations in Economic History*, 62, 2016, 1–25.

Beckett, S. *Empire of Cotton: A Global History*. London: Vintage, 2015.

Beinart, W. and P. Delius. The historical context and legacy of the Natives Land Act of 1913. *Journal of Southern African Studies*, 40 (4), 2014, 667–88.

Belini, C. Industrial exports and Peronist economic policies in post-war Argentina. *Journal of Latin American Studies*, 44 (2), 2012, 285–317.

Benguria, F., C. Vickers and N. L. Ziebarth. Labor earnings inequality in manufacturing during the Great Depression. *Journal of Economic History*, 80 (2), 2020, 531–63.

Berger, T. Railroads and rural industrialization: Evidence from a historical policy experiment. *Explorations in Economic History*, 74, 2019, 101277.

Bhagwati, J. *Termites in the Trading System: How Preferential Agreements Undermine Free Trade*. Oxford: Oxford University Press, 2008.

Blaydes, L. and C. Paik. The impact of Holy Land Crusades on state formation: War mobilization, trade integration, and political development in medieval Europe. *International Organization*, 70 (3), 2016, 551–86.

Bloch, M. *Feudal Society*, trans. L. A. Manyon, 2 vols. Chicago: University of Chicago Press, 1961.

Blouin, A. Axis-orientation and knowledge transmission: Evidence from the Bantu expansion. *Journal of Economic Growth*, 26, 2021, 359–84.

Boshoff, W. H. and J. Fourie. The significance of the Cape trade route to economic activity in the Cape Colony: A medium-term business cycle analysis. *European Review of Economic History*, 14 (3), 2010, 469–503.

Boshoff, W. H. and J. Fourie. The South African economy in the twentieth century. In *Business Cycles and Structural Change in South Africa*, edited by W. Boshoff. Cham: Springer, 2020, 49–70.

Boshoff, W. H. and J. Fourie. When did South African markets integrate into the global economy? *Studies in Economics and Econometrics*, 41 (1), 2017, 19–32.

Broadberry, S. and L. Gardner. Economic growth in Sub-Saharan Africa, 1885–2008: Evidence from eight countries. *Explorations in Economic History*, 83, 2022, 101424.

Broadberry, S., H. Guan and D. Li. China, Europe, and the Great Divergence: A restatement. *Journal of Economic History*, 81 (3), 2021, 958–74.

Buggle, J. C. and S. Nafziger. The slow road from serfdom: Labor coercion and long-run development in the former Russian Empire. *Review of Economics and Statistics*, 103 (1), 2021, 1–7.

Cagé, J. and V. Rueda. Sex and the mission: The conflicting effects of early Christian missions on HIV in sub-Saharan Africa. *Journal of Demographic Economics*, 86 (3), 2020, 213–57.

Carleton, T. A., A. Jina, M. T. Delgado, M. Greenstone, T. Houser, S. M. Hsiang, A. Hultgren, R. E. Kopp, K. E. McCusker, I. B. Nath and J. Rising. Valuing the global mortality consequences of climate change accounting for adaptation costs and benefits. National Bureau of Economic Research, working paper no. 27599, 2020.

Carlson, M.A., S. Correia and S. Luck. The effects of banking competition on growth and financial stability: Evidence from the national banking era. Working paper SSRN 3202489, 2019.

Chandler, A. D. *The Visible Hand: The Managerial Revolution in American Business*. Cambridge, MA: Belknap Press of Harvard University Press, 1977.

Chen, S. and X. Lan. There will be killing: Collectivization and death of draft animals. *American Economic Journal: Applied Economics*, 9 (4), 2017, 58–77.

Cherniwchan, J. and J. Moreno-Cruz. Maize and precolonial Africa. *Journal of Development Economics*, 136, 2019, 137–50.

Chiovelli, G., S. Michalopoulos and E. Papaioannou. Landmines and spatial development. National Bureau of Economic Research working paper no. w24758, 2018.

Clark, N. L. *Manufacturing Apartheid: State Corporations in South Africa.* New Haven: Yale University Press, 1994.

Clemens, M. A. and L. Pritchett. The new economic case for migration restrictions: An assessment. *Journal of Development Economics*, 138, 2019, 153–64.

Collier, P. and J. W. Gunning. Why has Africa grown slowly? *Journal of Economic Perspectives*, 13 (3), 1999, 3–22.

Danziger, K. The psychological future of an oppressed group. *Social Forces*, 42 (1), 1963, 31–40.

David, P. A. Computer and dynamo: The modern productivity paradox in a not-too-distant mirror. Working paper, 1989.

David, P. A. The dynamo and the computer: An historical perspective on the modern productivity paradox. *American Economic Review*, 80 (2), 1990, 355–61.

de Haas, M. Measuring rural welfare in colonial Africa: Did Uganda's smallholders thrive? *Economic History Review*, 70 (2), 2017, 605–31.

de Kock, M. H. *Selected Subjects in the Economic History of South Africa.* Cape Town: Juta & Co., 1924.

de Vries, J. The limits of globalization in the early modern world. *Economic History Review*, 63 (3), 2010, 710–33.

Dell, M. The persistent effects of Peru's mining mita. *Econometrica*, 78 (6), 2010, 1863–1903.

Depew, B., P. V. Fishback and P. W. Rhode. New Deal or no deal in the Cotton South: The effect of the AAA on the agricultural labor structure. *Explorations in Economic History*, 50 (4), 2013, 466–86.

Diamond, J. *Guns, Germs and Steel.* New York: Vintage, 1997.

Dinkelman, T. and M. Mariotti. The long-run effects of labor migration on human capital formation in communities of origin. *American Economic Journal: Applied Economics*, 8 (4), 2016, 1–35.

Dommisse, E. and W. P. Esterhuyse. *Anton Rupert: A Biography.* Cape Town: Tafelberg, 2005.

Donaldson, D. Railroads of the Raj: Estimating the impact of transportation infrastructure. *American Economic Review*, 108 (4–5), 2018, 899–934.

Donaldson, D. and R. Hornbeck. Railroads and American economic growth: A 'market access' approach. *Quarterly Journal of Economics*, 131 (2), 2016, 799–858.

Easterly, W. In search of reforms for growth: New stylized facts on policy and growth outcomes. National Bureau of Economic Research, working paper no. w26318, 2019.

Easterly, W. What did structural adjustment adjust? The association of policies and growth with repeated IMF and World Bank adjustment loans. *Journal of Development Economics*, 76 (1), 2005, 1–22.

Easterly, W. *The White Man's Burden: Why the West's Efforts to Aid the Rest Have Done So Much Ill and So Little Good.* London: Penguin, 2006.

Ehlers, A. Business, state and society – doing business apartheid style: The case of Pep Stores Peninsula Limited. *New Contree*, 63, 2012, 35–66.

Ehlers, A. Renier van Rooyen and Pep Stores Limited: The genesis of a South African entrepreneur and retail empire. *South African Historical Journal*, 60 (3), 2008, 422–51.

Eichengreen, B. Economic history and economic policy. *Journal of Economic History*, 72 (2), 2012, 289–307.

Ekama, K. Bondsmen: Slave collateral in the 19th-century Cape Colony. *Journal of Southern African Studies*, 47 (3), 2021, 437–53.

Ekama, K. Profiting from slavery after abolition: Emancipation and the business of compensation in the Cape Colony. Working paper, 2020.

Engerman, S. L. and K. L. Sokoloff. *Economic Development in the Americas since 1500: Endowments and Institutions.* Cambridge: Cambridge University Press, 2012.

Englebert, P. Solving the mystery of the AFRICA dummy. *World Development*, 28 (10), 2000, 1821–35.

Finn, A., M. Leibbrandt and I. Woolard. What happened to multidimensional poverty in South Africa between 1993 and 2010? SALDRU working paper no. 99, University of Cape Town, 2013.

Fishback, P. The newest on the New Deal. *Essays in Economic and Business History*, 36, 2018, 1–22.

Fitzgerald, F. S. *The Great Gatsby.* London: Penguin, 1974 [1926].

Fourie, J. The data revolution in African economic history. *Journal of Interdisciplinary History*, 47 (2), 2016, 193–212.

Fourie, J. An inquiry into the nature, causes and distribution of wealth in the Cape Colony, 1652–1795. PhD thesis, Utrecht University, 2012.

Fourie, J. The long walk to economic freedom after apartheid, and the road ahead. *Southern Journal for Contemporary History*, 42 (1), 2017, 59–80.

Fourie, J. The quantitative Cape: A review of the new historiography of the Dutch Cape Colony. *South African Historical Journal*, 66 (1), 2014, 142–68.

Fourie, J. The remarkable wealth of the Dutch Cape Colony: Measurements from eighteenth-century probate inventories. *Economic History Review*, 66 (2), 2013, 419–48.

Fourie, J. Who writes African economic history? *Economic History of Developing Regions*, 34 (2), 2019, 111–31.

Fourie, J. and F. Garmon. The settlers' fortunes: Comparing tax censuses in the Cape Colony and early American Republic. Mimeo, 2022.

Fourie, J. and E. Green. The missing people: Accounting for the productivity of indigenous populations in Cape colonial history. *Journal of African History*, 56 (2), 2015, 195–215.

Fourie, J., K. Inwood and M. Mariotti. Military technology and sample selection bias. *Social Science History*, 44 (3), 2020, 485–500.

Fourie, J. and N. Obikili. Decolonizing with data: The cliometric turn in African economic history. In *Handbook of Cliometrics*, edited by C. Diebolt and M. Haupert. Heidelberg: Springer Reference, 2019, 1–25.

Fourie, J. and J. L. van Zanden. GDP in the Dutch Cape Colony: The national accounts of a slave-based society. *South African Journal of Economics*, 81 (4), 2013, 467–90.

Fourie, J. and D. von Fintel, Settler skills and colonial development: The Huguenot wine-makers in eighteenth-century Dutch South Africa. *Economic History Review*, 67 (4), 2014, 932–63.

Frankema, E. and M. Jerven. Writing history backwards or sideways: Towards a consensus on African population, 1850–2010. *Economic History Review*, 67 (4), 2014, 907–31.

Frankema, E. and M. van Waijenburg. Africa rising? A historical perspective. *African Affairs*, 117 (469), 2018, 543–68.

Frankema, E. and M. van Waijenburg. Structural impediments to African growth? New evidence from real wages in British Africa, 1880–1965. *Journal of Economic History*, 72 (4), 2012, 895–926.

Frankema, E., J. Williamson and P. Woltjer. An economic rationale for the West African scramble? The commercial transition and the commodity price boom of 1835–1885. *Journal of Economic History*, 78 (1), 2018, 231–67.

Gallego, F. A. and R. Woodberry. Christian missionaries and education in former African colonies: How competition mattered. *Journal of African Economies*, 19 (3), 2010, 294–329.

Galofré-Vilà, G., C. M. Meissner, M. McKee and D. Stuckler. Austerity and the rise of the Nazi Party. *Journal of Economic History*, 81 (1), 2021, 81–113.

Garstang, M., A. D. Coleman and M. Therrell. Climate and the Mfecane. *South African Journal of Science*, 110 (5–6), 2014, 1–6.

Germond, R. *Chronicles of Basutoland: A Running Commentary on the Events of the Years 1830–1902*. Morija: Morija Sesuto Book Depot, 1967.

Green, E. *Creating the Cape Colony: The Political Economy of Settler Colonisation*. London: Bloomsbury, 2022.

Green, E. The economics of slavery in the eighteenth-century Cape Colony: Revising the Nieboer–Domar hypothesis. *International Review of Social History*, 59 (1), 2014, 39–70.

Green, E. *Production Systems in Pre-Colonial Africa* (online textbook). www.aehnetwork.org/textbook/production-systems-in-pre-colonial-africa/.

Grier, K. B. and R. M. Grier. The Washington Consensus works: Causal effects of reform, 1970–2015. *Journal of Comparative Economics*, 49 (1), 2021, 59–72.

Guedes, J. D. A., T. C. Bestor, D. Carrasco, R. Flad, E. Fosse, M. Herzfeld, C. C. Lamberg-Karlovsky, C. M. Lewis, M. Liebmann, R. Meadow and N. Patterson. Is poverty in our genes? A critique of Ashraf and Galor, 'The "Out of Africa" hypothesis, human genetic diversity, and comparative economic development', American Economic Review (forthcoming). *Current Anthropology*, 54 (1), 2013, 71–9.

Gwaindepi, A. and J. Fourie. Public sector growth in the British Cape Colony: Evidence from new data on expenditure and foreign debt, 1830–1910. *South African Journal of Economics*, 88 (3), 2020, 341–67.

Haidari, L. A., S. T. Brown, M. Ferguson, E. Bancroft, M. Spiker, A. Wilcox, R. Ambikapathi, V. Sampath, D. L. Connor and B. Y. Lee. The economic and operational value of using drones to transport vaccines. *Vaccine*, 34 (34), 2016, 4062–7.

Hamidullah, M. Muslim discovery of America before Columbus. *Journal of the Muslim Students' Association of the United States and Canada*, 4 (2), 1968, 7–9.

Hanushek, E. A. and L. Woessmann. Knowledge capital, growth, and the East Asian miracle. *Science*, 351 (6271), 2016, 344–5.

Harari, Y. N. *Sapiens: A Brief History of Humankind*. London: Random House, 2014.

Havemann, R. The South African small banks' crisis of 2002/3. *Economic History of Developing Regions*, 36 (2), 2021, 313–38.

Heilbroner, R. *The Worldly Philosophers: The Lives, Times, and Ideas of the Great Economic Thinkers*. New York: Simon & Schuster/Touchstone, 1999 [1953].

Hejeebu, S. The colonial transition and the decline of the East India Company, c.1746–1784. In *A New Economic History of Colonial India*, edited by L. Chaudhary, B. Gupta, T. Roy and A. V. Swamy. London: Routledge, 2015, 33–51.

Heldring, L. and J. Robinson. Colonialism and economic development in Africa. In *The Oxford Handbook of the Politics of Development*, edited by C. Lancaster and N. van de Walle. Oxford: Oxford University Press, 2018, 295–327.

Henshilwood, C. S., F. d'Errico, K. L. van Niekerk, L. Dayet, A. Queffelec and L. Pollarolo. An abstract drawing from the 73,000-year-old levels at Blombos Cave, South Africa. *Nature*, 562 (7725), 2018, 115–18.

Herranz-Loncán, A. The role of railways in export-led growth: The case of Uruguay, 1870–1913. *Economic History of Developing Regions*, 26 (2), 2011, 1–32.

Herranz-Loncán, A. and J. Fourie. 'For the public benefit'? Railways in the British Cape Colony. *European Review of Economic History*, 22 (1), 2018, 73–100.

Hillbom, E. Diamonds or development? A structural assessment of Botswana's forty years of success. *Journal of Modern African Studies*, 46 (2), 2008, 191–214.

Hochschild, A. *King Leopold's Ghost: A Story of Greed, Terror, and Heroism in Colonial Africa*. London: Folio Society, 2017 [1998].

Hopkins, A. G. Fifty years of African economic history. *Economic History of Developing Regions*, 34 (1), 2019, 1–15.

Hornbeck, R. and T. Logan. The great American productivity gain: Emancipation and aggregate productivity growth. Working paper, 2022.

Huillery, E. The black man's burden: The cost of colonization of French West Africa. *Journal of Economic History*, 74 (1), 2014, 1–38.

Jedwab, R. and A. Moradi. The permanent effects of transportation revolutions in poor countries: Evidence from Africa. *Review of Economics and Statistics*, 98 (2), 2016, 268–84.

Jedwab, R., F. Meier zu Selhausen and A. Moradi. Christianization without economic development: Evidence from missions in Ghana. *Journal of Economic Behavior and Organization*, 190, 2021, 573–96.

Jedwab, R., F. Meier zu Selhausen and A. Moradi. The economics of missionary expansion: Evidence from Africa and implications for development. *Journal of Economic Growth* (forthcoming, 2022).

Jerven, M. African growth recurring: An economic history perspective on African growth episodes, 1690–2010. *Economic History of Developing Regions*, 25 (2), 2010, 127–54.

Kamarck, A. *The Economics of African Development*. New York: Praeger, 1967.

Kerby, E. Bamboo shoots: Asian migration, trade and business networks in South Africa. *Studies in Economics and Econometrics*, 42 (2), 2018, 103–37.

Krell, N. T., S. A. Giroux, Z. Guido, C. Hannah, S. E. Lopus, K. K. Caylor and T. P. Evans. Smallholder farmers' use of mobile phone services in central Kenya. *Climate and Development*, 2020, 1–13.

Lamoreaux, N. R., D. M. Raff and P. Temin. Beyond markets and hierarchies: Toward a new synthesis of American business history. *American Historical Review*, 108 (2), 2003, 404–33.

Landes, D. S. *The Wealth and Poverty of Nations: Why Some Are so Rich and Some so Poor*. New York: W. W. Norton, 1998.

Levine, R., C. Lin and W. Xie. The African slave trade and modern household finance. *Economic Journal*, 130 (630), 2020, 1817–41.

Levinson, M. *The Box: How the Shipping Container Made the World Smaller and the World Economy Bigger*. Princeton: Princeton University Press, 2016.

Lewis, W. A. Economic development with unlimited supplies of labour. *Manchester School*, 22 (2), 1954, 139–91.

Lipton, M. *Capitalism and Apartheid: South Africa, 1910–1986*. Cape Town: David Philip, 1986.

Lovejoy, P. E. Long-distance trade and Islam: The case of the nineteenth-century Hausa kola trade. *Journal of the Historical Society of Nigeria*, 5 (4), 1971, 537–47.

Lowenberg, A. D. Why South Africa's apartheid economy failed. *Contemporary Economic Policy*, 15 (3), 1997, 62–72.

Lowes, S. and E. Montero. Concessions, violence, and indirect rule: Evidence from the Congo Free State. *Quarterly Journal of Economics*, 136 (4), 2021, 2047–91.

Lundahl, M. O. *Apartheid in Theory and Practice: An Economic Analysis*. London: Routledge, 2019.

Luthuli, A. *Let My People Go*. London: Fontana, 1982.

Malthus, T. R. *An Essay on the Principle of Population As It Affects the Future Improvement of Society, with Remarks on the Speculations of Mr. Goodwin, M. Condorcet and Other Writers*. London: J. Johnson in St Paul's Church-yard, 1798.

Manning, P. African population: Projections, 1850–1960, in *The Demographics of Empire: The Colonial Order and the Creation of Knowledge*, edited by K. Ittmann, D. D. Cordell and G. H. Maddox. Athens: Ohio University Press, 2010, 245–75.

Manning, P. *Slavery and African Life: Occidental, Oriental, and African Slave Trades*. Cambridge: Cambridge University Press, 1990.

Maravall, L. The impact of a 'colonizing river': Colonial railways and the indigenous population in French Algeria at the turn of the century. *Economic History of Developing Regions*, 34 (1), 2019, 16–47.

Mariotti, M. Fathers' employment and sons' stature: The long-run effects of a positive regional employment shock in South Africa's mining industry. *Economic Development and Cultural Change*, 63 (3), 2015, 485–514.

Mariotti, M. Labour markets during apartheid in South Africa 1. *Economic History Review*, 65 (3), 2012, 1100–22.

Marks, S. G. *The Information Nexus: Global Capitalism from the Renaissance to the Present*. Cambridge: Cambridge University Press, 2016.

Marx, K. *Critique of the Gotha Programme*, edited by C. P. Dutt. New York: International Publishers, 1938.

Mbiti, I. and D. N. Weil. The home economics of e-money: Velocity, cash management, and discount rates of M-Pesa users. *American Economic Review*, 103 (3), 2013, 369–74.

McCloskey, D. N. *Bourgeois Dignity: Why Economics Can't Explain the Modern World*. Chicago: University of Chicago Press, 2010.

McCloskey, D.N. The great enrichment: A humanistic and social scientific account. *Social Science History*, 40 (4), 2016, 583–98.

McNeill, W. H. *Plagues and Peoples*. Garden City, NJ: Anchor Press, 1976.

Meredith, M. *The State of Africa: A History of the Continent since Independence*. New York: Simon & Schuster, 2011.

Michalopoulos, S. and E. Papaioannou. The long-run effects of the Scramble for Africa. *American Economic Review*, 106 (7), 2016, 1802–48.

Miguel, E. and G. Roland. The long-run impact of bombing Vietnam. *Journal of Development Economics*, 96 (1), 2011, 1–15.

Mokyr, J. *A Culture of Growth: The Origins of the Modern Economy*. Princeton: Princeton University Press, 2016.

Moyo, D. *Dead Aid: Why Aid Is Not Working and How There Is a Better Way for Africa*. New York: Farrar, Straus & Giroux, 2009.

Mpeta, B., J. Fourie and K. Inwood. Black living standards in South Africa before democracy: New evidence from height. *South African Journal of Science*, 114 (1–2), 2018, 1–8.

Nattrass, N. Deconstructing profitability under apartheid: 1960–1989. *Economic History of Developing Regions*, 29 (2), 2014, 245–67.

Nattrass, N. and J. Seekings. 'Two nations'? Race and economic inequality in South Africa today. *Daedalus*, 130 (1), 2001, 45–70.

Norberg, J. *Progress*. London: Oneworld, 2016.

Norris, C. J. The negativity bias, revisited: Evidence from neuroscience measures and an individual differences approach. *Social Neuroscience*, 16 (1), 2021, 68–82.

Nunn, N. Culture and the historical process. *Economic History of Developing Regions*, 27 (sup-1), 2012, 108–26.

Nunn, N. The long-term effects of Africa's slave trades. *Quarterly Journal of Economics*, 123 (1), 2008, 139–76.

Nunn, N. and D. Puga. Ruggedness: The blessing of bad geography in Africa. *Review of Economics and Statistics*, 94 (1), 2012, 20–36.

Nunn, N. and L. Wantchekon. The slave trade and the origins of mistrust in Africa. *American Economic Review*, 101 (7), 2011, 3221–52.

Nyika, F. and J. Fourie. Black disenfranchisement in the Cape Colony, c.1887–1909: Challenging the numbers. *Journal of Southern African Studies*, 46 (3), 2020, 455–69.

O'Rourke, K. H. and J. Williamson. When did globalisation begin? *European Review of Economic History*, 6 (1), 2002, 23–50.

Obikili, N. The trans-Atlantic slave trade and local political fragmentation in Africa. *Economic History Review*, 69 (4), 2016, 1157–77.

Ogilvie, S. The economics of guilds, *Journal of Economic Perspectives*, 28 (4), 2014, 169–92.

Okoye, D. Things fall apart? Missions, institutions, and interpersonal trust. *Journal of Development Economics*, 148, 2021, 102568.

Olmstead, A. L. and P. W. Rhode, Biological innovation and productivity growth in the antebellum cotton economy. *Journal of Economic History*, 68 (4), 2008, 1123–71.

Olmstead, A. L. and P. W. Rhode. Cotton, slavery, and the new history of capitalism. *Explorations in Economic History*, 67, 2018, 1–17.

Olsson, O. and C. Paik. Long-run cultural divergence: Evidence from the Neolithic Revolution. *Journal of Development Economics*, 122, 2016, 197–213.

Olsson, O. and C. Paik. A western reversal since the Neolithic? The long-run impact of early agriculture. *Journal of Economic History*, 80 (1), 2020, 100–35.

Paik, C. and J. Vechbanyongratana. Reform, rails and rice: Thailand's political railroads and economic development in the 20th century. Working paper, 2021.

Pak, S. The biological standard of living in the two Koreas. *Economics and Human Biology*, 2 (3), 2004, 511–21.

Palma, N., A. Papadia, T. Pereira and L. Weller. Slavery and development in nineteenth century Brazil. *Capitalism: A Journal of History and Economics*, 2 (2), 2021, 372–426.

Pascali, L. The wind of change: Maritime technology, trade, and economic development. *American Economic Review*, 107 (9), 2017, 2821–54.

Peterson, E. W. F. *A Billion Dollars a Day: The Economics and Politics of Agricultural Subsidies*. Oxford: John Wiley & Sons, 2009.

Pierce, L. and J. A. Snyder. The historical slave trade and firm access to finance in Africa. *Review of Financial Studies*, 31 (1), 2018, 142–74.

Pinilla, V. and A. Rayes. How Argentina became a super-exporter of agricultural and food products during the First Globalisation (1880–1929). *Cliometrica*, 13 (3), 2019, 443–69.

Pinker, S. *Enlightenment Now*. New York: Viking, 2018.

Plaatje, S. *Native Life in South Africa*. Johannesburg: Picador Africa, 2007.

Pollard, E. and O. C. Kinyera. The Swahili coast and the Indian Ocean trade patterns in the 7th–10th centuries CE. *Journal of Southern African Studies*, 43 (5), 2017, 927–47.

Quinn, W. and J. D. Turner. *Boom and Bust: A Global History of Financial Bubbles*. Cambridge: Cambridge University Press, 2020.

Rauchway, E. *The Great Depression and the New Deal: A Very Short Introduction*. Oxford: Oxford University Press, 2008.

Rodney, W. *How Europe Underdeveloped Africa*. Dar es Salaam: Tanzania Publishing House, 1972.

Rodrik, D. East Asian mysteries: Past and present, National Bureau of Economic Research, The Reporter, no 2. www.nber.org/reporter/spring-1999/east-asian-mysteries-past-and-present.

Rodrik, D. Goodbye Washington Consensus, hello Washington confusion? A review of the World Bank's economic growth in the 1990s: Learning from a decade of reform. *Journal of Economic Literature*, 44 (4), 2006, 973–87.

Rodrik, D. Populism and the economics of globalization. *Journal of International Business Policy*, 1 (1), 2018, 12–33.

Rosenberg, N. and M. Trajtenberg. A general-purpose technology at work: The Corliss steam engine in the late-nineteenth-century United States. *Journal of Economic History*, 64 (1), 2004, 61–99.

Rosling, H. *Factfulness*. New York: Flatiron Books, 2018.

Ross, R. and L.-C. Martin. Accommodation and resistance: The housing of Cape Town's enslaved and freed population before and after emancipation. *Journal of Southern African Studies*, 47 (3), 2021, 417–35.

Rubin, J. Printing and Protestants: An empirical test of the role of printing in the Reformation. *Review of Economics and Statistics*, 96 (2), 2014, 270–86.

Rubin, J. *Rulers, Religion, and Riches: Why the West Got Rich and the Middle East Did Not*. Cambridge: Cambridge University Press, 2017.

Sachs, J. D. *The End of Poverty: Economic Possibilities for Our Time*. London: Penguin, 2006.

Saleh, M. On the road to heaven: Taxation, conversions, and the Coptic–Muslim socioeconomic gap in medieval Egypt. *Journal of Economic History*, 78 (2), 2018, 394–434.

Scott, J. C. *Against the Grain: A Deep History of the Earliest States*. New Haven: Yale University Press, 2017.

Shell, R. C. H. *Children of Bondage: A Social History of the Slave Society at the Cape of Good Hope, 1652–1838*. Hanover, NH, and London: Wesleyan University Press, 1994.

Singhal, S. Early life shocks and mental health: The long-term effect of war in Vietnam. *Journal of Development Economics*, 141, 2019, 102244.

Smith, A. *An Inquiry into the Nature and Causes of the Wealth of Nations*, edited by E. Cannan. London: Methuen & Co., 1904.

Sokoloff, K. L. and S. L. Engerman. Institutions, factor endowments, and paths of development in the New World. *Journal of Economic Perspectives*, 14 (3), 2000, 217–32.

Sparks, S. J. Apartheid modern: South Africa's oil from coal project and the history of a company town. PhD thesis, University of Michigan, 2012.

Sparks, S. J. Between 'artificial economics' and the 'discipline of the market': Sasol from parastatal to privatization. *Journal of Southern African Studies*, 42 (4), 2016, 711–24.

Steinbeck, J. *The Grapes of Wrath*. New York: Viking, 1939.

Swilling, M. Betrayal of the promise: How South Africa is being stolen. State Capacity Research Project, 2017.

Tang, J. P. Railroad expansion and industrialization: Evidence from Meiji Japan. *Journal of Economic History*, 74 (3), 2014, 863–86.

Tang, J. P. Technological leadership and late development: Evidence from Meiji Japan, 1868–1912. *Economic History Review*, 64 (1), 2011, 99–116.

Taylor, A. M. External dependence, demographic burdens, and Argentine economic decline after the Belle Epoque. *Journal of Economic History*, 52 (4), 1992, 907–36.

Terkel, S. *Hard Times: An Oral History of the Great Depression*. New York: The New Press, 2000.

Tignor, R. L. *W. Arthur Lewis and the Birth of Development Economics*. Princeton: Princeton University Press, 2006.

Toye, J. F. and R. Toye. The origins and interpretation of the Prebisch–Singer thesis. *History of Political Economy*, 35 (3), 2003, 437–67.

Tumbe, C. *The Age of Pandemics, 1817–1920: How They Shaped India and the World*. New Delhi: HarperCollins India, 2020.

Valencia Caicedo, F. The mission: Human capital transmission, economic persistence, and culture in South America. *Quarterly Journal of Economics*, 134 (1), 2019, 507–56.

van der Berg, S. Apartheid's enduring legacy: Inequalities in education. *Journal of African Economies*, 16 (5), 2007, 849–80.

van Duin, P. and R. Ross. *The Economy of the Cape Colony in the 18th Century*. Leiden: Centre for the Study of European Expansion, 1987.

van Onselen, C. *The Night Trains: Moving Mozambican Miners to and from the Witwatersrand Mines, circa 1902–1955*. Cape Town: Jonathan Ball, 2019.

van Waijenburg, M. Financing the African colonial state: The revenue imperative and forced labor. *Journal of Economic History*, 78 (1), 2018, 40–80.

van Waijenburg, M. and E. Frankema. Structural impediments to African growth? New evidence from real wages in British Africa, 1880–1965. CGEH Working Paper no. 24, 2011.

Vermeulen, D. The remarkable Dr Hendrik van der Bijl. *Proceedings of the IEEE*, 86 (12), 1998, 2445–54.

Voigtländer, N. and H. J. Voth. Persecution perpetuated: The medieval origins of anti-Semitic violence in Nazi Germany. *Quarterly Journal of Economics*, 127 (3), 2012, 1339–92.

von Fintel, D. and J. Fourie. The great divergence in South Africa: Population and wealth dynamics over two centuries. *Journal of Comparative Economics*, 47 (4), 2019, 759–73.

Wade, R. H. East Asia. In *Asian Transformations*, edited by D. Nayyar. Oxford: Oxford University Press, 2019, 477–503.

Wanamaker, M. H. 150 years of economic progress for African American men: Measuring outcomes and sizing up roadblocks. *Economic History of Developing Regions*, 32 (3), 2017, 211–20.

Wang, T. Media, pulpit, and populist persuasion: Evidence from Father Coughlin. *American Economic Review*, 111 (9), 2021, 3064–92.

Whatley, W. C. The gun–slave hypothesis and the 18th century British slave trade. *Explorations in Economic History*, 67, 2018, 80–104.

Whiteford, A. and D. van Seventer. Understanding contemporary household inequality in South Africa. *Studies in Economics and Econometrics*, 24 (3), 2000, 7–30.

Wickramasinghe, N. *Slave in a Palanquin: Colonial Servitude and Resistance in Sri Lanka*. New York: Columbia University Press, 2020.

Wilson, J. H. *Herbert Hoover: Forgotten Progressive*. Long Grove: Waveland Press, 1992.

Wood, G. D. A. *Tambora: The Eruption that Changed the World*. Princeton: Princeton University Press, 2014.

Wragg Sykes, R. M. *Kindred: Neanderthal Life, Love, Death and Art*. London: Bloomsbury, 2020.

Wright, G. Slavery and Anglo-American capitalism revisited. *Economic History Review*, 73 (2), 2020, 353–83.

Yanagizawa-Drott, D. Propaganda and conflict: Evidence from the Rwandan genocide. *Quarterly Journal of Economics*, 129 (4), 2014, 1947–94.

Zuboff, S. Big other: Surveillance capitalism and the prospects of an information civilization. *Journal of Information Technology*, 30 (1), 2015, 75–89.

Index

Printed in the United States
by Baker & Taylor Publisher Services